Ah, What Is It? – That I Heard

COSTERUS NEW SERIES 204

Series Editors:
C.C. Barfoot, László Sándor Chardonnens
and Theo D'haen

Cover image: *Esquisse en mouvement / Sketch in movement,* by Anne
Mounic. Gouache, 32,5 x 25 cm, 2012.
Back cover image and page viii: *Katherine Mansfield,* by Anne Mounic.
Pencil, April 2014.

Cover design: Aart Jan Bergshoeff

ISBN: 978-90-420-3864-6
E-Book ISBN: 978-94-012-1106-2
©Editions Rodopi B.V., Amsterdam - New York, NY 2014
Printed in the Netherlands

Ah, What Is It? – That I Heard
Katherine Mansfield's Wings of Wonder

Anne Mounic

Foreword by
Vincent O'Sullivan

Rodopi Amsterdam-New York, NY 2014

But isn't it extraordinary that under his sweet, joyful little singing it was just this – sadness? – Ah, what is it? – that I heard.[1]

The pursuit of experience is the pursuit of the unimaginative.[2]

Far away lightning flutters – flutters like a wing – flutters like a broken bird that tries to fly and sinks again and again struggles.[3]

... for it is great to give up one's desire, but it is greater to hold fast to it after having given it up; it is great to lay hold of the eternal, but it is greater to hold fast of the temporal after given it up.

Then came the fullness of time.[4]

For someone living aesthetically the mood is always eccentric, because he has his centre at the periphery. Personal being has its centre in itself, and someone who does not have himself is eccentric. Someone living ethically, however, has his mood centralized, he is not inside the mood, he is not the mood itself, he has mood and has the mood in him. What he works for is continuity and that is always master over mood.[5]

---

[1] Katherine Mansfield, "The Canary" (1922), in *The Edinburgh Edition of the Collected Works of Katherine Mansfield*, II, The Collected Fiction of Katherine Mansfield, 1916-1922, eds Gerri Kimber and Vincent O'Sullivan, Edinburgh: Edinburgh University Press, 2012, 514; *The Collected Stories*, London: Penguin, 2011, 422.

[2] Katherine Mansfield, *Notebook 2* (1907), in *The Katherine Mansfield Notebooks*, ed. Margaret Scott, Minneapolis: University of Minnesota Press, 1997, I, 158.

[3] "The Man Without a Temperament" (1920), in *The Edinburgh Edition of the Collected Works of Katherine Mansfield*, II, 208; *The Collected Stories*, 142.

[4] Søren Kierkegaard, *Fear and Trembling* (1843), in *Fear and Trembling, Repetition*, ed. and trans. Howard V. Hong and Edna H. Hong, Princeton, NJ: Princeton University Press, 1983, 18.

[5] Søren Kierkegaard, *Either... or...* (1843), trans. with an Introduction by Alastair Hannay, London: Penguin, 2004, 528.

CONTENTS

to Vincent O'Sullivan

MOUNIC
7.4.14

FOREWORD

VINCENT O'SULLIVAN

At least for some readers, the insistent tolling behind the title of *La Recherche du Temps Perdu* is that for all the novel's triumphal claim for art, for most of us time is not retrieved, and the possibilities of life are the finer for their occurring, as most of us believe, just this once. Yet Proust's defiance of that truism chimed with what had been in the air for much of the nineteenth century. Katherine Mansfield, as a young woman on the far side of the world from Europe, was in thrall as so many of her generation were to Walter Pater's celebrated dictum that it was art and art alone that gave "the highest quality to your moments as they pass",[1] while the current hurries us down stream to an inevitable Niagara. For the later Mansfield, goaded by her early and fatal illness, an abiding challenge was how not to despair that the river ran always faster than one seemed prepared for?

Mansfield was among the first of her contemporaries to take on board quite what a later generation, in France especially, would mean by "authenticity", and did so before the resonant language of Existentialism was available to her. So much of what she wrote in her short stories, in her precise and fearless journals, and in her scintillating letters, might now be read as counterpoint to what her contemporary, Martin Heidegger, was finding a way to speak of with the cooler distancing of philosophy. The creative writer, with her innate suspicion of formula and precept, would engage more sensuously with image and pattern, with what Maurice Blanchot called "the shiver of rhythm, the call of a cadence",[2] that attends them. It is there, in the textures of her fiction and her self-examining, that

---

[1] Walter Pater, "Conclusion", in *The Renaissance: Studies in Art and Literature* (1868), Oxford: Oxford University Press, 1998, 153.
[2] Maurice Blanchot, "The Novel and Poetry", in *Faux Pas* (1943), trans. Charlotte Mandell, Stanford, CA: Stanford University Press, 2001, 203.

Mansfield addresses both entrapment and the compelling urgencies to freedom.

Two key tropes leap at one from her writing, as each puts with defining clarity quite how the courage of defiance, and the hard demands of accepting contingency, are central to her as an artist. The first concludes "The Man without a Temperament", a story she wrote in 1919 about a seriously ill woman; the second is from a letter to her husband a year later, when it already was clear to her that recovery from tuberculosis was less likely by the month. In the fiction a remote and enigmatic husband cares for his ailing wife on the Riviera. She disturbs him during the night to attend to her in his role of nursing spouse. Her regret for what she demands of him is set against his deeply ironical reply, dismissing her distress, and possibly her life as well, with unbridled force:

> "I sometimes wonder – do you mind awfully being out here with me?"
> He bends down. He kisses her. He tucks her in, he smooths the pillow. "Rot!", he whispers.[3]

As Mansfield addresses her physical condition and the mental state it promotes, a startling image embodies what will later become that clichéd phrase, "existential dread":

> It has taken me three years to understand this – to come to see this. We resist – we are terribly frightened. The little boat enters the dark fearful gulf and out only cry is to escape – "put me on land again". But it is useless. Nobody listens. The shadowy figure rows on. One ought to sit still and uncover one's eyes.[4]

It is this deft weaving of biography and imaginative text into the fabric of what we mean by "Mansfield", that Anne Mounic's volume so adventurously spells out.

Anne Mounic, a critic steeped in her country's various intellectual currents, is also a poet whose engagement with the enchantments and entrapments of language allows her to approach Mansfield as an

---

[3] Katherine Mansfield, "The Man Without a Temperament", in *The Collected Stories*, 143; in *The Collected Fiction of Katherine Mansfield*, II, 2012, 209.
[4] *The Collected Letters of Katherine Mansfield*, eds Vincent O'Sullivan and Margaret Scott, 5 Volumes, Oxford: Clarendon Press, 1984-2008, IV, 75.

informed academic mind, and as importantly, as a reader grounded in the relaxed openness of a fellow writer. In the tradition of Kierkegaard, her acknowledged and abiding mentor, she is too adroit a critic, and too flexible as a writer, to be much interested in easy categorizing or modish currencies. Her method as a thinker is an adventurous one, admirably suspicious of dictates, equally cautious of easy conclusions, while so often she brings to whatever text she attends, her involvement with other texts that are deeply important to her. Her reading of a story, or of a sentence even, is very much that of a frank temporal meeting – the implication is that the next such occasion may carry other valencies than those of today. This is as it were a mind's pulse monitored as it occurs. Just as, in John Donne's phrase, "no man is an island", no supposed reader is a solitary unsharing mind. Mounic places herself where a skein of voices converge, as if in some complex motet. There are numerous points in her essays where the reader is enlivened by seemingly chance conjunctions, which in fact turn out to be instructive flares, as Mansfield is paired with Baudelaire or Lawrence, with Colette or Catherine Pozzi, with Bergson or the Bible.

How much of Mansfield seems preoccupied with gradation, with scale, with how to turn the intractable to a point of illumination. At times it may seem that the legend inscribed above the entrance to so much Modernist literature, as forbidding almost as that to the entrance of Dante's *Inferno,* are those lines from the end of *Oedipus Rex,* baldly advising to "call no man happy till he dies, free of pain at last". Yet as Mansfield's image of the small boat approaching the gulf vividly declared, her response, like Beckett's when Godot does not arrive, is the choice still to go on.

By the time Mounic has covered the terrain of her author's *oeuvre,* she assures us of Mansfield's insistence that freedom flares the brighter for the constraints that bracket it. That is what she so compellingly attends to, the possibilities in that space "between", where, as in fairy stories, miracles may occur as naturally as rain. ("It's only the fairy tales we *really* live by", as she told her husband.[5]) Mounic draws attention especially to gardens, to those expansive Edenic echoes in Virginia Woolf as well as in Mansfield herself – "The garden is the place of renewal since it is the place of origins".[6]

---

[5] *Ibid.*, 75.
[6] Chapter 9, p. 164, in this volume.

While flowers, those by-words for evanescence, trail their pervasive veils of myth, teleology, the refusal to accept confinement, as much as they do the effortless clamour of colour and design. We are back with Pater's 'tremulous wisp constantly reforming itself on the stream ... that strange, perpetual weaving and unweaving of ourselves",[7] the fragmentary as complete as we are likely to know experience to be. As artists, we are each a variant of "the supreme fiction", in Wallace Stevens' shimmering phrase.

As Mounic deftly argues, time and again, and with quiet confidence in her storehouse of rich distractions and asides, it is the notion of "performance" that distributes vivacity and depth throughout so much of Mansfield: "The narrator gives the impression of being in a world of make-believe, a stage on which human passions are being dramatized."[8] To act out one's own reality, to fashion one's own script in doing so, is to assert being itself as freedom, so that even the cage-bars of necessity may serve their turn as props. And how this then finds its route back towards Proust's first and final concern – that we do not lose what mere mechanical time so insists we cannot retrieve.

Near the end of her book, Mounic quotes from a late Mansfield letter, "If I were allowed one single cry to God that cry would be *I want to be* REAL".[9] She goes on to note "Being 'REAL' means being able to convert the ambivalence of joy and fear into a work of art through what Kierkegaard, thinking of Job, called 'repetition' – a renewal of life in art".[10] At the last, the ethical and the aesthetic tend towards the same conclusion, where the plaiting of one within the other is complete. Just as Mansfield had written that she knew in her own ailing body the moral implications of corruption, it was there too, in her troubled breathing, that she understood what she aspired to, and that health and ethical meaning might be spoken of together. One's next breath may be the prelude, not to some all-encompassing "answer", but at least to a further stage of clarity we can only think of as moving *towards*. Her last story, "The Canary", in which a lonely woman mourns the death of her pet canary, concludes with that

---

[7] Pater, "Conclusion", 152.
[8] Chapter 10, p. 180, in this volume.
[9] *The Collected Letters of Katherine Mansfield*, V, 1922-1923, eds Vincent O' Sullivan and Margaret Scott, 2008, 341.
[10] Chapter 10, p. 189, in this volume.

physical and spiritual drive – for they are no longer separate things – toward the embodiment of what, so elusively, is *almost* within grasp:

> It is there, deep down, deep down, part of one, like one's breathing. However hard I work and tire myself I have only to stop to know it is there, waiting. I often wonder if everybody feels the same. One can never know. But isn't it extraordinary that under his sweet, joyful little singing it was just this – sadness? – Ah, what is it? – that I heard.[11]

A few weeks before her death, Mansfield spoke of how tired she was of her own little stories, "like birds bred in cages", as she put it.[12] Yet even if to be free might mean simply to change one cage for another, that too is a matter of willing what is new, as much as accepting a sentence. And as any writer, as any performer, knows, "sentence" itself remains an open possibility, until breath determines how it will be said.

---

[11] Katherine Mansfield, "The Canary", in *The Edinburgh Edition of the Collected Works of Katherine Mansfield*, II, 514.
[12] *The Collected Letters of Katherine Mansfield*, V, 346.

INTRODUCTION

This book started with my idea of collecting the essays I had written in English on Katherine Mansfield's work for several conferences, books, and reviews, and especially for *Katherine Mansfield Studies: The Journal of the Katherine Mansfield Society*. Yet each of them had to be adapted for the coherence of the whole and I found that I needed to add two chapters devoted to the Biblical allusions and their import in Katherine Mansfield's work and to the comparison with Virginia Woolf through *Mrs. Dalloway*. The idea of collecting those essays occurred to me once I had completed the item on the newly discovered stories (Chapter 1) for a conference to be held in Paris at the occasion of the publication of the two volumes of the Collected Fiction, 1898-1915 and 1916-1922, edited by Gerri Kimber and Vincent O'Sullivan. Until then my reference book as far as the stories are concerned was the Penguin edition of the *Collected Stories*; from then on I have used the 2012 complete edition. However the reference edition throughout this book remains the Penguin edition of the *Collected Stories*. I am referring to it in each chapter except when the stories, scattered in the *Notebooks*, or yet undiscovered, are only to be found in the Edinburgh edition.

I started studying Katherine Mansfield's work in 2003 and the first result was a chapter dedicated to her in *Psyché et le secret de Perséphone*: "Katherine Mansfield: Au souffle du vent, les métamorphoses du rêve, un art de la mémoire" followed by a comparative study, "Du jardin de juillet aux fruits d'automne: de Katherine Mansfield à Catherine Pozzi. Pourquoi écrire?".[1] Then a detailed study of two of her stories, "An Indiscreet Journey" and "The Fly", was published in *Monde terrible où naître: La voix singulière face à l'Histoire*.[2] Katherine Mansfield's work and outlook have

---

[1] Anne Mounic, *Psyché et le secret de Perséphone*, Paris: L'Harmattan, 2004, 19-134.
[2] Anne Mounic, Chapter 6, "'An Indiscreet Journey': Katherine Mansfield et la Grande Guerre" and Chapter 7, "'... he felt a real admiration for the fly's courage .... il ressentit une réelle admiration pour le courage de la mouche': Katherine Mansfield et

helped me to take further my own reflection on poetry and literature. I connect her writings with several notions – memory, communication between people, the sense of wonder, wrestling with negativity, the ethical choice, the spiritual achievement of joy, the song as an "active state of grace".[3] It seems that from a very early age she was aware of her own spiritual power which she compares to "sunbeams" filling "the whole house".[4] Her outlook bears out my view of art as the outcome of an ethical choice, a choice of oneself, a choice of life, derived from Kierkegaard's definition to be found in *Either... or...* (1843).

The philosopher insists that choosing oneself does not mean choosing this "thing or that" but "the absolute, and what is the absolute? It is myself in my eternal validity." Choosing oneself does not mean creating oneself; it means transcending one's "immediate personal existence",[5] which has "been created out of nothing". It does not mean knowing oneself either. Knowing oneself "cannot be the goal unless at the same time it is the beginning .... Through the individual's intercourse with himself the individual gets himself with child and gives himself birth."[6] If knowing oneself was only a goal and "mere contemplation", the duality between subject and object would crop up, breaking the sense of continuity. Kierkegaard affirms that the "ethical individual is transparent to himself"; he "has seen himself, knows himself, permeates his own concretion with his consciousness"; he "has himself as a task, not as a possibility, not as a plaything for his caprice to sport with".

Very soon in her life, Katherine Mansfield thought she had a task to perform and that feeling became even stronger around 1915 and after her brother's death. The task is existential: it means adding new chapters to the human epic. An important consequence of the ethical choice is the individual's awareness of his own history and the history

---

le destin", in *Monde terrible où naître: La voix singulière face à l'Histoire*, Paris: Honoré Champion, 2011, 193-224.
[3] *The Katherine Mansfield Notebooks*, II, 58.
[4] Katherine Mansfield, "The Thoughtful Child", in *The Edinburgh Edition of the Collected Works of Katherine Mansfield*, I, The Collected Fiction of Katherine Mansfield, 1898-1915, eds Gerri Kimber and Vincent O'Sullivan, Edinburgh: Edinburgh University Press, 2012, 127. See Chapter 1.
[5] Kierkegaard, *Either... or...*, 516-17.
[6] *Ibid.*, 549.

of "other individuals":[7] "He can only choose himself ethically when he chooses himself in continuity, and so he has himself as a multiply specified task."[8] Borrowing from Thomas Mann and Imre Kertész,[9] I call that awareness of oneself and of one's history the "spirit of the narrative", that is the feeling of continuity of the human epic, which is individual. Each singular voice contributes to the long account of our existence. It means facing the immediacy of the present moment and elevating it to the dimension of the instant set in the infinite of becoming, which Kierkegaard expressed in *Fear and Trembling* (1843), as appears among the epigraphs:

> ... for it is great to give up one's desire, but it is greater to hold fast to it after having given it up; it is great to lay hold of the eternal, but it is greater to hold fast of the temporal after given it up.
> Then came the fullness of time.[10]

Time prevails over space just as the feeling of empathy replaces the cathartic effect of tragedy – a purgation of the emotions of pity and fear. The compassionate character is reluctant to get rid of such emotions. Jon Silkin led me to question the notion of catharsis, as he said he did in his anthology of First World War Poetry (see Chapter 8). Those opposite notions, empathy versus catharsis, are relevant in the contrastive study of Katherine Mansfield and Virginia Woolf. And we read differently when we absorb the others' suffering instead of dispelling it.

Katherine Mansfield's own mood is filled with empathy. It is a choice of life. Tragedy chooses the other's death and sacrifice. It breaks the sense of continuity. Kierkegaard's principle of repetition, or renewal, is a choice of life. It means accepting our essential passivity as our original power to achieve our task, not as the irresistible force Schopenhauer called the "Will" and which

---

[7] *Ibid.*, 518.

[8] *Ibid.*, 549.

[9] Imre Kertész, *L'Holocauste comme culture*, Preface by Péter Nádas, trans. Natalia Zaremba-Huzsvai and Charles Zaremba, Arles: Actes Sud, 2009, 43-44; Thomas Mann, *Joseph et ses frères: Les Histoires de Jacob* (1933), trans. L. Vic, Paris: Gallimard L'Imaginaire, 1985, 47. See Anne Mounic, *L'Esprit du récit ou La chair du devenir: Ethique et création littéraire*, Paris: Champion, 2013, Introduction, 13.

[10] Kierkegaard, *Fear and Trembling* (1843), in *Fear and Trembling, Repetition*, 18. See Chapter 2 in the present volume, 22.

determines our lives in the same way as Nemesis, the Greek Necessity ruling over tragedy, does. Freedom is a question of choice and of confidence in our subjective power. In 1906, the young Katherine Mansfield wrote in her Notebooks, among many quotations by Oscar Wilde, Henrik Ibsen, Montaigne and La Rochefoucauld: "To acknowledge the presence of Fear is to give birth to Failure."[11] A quote attributed to a certain "A.H.H." asserts the importance of subjectivity: "People who learn from experience do not allow for intuition."[12] She also quotes Oscar Wilde: "To realise one's nature perfectly – that is what each of us is here for."[13] One obviously thinks of Spinoza.

The process of repetition, of a return to oneself in the infinite, is linked to the notion of the Open, so cherished by Rilke in his Eighth Duino Elegy, dedicated to Rudolf Kassner. In the essay on universal physiognomony[14] which Kassner had read to Rilke before he wrote that Elegy, that very original thinker distinguished between the return (*Umkehr*) on oneself in the movement of the infinite and the return on oneself to gain something else. The movement is the meaning, and means freedom; while the movement which is alienated from its goal encloses the individual within the finite world of dogma. Rilke opposes the Open, which is freedom, to the tragic closure of fate. In his famous ode "Brot und Wein", Hölderlin connects the Open and the living: "So komm! daß wir das Offene schauen, / Daß Lebendiges wir suchen, so weit es auch ist."[15] The sense of freedom and continuity leads to such achievement, which means unhampered breathing.

We find a strong sense of continuity in Katherine Mansfield's early stories of the "Thoughtful Child" (Chapter 1). I wish to emphasize her sense of wonder in the second chapter, focusing on such stories as "Bliss", "Prelude" or "The Wind Blows", without forgetting the poems. Her few direct references to the Bible add to the existential resonance of her genius for the marvellous (Chapter 3). Her art of

---

[11] *The Katherine Mansfield Notebooks*, I, 94

[12] *Ibid.*, 96.

[13] *Ibid.*, 97.

[14] See Anne Mounic, *L'inerte ou l'exquis: Pensée poétique, pensée du singulier*, Paris: Champion, 2014, Chapter 2; Rudolf Kassner, *Esquisse d'une physiognomonie universelle, Evocations et paraboles*, trans. Geneviève Bianquis, Paris: Plon, 1956, 8.

[15] Friedrich Hölderlin, "Brot und Wein", 3, Second version, in *Œuvre poétique complète*, trans. François Garrigue, A German/French edition, Paris: La Différence, 2005, 697-99.

memory has to be contemplated in the light of Marcel Proust's endeavour in *La recherche du temps perdu* (*In Search of Lost Time*). In Chapter 4 I shall consider more particularly "Feuille d'Album". Through the study of her allusions to birds, I wish to highlight her response to the pessimistic outlook spread in the wake of Schopenhauer's philosophy of the relentless Will (Chapter 5). Trains and other means of transportation play a great part in stimulating her narrative faculties, which I tried to show in Chapter 6. The next three chapters are comparative studies: Katherine Mansfield and D.H. Lawrence in Chapter 7; Katherine Mansfield and Virginia Woolf in Chapter 8; Katherine Mansfield, Colette, Catherine Pozzi and Dorothy Richardson in Chapter 9. In Chapter 10, I shall highlight her connections with Paris, while in Chapter 11, I shall consider the development – and personal initiation – of the narrative subject, or author, within the perspective of the spirit of the narrative. Finally I shall consider her achievement in connection with the art of Proust and Baudelaire (Chapter 12), emphasizing the significance of night and the essential contrast of light and darkness.

A survey of the critical response to Katherine Mansfield's work would certainly belong to the "spirit of the narrative" since each point of view renews the work considered. Moreover it tells as much on the period in which it occurs and the critic's outlook as on the author him/herself. The task was undertaken by Jan Pilditch until 1991. *The Critical Response to Katherine Mansfield*[16] was published in 1996. Since then, a lot has been written on her especially since the Katherine Mansfield Society was founded, in 2008. During the Katherine Mansfield conference in Paris X Nanterre in June 2013, Anne Besnault-Levita made an interesting inventory of the recent critical approaches to Katherine Mansfield's work, which led her to "distinguish the scholarly fields in which she appeared as a central figure – mainly Short Story Theories – from the fields that still neglect her influence: modernist studies, new modernist studies, and to a lesser extent, feminist studies".[17] However I shall restrict my study to my reading of Katherine Mansfield's work in the perspective I have

---

[16] *The Critical Response to Katherine Mansfield*, ed. Jan Pilditch, Westport, CT: Greenwood Press, 1996.
[17] From Anne Besnault-Levita's abstract for the 21 June 2013 Katherine Mansfield Conference organized by Valérie Baisnée and Dunstan Ward in Paris X Nanterre.

just sketched. A bibliography of the critical work on Katherine Mansfield is to be found on the site of the Katherine Mansfield Society[18] as well as a list of some of the books containing chapters on Katherine Mansfield.[19]

---

[18] http://www.katherinemansfieldsociety.org/critical-works-on-mansfield-in-english/
[19] http://www.katherinemansfieldsociety.org/books-containing-chapters-on-mansfield/

CHAPTER 1

THE "THOUGHTFUL CHILD" IN LOVE WITH WORDS:
KATHERINE MANSFIELD'S ACHIEVEMENT OF JOY

The four stories newly discovered by Chris Mourant in the King's College London Archives are absolutely in keeping with the general tone and concerns of their author in the rest of her work, whether it be stories, poems, letters, or diary notes. Vincent O'Sullivan and Gerri Kimber tell us[1] that the three tales concerning the "Thoughtful Child" should be read in connection with "The Thoughtful Child. Her Literary Aspirations",[2] which was formerly published in her Notebooks.[3] We should also refer to "The Thoughtful Child", also published in the *Notebooks*.[4] Those tales were part of the project of a children's book which was abandoned. The fourth story, "A Little Episode" (1909), belongs to the same period as "His Sister's Keeper", also published in the *Notebooks*.[5] Both stories tell of her disillusionment after her love affair with Garnet Trowell and her "brief relationship with George Bowden, her husband of convenience".[6] All those writings precede the first collection of her work, *In a German Pension*, published in December 1911.

I think that those four stories emphasize a quality to be found in the rest of her work, or a sense of continuity from childhood to the mature writer's capacity for wonder, paralleled with a sense of continuity within what I call, after Imre Kertész and Thomas Mann, "the spirit of

---

"The 'Thoughtful Child' in Love with Words: Katherine Mansfield's Achievement of Joy" was written for the Katherine Mansfield conference in Paris X Nanterre on 21 June 2013.
[1] *The Edinburgh Edition of the Collected Works of Katherine Mansfield*, I, 531 (note).
[2] *Ibid.*, 119-22.
[3] *The Katherine Mansfield Notebooks*, I, 204-206.
[4] *Ibid.*, 126-29.
[5] *Ibid.*, 228-34; and *The Edinburgh Edition of the Collected Works of Katherine Mansfield*, I, 150-57.
[6] *The Edinburgh Edition of the Collected Works of Katherine Mansfield*, I, 544 (note).

the narrative"[7] (see Introduction): what she has read, which nurtures
her own work, also kindles her sense of wonder through a feeling of
belonging. The result is that the experience of writing, whether it deals
with pain and disillusion, or with delightful moments, is an
achievement of joy, making up for the dry indifference of reality. Her
love of words enables her to create for herself and for us some sort of
a floating abode of nowhere, an utopian place, in the original meaning
of the term, which says what she longs for – loving and breathing, a
sense of freedom and the enjoyment of life, in spite of all.

A sense of continuity

"What is the fascination and the charm in these old, old rhymes?" the
Thoughtful Child's father wonders in "Hand-in-Hand with the
Thoughtful Child" (1908). And some nursery rhymes are hinted at or
even quoted in the tale, as well as the poem about the man "with a
bird's nest in his beard" in *Cole's Picture Book Annual* (1883)[8] and
Stevenson's *A Child's Garden of Verses* (1885), which is also
mentioned in "The Thoughtful Child: Her Literary Aspirations"[9]
through the reference to "the friendly cow":

> The friendly cow, all red and white,
>   I love with all my heart:
> She gives me cream with all her might,
>   To eat the apple-tart.[10]

The "Thoughtful Child" even seems to belong to this spirit of the
narrative which transcends her own being:

> The next day at dinner – there was apple-tart. 'Won't you have
> some of the friendly cow, Uncle Peter?' asked my daughter, waving
> her teaspoon airily at the cream jug.
>   'Bless me, you're a very smart young lady.'

---

[7] See Mounic, *L'Esprit du récit ou La chair du devenir: Ethique et création littéraire*,
Introduction, 13-35.

[8] Katherine Mansfield, "Hand-in-hand with the Thoughtful Child" (1908), in *The
Edinburgh Edition of the Collected Works of Katherine Mansfield*, I, 535, and note,
537.

[9] Katherine Mansfield, "The Thoughtful Child. Her Literary Aspirations" (1908), in
ibid., 120.

[10] Robert Louis Stevenson, *The Child's Garden of Verses* (1885), Ware: Wordsworth
Edition, 1994, 49.

'Oh, it's not *me*, Uncle Peter – Mr Stevenson, you know.' But he did not know – and she was amazed. 'Oh, I knew that years ago,' she cried. 'years and years before I was born even. Why I remember –' 'Yes, dear, that's enough' said Mother, looking at me and I smiled back at her.

The "private and particular language of the Secret Society",[11] which transfigures the inert reality into a marvel of a living world ("They must learn, too, that there are no such things as dolls – they are fairy babies"[12]), is known only to "the right sort of people",[13] those on whom, as a child, you can sit. It means that the world of story-telling gives evidence of a strong relationship between parents and children. It is certainly the reason why the father is the narrator in "The Thoughtful Child. Her Literary Aspirations" and in the three newly discovered stories. In the former he is also the one who tells the stories to the child, then awakening her "literary aspirations" – "to write a book for all those Poor Things who have no babies of their own to look after but other people's children"[14] – and connecting her with such people as "Mr Stevenson", who lived and wrote "years before I was born even". In other words, the "Thoughtful Child" aims at initiating ignorant grown-ups to the art of wishful transfiguring of reality. In May 1913, she wrote to J.M. Murry:

> Thank you for Pa's letter. He was cheerful and poetic, a trifle puffed up but very loving. I feel towards my Pa man like a little girl. I want to jump and stamp on his chest and cry 'you've got to love me'. When he says he does, I feel quite confident that God is on my side.[15]

She also refers to a Russian legend, "The Sea King's Daughter",[16] the story of a Russian merchant made wealthy by the Sea King who wanted him to marry one of his daughters and remain at the bottom of the sea forever. But he managed to escape and go back to Novgorod.

---

[11] Mansfield, "The Thoughtful Child. Her Literary Aspirations", in *The Edinburgh Edition of the Collected Works of Katherine Mansfield*, I, 119.

[12] *Ibid.*, 120.

[13] *Ibid.*, 121.

[14] *Ibid.*, 119.

[15] To J.M. Murry, [early May 1913], in *The Collected Letters of Katherine Mansfield*, I, 120.

[16] Katherine Mansfield, "The Thoughtful Child. In Autumn" (1908), in *The Edinburgh Edition of the Collected Works of Katherine Mansfield*, I, 532.

In some ways, the tale recalls the *Arabian Nights*, a book which Proust refers to, and takes as a model, to a certain extent, in *In Search of Lost Time*.

"What is the fascination and the charm in these old, old rhymes?" For a New Zealander longing to become a writer, they are the first words providing her with a sense of belonging to the English literary tradition. Moreover, and more generally, connecting the child with the "years before [she] was born even", those first poems introduce her to the spirit of the narrative and the notion of a special language going beyond the appearances and bestowing subjective life to the world around her. "But the best times she had were with the Shadow Children in the wood at the bottom of the garden":[17] the process which is described in this tale, "The Thoughtful Child", is particularly interesting. Questioning the "Shadow Children" about their identity, she loses them and gains "a real brother"[18] who is something of a nuisance until he dies and re-appears among the "Shadow Children", offering her to "go sunbeam-catching".[19] The imaginary creatures sing the "Fairy Song" and are connected with the "'inside' voice". They figure the power of the reflexive consciousness to descend into the self (Kassner's return, or Kierkegaard's repetition) and find the subjective energy at the core to animate the world: "And the sunbeams that she had swallowed grew so big that when she started laughing they flew out – all except one, and filled the whole house." The "Thoughtful Child" then becomes a centre of radiating power. D.H. Lawrence evinced the same feeling a few years later in "The Thorn in the Flesh": "The doing came from within her without call or command. It was a delicious outflow, like sunshine, the activity that flowed from her and put her tasks to right."[20]

It is strange how "The Thoughtful Child" foreshadows what shall be her reaction to her brother's death in October 1915 – looking back on their childhood and endeavouring to "renew"[21] it for future readers, which she had actually started doing before he died. But what she says

---

[17] Mansfield, "The Thoughtful Child. Her Literary Aspirations", in *ibid.*, 125.
[18] *Ibid.*, 126.
[19] *Ibid.*, 127.
[20] D.H. Lawrence, "The Thorn in the Flesh" [written as "Vin Ordinaire" in May-June 1913], in *The Prussian Officer and Other Stories* (1914), London: Panther Books, 1985, 45.
[21] "I long to renew them in writing" (*The Katherine Mansfield Notebooks*, ed. Margaret Scott, Minneapolis: University of Minnesota Press, 2002, II, 32).

after her brother's death shows how her mind's power of transfiguration is so intense that reality without the right words to animate it sounds inert, or lifeless, to her:

> I hear his voice in trees and flowers, in scents and light and shadow. Have people, apart from those far away people, ever existed for me? Or have they failed me, and faded because I denied them reality?[22]

She captures the trees and flowers' power to resurrect in spring and remembers only to "renew": "The words are like flowers."[23] The past revives into the future – an instance of "repetition" to use Kierkegaard's word, but it does not mean repeating but resuming. The Danish philosopher found the notion when talking about Job. Katherine Mansfield chose Kezia, Job's daughter's name, to speak of her childhood (see Chapter 3). Writing opens an enchanted world, not only when she writes children's stories. And her sense of continuity includes Shakespeare. When she writes: "The thoughtful child knew 'most everything about Fairies. She had been one herself once, and lived in a crocus on the lawn",[24] we obviously think of Shakespeare's fairies in *A Midsummer Night's Dream* (1596). In her Notebooks and letters, she keeps praising Shakespeare and, in December 1915, wrote to her husband that she loved him so much, and she added: "There are faeries, faeries everywhere. I would not be surprised if I were to find them putting fir boughs in the hall, and wreaths upon the door handles and swags and garlands over the windows."[25]

"What is the fascination and the charm in these old, old rhymes?" If we consider the musicality of their rhythm, we may also think of a very influential book in English literature, the Book of Psalms,[26] which Katherine Mansfield mentions in a letter to her husband in December 1915: "The rain is pouring down & the sea is roaring down

---

[22] *Ibid.*, 16.
[23] *Ibid.*, 33.
[24] Mansfield, "The Thoughtful Child. Her Literary Aspirations", in *The Edinburgh Edition of the Collected Works of Katherine Mansfield*, I, 124.
[25] To J.M. Murry, [27 December 1915], in *The Collected Letters of Katherine Mansfield*, I, 236.
[26] In her poems, Stevie Smith (1902-1971) borrowed both from nursery rhymes and the Psalms in her search for rhythm.

the Psalms."[27] Biblical awareness (see Chapter 3) also partakes of the sense of continuity and a common ground, "years before I was born even". In the Psalms, the poet is close to God, speaking to Him and asking Him to listen. The "inside" voice seeks its response in its own words, which create an "inside" relationship. We find such a relationship in Katherine Mansfield's 1908 stories, particularly in the last two, "The Thoughtful Child. In Autumn" and "Hand-in-Hand with the Thoughtful Child". The sense of belonging is dependent on this I and You relationship. In "The Doll's House", she associates the moment of tremendous enchantment with the character of God opening all houses at night like a doll's house and emphasizes the presence of the lamp at the centre of the house, stressing the fact that the lamp belonged: "It seemed to smile at Kezia, to say, 'I live here.' The lamp was real."[28] The sense of continuity goes with the sense of belonging. "The strongest man is he who stands most alone",[29] she wrote down in her *Notebooks*, in 1906, quoting Ibsen.

A sense of belonging
The epigraph to "A Little Episode" (1909) is a quote from Oscar Wilde's *Picture of Dorian Gray* (1891): "The one charm of the past is that it is past. But women never know when the curtain has fallen."[30] Yvonne, the main protagonist in "A Little Episode", wishes to prolong the enchantment of love when she meets again Jacques Saint Pierre, "the symbol of all her happy life – her Paris days".[31] If Oscar Wilde is an influence, her Paris recollections recall George Du Maurier's *Trilby* (1894). He is mentioned in the story as a cartoonist but the Paris *Bohème*, the Paris Bohemia, Katherine Mansfield describes – her "studio days"[32] – recalls *Trilby*: "Trilby, tall, graceful, and stately, and also swift of action, though more like Juno or Diana than Hebe, devoted herself more especially to her own particular favourites –

---

[27] To J.M. Murry, [25 December 1915], in *The Collected Letters of Katherine Mansfield*, I, 229.
[28] *The Edinburgh Edition of the Collected Works of Katherine Mansfield*, II, 415.
[29] *The Katherine Mansfield Notebooks*, I, 95.
[30] Katherine Mansfield, "A Little Episode" (1909), in *The Edinburgh Edition of the Collected Works of Katherine Mansfield*, I, 538. Oscar Wilde, *The Picture of Dorian Gray* (1891), Harmondsworth: Penguin, 1986, 131.
[31] Mansfield, "A Little Episode", in *The Edinburgh Edition of the Collected Works of Katherine Mansfield*, I, 541.
[32] *Ibid.*, 540.

Durien, Taffy, the laird, Little Billee – and Dodor and Zouzou, whom she loved, and *tutoyé'd en bonne camarade* as she served them with all there was of the choicest."[33] On 24 October 1908, Katherine Mansfield wrote to Garnet Trowell, to whom she says she felt "married":[34]

> I am more than sorry to leave Paris. Indeed it is easy to realise what Paris means – And she is a city for – – – – you & I. The picturesque aspect of it all – the people – and at night from the top of a tram – the lighted interiors of the houses – you know the effect – people gathered round a lamp lighted table – a little homely café – a laundry – a china shop – or at the corners the old chestnut sellers – the Italians selling statuettes of the Venus de Milo – & Napoleon encore Napoleon.[35]

What is striking is that the following remark in "A Little Episode" anticipates on John Middleton Murry's creation of the magazine *Rhythm* after an encounter with the Scottish painter J.D. Fergusson in Paris in 1910, and foreshadows her getting in touch with him and contributing to it: "Primitive woman she felt – with primitive impulses – primitive needs – all conventions – all scruples were thrown to the four winds."[36] Angela Smith quotes Frederick Goodyear on "the magazine's rejection of artistic and philosophical conservatism: 'a true impulse towards conscious freedom ... comes to men who see instinctively that no man is certainly free till all men are free ... it is the neo-barbarians, men and women who to the timid and unimaginative seem merely perverse and atavistic, that must familiarize us with our outcast selves'."[37]

Katherine Mansfield, born in New Zealand, was aware that there were other modes of living apart from the Western world's (see Chapter 6). These lines in her Notebooks give an account of the variety of her cultural background:

---

[33] George Du Maurier, *Trilby* (1894), London: Everyman, 1992, 94.
[34] To Garnet Trowell, [24 October 1908], in *The Collected Letters of Katherine Mansfield*, I, 76.
[35] *Ibid.*, 77-78.
[36] Mansfield, "A Little Episode", in *The Edinburgh Edition of the Collected Works of Katherine Mansfield*, I, 543.
[37] Angela Smith, "Paris Is Simply a Place of Freedom", *Temporel* n° 7, May 2009, http://temporel.fr/Rhythm-par-Angela-Smith.

> ... Wahi brings us a great bowl of milk & a little cup of cream. Also a
> cup of curd. She dines with us, teaches me Maori & smokes a cigaret.
> Johanna is rather silent, reads Byron & Shakespeare & wants to go
> back to school. W. teaches her fancy work. At night we go & see her–
> the clean place, the pictures, the beds, Byron & the candle-like flowers
> in a glass– sweet – the paper & pens, photos of Maories & whites
> too.[38]

Against "all those fat, stolid Philistines",[39] the artists stand out as
members of the "Secret Society" speaking with the "inside voice", as
the "Thoughtful Child" would have it: "She was half laughing, half
crying, inexpressibly, intoxicatingly beautiful ... the little charming
chrysalis of studio days had become this fascinating Society butterfly
– and to her – this dear affectionate boy had become ideal man – ideal
musician – the symbol of all her happy life – her Paris days."

This joy at listening to music calls for family recollections which
tell of strong peaceful relations with the girl's father:

> A sudden wave of colour flooded her face – as he began to play.
> Recollections – exquisite bitter sweet memories began to flock
> past her – a motley – sad, fascinating troupe. She closed her eyes ...
> Back again in her Father's rooms – Jacques at the piano – Emil, half
> lying across the table – Jean by the fire – sketching them all ... She,
> sitting huddled up by her Father – his arm around her, cheek to cheek,
> heart to heart.[40]

We remember "The Wind Blows" and the piano lesson, the very
sensitive account of Mr Bullen, the piano teacher, and the suggestion
that rhythm may counteract the destructive effects of time passing. In
The Picture of Dorian Gray, Oscar Wilde wrote: "Yet one had
ancestors in literature, as well as in one's own race, nearer perhaps in
type and temperament, many of them, and certainly with an influence
of which one was more absolutely conscious."[41] In her Notebooks, in
a story entitled "In a Café", which was published in 1907 in *The
Native Companion*, she wrote: "Life to a girl who had read Nietzsche,

---

[38] *The Katherine Mansfield Notebooks*, I, 141.
[39] Mansfield, "A Little Episode", in *The Edinburgh Edition of the Collected Works of Katherine Mansfield*, I, 541.
[40] *Ibid.*, 540-41.
[41] Wilde, *The Picture of Dorian Gray*, 176.

Eugene Sue, Baudelaire, D'Annunzio, Georges Barres, Catulle Mendes, Sudermann, Ibsen, Tolstoi, was, in her opinion, but a trifle obvious."[42]

In "His Sister's Keeper", (an adapted allusion to the biblical episode of Cain and Abel, Genesis, 4, 9), the girl who "was sick of existing" was reading A.E. Housman's *Shropshire Lad* (1896), a collection of poems, so popular with the Georgian poets, in which the poet recalls his native region in a pessimistic tone:

> With rue my heart is laden
>   For golden friends I had,
> For many a rose-lipt maiden
>   And many a lightfoot lad;
>
> By brooks too broad for leaping
>   The lightfoot boys are laid;
> The rose-lipt girls are sleeping
>   In fields where roses fade.[43]

The reference to Housman gives a clue to the author's and her characters' moods. I found no mention of Housman in the Notebooks and letters of the period but Oscar Wilde played a significant role in her initiation to literature. In May 1908, she wonders: "Does Oscar – and there is a gardenia yet alive beside my bed – does Oscar still keep so firm a stronghold in my soul?"[44] Her answer is negative and she also quotes Arthur Symons, Ibsen, Tolstoy, Shaw, D'Annunzio or Meredith. She goes on:

> To weave the intricate tapestry of one's own life it is well to take a thread from many harmonious skeins, and to realise that there must be harmony. Not necessary to grow the sheep, comb the wool, colour and brand it, but joyfully take all that is ready and with that saved time go a great way further. Independence, resolve, firm purpose and the gift of discrimination, <u>mental clearness</u>, – here are the inevitables. Again, Will – the realisation that Art is absolutely self development. The knowledge that genius is dormant in every soul, that that very

---

[42] *The Katherine Mansfield Notebooks*, I, 172 (Hermann Sudermann [1857-1928] was a German playwright).
[43] A.E. Housman, "With Rue My Heart Is Laden" (1896), in *The Norton Anthology of Poetry*, Fourth Edition, New York and London: W.W. Norton, 1996, 1072.
[44] *The Katherine Mansfield Notebooks*, I, 110.

individuality which is at the root of our being is what matters so poignantly.

At the same time she evinces a sense of continuity as regards her literary predecessors, a sense of belonging to a coherent tradition of individual development. The spirit of the narrative has to do with individual achievement of plenitude. "The aim of life is self-development",[45] said Lord Henry to Dorian Gray. Being chased from such poetic abode is to leave all hope:

> She put her hand on his sleeve – 'They crushed all my ideals – all my hopes – they made me think of Paris – as hell the fools – and Father the Arch Fiend. Bon Dieu – I was friendless – homeless – helpless – Then Lord Mandeville came – and engaged himself to me – yes, that's the way to put it – and we've been married nine months.'[46]

And she feels "caged" instead of feeling "alive"[47] and carried away by "the adorable irresponsibility of everything".[48]

Joy and hope

The "Secret Society" cannot survive in good health among the Philistines: "She sprang into bed – and suddenly, instinctively with a little childish gesture – she put one arm over her face – as though to hide something hideous and dreadful – as her husband's heavy ponderous footsteps sounded on the stairs ...."[49] The pianist plays Beethoven's *Appassionata* sonata in F minor written in 1804-1805. Although the title was not given to the piece by Beethoven himself it is not completely inappropriate: "Seized by an ungovernable impulse she rose and swiftly passed out of the hall."[50]

Jacques' betrayal foreshadows the disillusionment as regards the Bohemia of artists and writers Katherine Mansfield will express in stories such as "Bliss" (1918) or "Marriage à la Mode" (1921). In the first of these stories the figure of the blossoming pear tree, still an

---

[45] Wilde, *The Picture of Dorian Gray*, 41.
[46] Mansfield, "A Little Episode", in *The Edinburgh Edition of the Collected Works of Katherine Mansfield*, I, 541.
[47] *Ibid.*, 543.
[48] *Ibid.*, 542.
[49] *Ibid.*, 543-44.
[50] *Ibid.*, 540.

image of wonder, stands against the bitterness of betrayal. The same importance is given by Oscar Wilde to blossoming trees, such as the lilac at the beginning of *The Picture of Dorian Gray*: "The studio was filled with the rich odour of roses, and when the light summer wind stirred amidst the trees of the garden, there came through the open door the heavy scent of the lilac, or the more delicate perfume of the pink-flowering thorn."[51] As it is in Baudelaire's poems, an influence on Wilde and on Katherine Mansfield, the scent is particularly stressed: "From early morning the lilac tosses its beautiful plumes and the scent – which is the very quintessence of Spring – floats like a pale mist across the lawn over the garden, and in through the muslin curtains ...."[52]

In "Marriage à la Mode", William feels estranged from his wife, the "new Isabel"[53] and her "young poets"[54] are only conceited scroungers. She is also sarcastic as regards the character of Raoul Duquette in "Je ne Parle Pas Français". However, in spite of all hindrances and disappointments, there seems to be a "thread" which helped her "weave the intricate tapestry of [her] own life"[55] (see above on page 15):

> In this Spring weather a bird in the lilac tree on the lawn sings each day – a little brown bird – its song is about a fairy stream running through a dream forest.
> Nothing has ever enchanted the Thoughtful Child so much. She is transfigured this Spring and I look at her radiant face with awe.[56]

Any reader familiar with Katherine Mansfield will think of her last story, "The Canary" (1922), when the bird's song, "his sweet, joyful singing",[57] takes an existential meaning.

---

[51] Wilde, *The Picture of Dorian Gray*, 23.

[52] Katherine Mansfield, "The Thoughtful Child and the Lilac Tree" (1908), in *The Edinburgh Edition of the Collected Works of Katherine Mansfield*, I, 530.

[53] Katherine Mansfield, "Marriage à la Mode" (1921), in *The Edinburgh Edition of the Collected Works of Katherine Mansfield*, II, 330; in *The Collected Stories*, 309.

[54] *Ibid.*, 331, 310.

[55] *The Katherine Mansfield Notebooks*, I, 110.

[56] Mansfield, "The Thoughtful Child and the Lilac Tree", in *The Edinburgh Edition of the Collected Works of Katherine Mansfield*, I, 529.

[57] Mansfield, "The Canary" (1922), in *The Edinburgh Edition of the Collected Works of Katherine Mansfield*, II, 514; in *The Collected Stories*, 422.

In the 1908 story, she is already aware of the capacity of art to transfigure reality:

> So you find the world a kind place, little daughter. You are not haunted by the decay of Autumn, you are not chilled by the paralysis of Winter. To you it is firelight, then the softest, gentlest sleep .... And the white shroud is only a night gown – the bare earth – a bed for my little girl.[58]

In her letters and Notebooks she wrote beautifully about autumn:

> Big red pears – monsters jostle in Ernestine's apron. Yes, ça commence, ma chere. And I feel as I always do that autumn is loveliest of all.[59]

We think of Keats' "Ode to Autumn" when reading the following notation:

> Its autumn. Now Jack brings home from his walks mushrooms and autumn crocuses. Little small girls knock at the door with pears to sell and blue black plums. The hives have been emptied; there's new honey and the stars look almost frosty.[60]

Autumn fully satisfied her sense of wonder: "Lo! it is Autumn. What is the magic of that? It is magic to me."[61]

In "An Indiscreet Journey", she transforms what she sees:

> What beautiful cemeteries we are passing! .... But they are not flowers at all. They are bunches of ribbons tied to the soldiers' graves.[62]

Such determination to overcome despair culminates in "The Fly" (1922). Old Woodifield describes the military cemetery as "a garden"

---

[58] Mansfield, "The Thoughtful Child. In Autumn", in *The Edinburgh Edition of the Collected Works of Katherine Mansfield*, I, 533.

[59] *The Collected Letters of Katherine Mansfield*, IV, 269.

[60] *Ibid.*, 275.

[61] *Letters between Katherine Mansfield and John Middleton Murry*, ed. Cherry A. Hankin, New York: New Amsterdam Books, 1988, 372.

[62] Katherine Mansfield, "An Indiscreet Journey" (1915), in *The Edinburgh Edition of the Collected Works of Katherine Mansfield*, I, 441; in *The Collected Stories*, 619.

with "Nice broad paths".[63] And then the fly makes a desperate effort to survive the boss' "idea".[64] Katherine Mansfield hated writing this story.[65] However she kept her determination until the very end of her life, it seems. After telling her husband she wanted *"to be REAL"*,[66] in December 1922, she wrote: "But this place has taught me so far how unreal I am. It has taken from me one thing after another (the things were never mine) until at this present moment all I know really really is that I am not annihilated and that I hope – more than hope – believe."

This is the radiating power of the "inside voice" to deduce from one's individual energy of being a strong sense of continuity, "years before I was born even", creating a sense of belonging through words and rhythm. Hope and joy may withstand disillusion and pain through a deep-rooted sense of wonder. Those four newly discovered tales bring further evidence of Katherine Mansfield's "very individuality which is at the root of our being" and which is "what matters so poignantly". Thinking of what Kierkegaard called his "ethical choice" in *Either... or...*, we may say that Katherine Mansfield very early went through the same type of awareness, which brings loneliness only apparently since it connects the individual with his own history "years before [he] was born even". It is worth quoting Kierkegaard:

> He now discovers that the self he chooses contains an infinite multiplicity inasmuch as it has a history, a history in which he acknowledges identity with himself. This is history of a different sort, for in this history he stands in relation to other individuals of the race and to the race as a whole, and in this history there is something painful, yet he is only the one he is, with this history. Therefore it needs courage to choose oneself, for just when he seems to be becoming more isolated, he is entering most deeply than ever the roots through which he is linked with the whole.[67]

---

[63] Katherine Mansfield, "The Fly" (1922), in *The Edinburgh Edition of the Collected Works of Katherine Mansfield*, II, 477; in *The Collected Stories*, 414.
[64] *Ibid.*, 479, 417.
[65] To William Gerhardi, 14 June 1922, in *The Collected Letters of Katherine Mansfield*, V, 206. See Chapters 8 and 9 in the present volume.
[66] To J.M. Murry, [26 December 1922], in *ibid.*, 341.
[67] Kierkegaard, *Either... or...*, 518.

With that in mind, we should no longer find it astonishing that earlier works might foreshadow future writings or even future events since they prove to be in keeping with the individual's awareness of himself. The person who has found his centre in himself is consistent throughout and transcends the wanderings in the labyrinth of immediate life. Katherine Mansfield was a reader of Ibsen, who dramatized very strong female characters, such as Hedda Gabler in the eponymous play (1890) or, closer to our author in the title of the play itself, Nora in *A Doll's House* (1879), and Ibsen was an attentive reader of Kierkegaard:

> Oh, I want for one moment to make our undiscovered country leap into the eyes of the old world. It must be mysterious, as though floating – it must take the breath. It must be 'one of those islands' ... I shall tell everything, even of how the laundry basket squeaked at '75' – but all must be told with a sense of mystery, a radiance, an after glow because you, my little sun of it, are set. You have dropped over the dazzling brim of the world. Now I must play my part – –[68]

Thanks to the "private and particular language of the Secret Society" of writers and poets, time past radiates into the future. "Then came the fullness of time", wrote Kierkegaard quoting Paul (*Galatians* 4: 4), in *Fear and Trembling* (1843). "Do you remember? I cried at my music lesson that day – how many years ago!"[69]

---

[68] *The Katherine Mansfield Notebooks*, II, 32.
[69] Katherine Mansfield, "The Wind Blows" (1920), in *The Edinburgh Edition of the Collected Works of Katherine Mansfield*, II, 229; in *The Collected Stories*, 110.

CHAPTER 2

"AH, WHAT IS IT? – THAT I HEARD": THE SENSE OF WONDER IN KATHERINE MANSFIELD'S STORIES AND POEMS

In April 1920, Katherine Mansfield wrote to her husband John Middleton Murry:

> If you knew how full my mind is of Shakespeare! It's a perfect world – his pastoral world. I roam through the forest of Arden & sit on the spiced Indian sands laughing with Titania.[1]

Everybody will have recognized her allusion to *A Midsummer Night's Dream* (II, 1, 124-25):

> And in the spiced Indian air, by night,
> Full often hath she gossip'd by my side.[2]

Katherine Mansfield's pastoral world is an enchanted world, a world of wonder, since, as it used to be in Shakespeare's time, before the "dissociation of sensibility",[3] as T.S. Eliot called it, in the seventeenth century, between man and the world there was a sense of "participation", Lucien Lévy-Bruhl's word for the intimate contact between man and reality, a metaphysical outlook, different from the duality between subject and object required by modern science. From this perspective, we could call Katherine Mansfield's work "transitive", which means that her stories and poems set up a link, or

---

"'Ah, what is it? – that I heard': The Sense of Wonder in Katherine Mansfield's Stories and Poems" was originally written for the 2008 London Conference and published in *Celebrating Katherine Mansfield: A Centenary Volume of Essays*, eds Gerri Kimber and Janet Wilson, Basingstoke: Palgrave Macmillan, 2011, 144-57.
[1] *The Collected Letters of Katherine Mansfield*, III, 282.
[2] William Shakespeare, *A Midsummer Night's Dream* (1595-1596), ed. Harold F. Brooks, London: Routledge, 1993, 35.
[3] T.S. Eliot, "The Metaphysical Poets" (1921), in *Selected Prose*, ed. Frank Kermode, London: Faber, 1984, 64.

even a communion, between the self and the world. The real things –
trees and flowers most often, but also the lamp in "The Doll's House"
– that she uses as images of being, are not emptied of life as sheer
signs or even concepts, but are shown as things of wonder with a life
of their own and an existential radiance due to that transitive quality.
As Claude Vigée writes in *L'art et le démonique* (*Art and the
Demonic*), quoting Goethe and Baudelaire, "the aesthetic expression is
possible only when the subject-object network has taken some new
solid unity, beyond its two original components".[4] The world
therefore is no longer lost to the poet who acknowledges, as
Shakespeare did, the correspondences between man's soul and the
outer reality of the world. The subject cannot be cut off from the
world in which he is rooted and acts. This ethical move creates a new
enchantment and a sense of wonder, based upon a full plenitude of
being, and therefore creating one's own inner world.

A transitive outlook, or the "fullness of time"
To describe this process in Katherine Mansfield's work, we may use
three words: "love", "distance", and "memory". The reality of love
has to be recreated in the mind to become acceptable and full, as she
writes to "dearest Bogey", her husband, in October 1922:

> But then I remember what we really felt there, the blanks, the silences,
> the anguish of continual misunderstanding. Were we positive, eager,
> real – alive? No, we were not. We were a nothingness shot with
> gleams of what might be. But no more.[5]

The process is akin to what Kierkegaard called "repetition", which is
thus defined in *Fear and Trembling*, the book he published in 1843,
the same year as *Repetition* itself:

> For it is great to give up one's wish, but it is greater to keep a firm
> grip on it after having given it up; it is great to lay hold of the eternal,
> but it is greater to stick doggedly to the temporal after having given it
> up. – Then came the fullness of time.[6]

---

[4] Claude Vigée, *L'art et le démonique*, Paris: Flammarion, 1978, 250 (my translation).
[5] *Letters between Katherine Mansfield and John Middleton Murry*, 371.
[6] Søren Kierkegaard, *Fear and Trembling*, eds C. Stephen Evans and Sylvia Walsh,
Cambridge: Cambridge University Press, 2006, 15. See also Introduction in the
present volume, 3. As far as this special passage is concerned, there is a slight

The Danish philosopher quotes *Galatians* (4, 4), referring to the coming of the Messiah, which means that in the process of recreating what has been lost, we reach a new dimension in time, which we could call messianic[7] – an appropriation of time as experienced by the inner soul, by the subject, or the subjective time of creation, *kairos* as opposed to *chronos*. "Only through time is time conquered", T.S. Eliot wrote.[8] In another letter to her husband, in October 1920, Katherine Mansfield wrote: "Looking back at our time in the Villa Pauline when the almond tree was in flower remembering how I saw you come out of the cave in your soft leather boots carrying logs of wood … it is all a dream."[9] In her poem, written in 1916, she speaks of "Our childish happiness".[10]

Both love and memory involve the work of the imagination and this is indeed what Katherine Mansfield describes in "Psychology". The male character, "He", says that everything in his life is indifferent to him except the female character's studio. She is called "She". He remembers the place and can even "touch, very lightly, that marvel of a sleeping boy's head".[11] In this remark, we find a striking combination of distance and closeness, with the reference to the hand touching the symbolic object while seeing it only in the mind's eye. Then the character says: "I love that little boy." What D.W. Winnicott calls "potential", or "transitional" space is created between the two lovers with the "little boy sleeping" as a transitional object, both separating and uniting them. In Katherine Mansfield's writing, this ambivalence is symbolized by the numerous dashes and suspension points she uses. These punctuation marks also have a deeper poetic resonance as the manifestation of the radiating but inarticulate origin of poetry.

---

difference in the translation, which I think is clearer in the edition of the book quoted in this chapter.

[7] See Giorgio Agamben, *Le temps qui reste* (2000), Paris: Rivages Poche, 2004, 125-26.

[8] T.S. Eliot, *Four Quartets* ("Burnt Norton"), in *Collected Poems*, London: Faber, 1974, 192.

[9] *The Collected Letters of Katherine Mansfield*, IV, 65.

[10] Katherine Mansfield, *Poems*, ed. Vincent O'Sullivan, Oxford: Oxford University Press, 1988, 46.

[11] Mansfield, *The Collected Stories*, 114.

In *Stanze*,[12] the Italian philosopher Giorgio Agamben explains that in the Middle Ages love was seen as the labour of the imagination. It was only thought possible to fall in love with an image recreated by memory. Therefore the world of Eros is the world of the imagination since the lover is in love with the image he has formed in his heart. This capacity to dream finds its origin in the vital breath which animates both the whole universe and the individual soul, in perfect unity of being.

Therefore the imagination, made of memory and desire, is ambivalent: it looks back into the past to flourish into the future. The image it creates is an epiphany of this new dimension of time which St Paul refers to as "fullness of time" (as quoted in the title to this section). This is the time as we experience it inside, the subjective time of personal feelings, the time to which we give an outward form through the work of art. The subject converts the destructive time of outer loss into the inner feeling of life passing but being constantly recreated, or renewed, and therefore deeply enjoyed. The enchantment is the awareness of such a full capacity of being, which makes up for the ever-impending threat of death. It is a constant struggle with the negative. At the end of "Psychology", the female character recovers her joy through looking at the violets brought by the "good friend"[13] – some sort of transitional object: "Even the act of breathing was a joy." Knowing about the author's biography (tuberculosis was diagnosed in 1917), we are aware of the full significance of her reference to breathing. It is really the fullness of life, the fullness of time appropriated through the work of creation.

Et in Arcadia ego ...

In Katherine Mansfield's work, the pastoral element keeps all its ambivalence, joy and anguish, life and death and, in her special predicament, breathing and aching. In her Notebooks,[14] she writes, in December 1915, remembering her dead brother, *"Et in Arcadia ego"*, which was the inscription on Poussin's painting (1638-40) *The Shepherds of Arcadia* – a phrase reminiscent of Virgil's Arcadia and meaning that death also dwells in this pastoral setting. Walter Pater, a

---

[12] Giorgio Agamben, *Stanze* (1981), trans. Yves Hersant, Paris: Rivages, 1998, 136-37, and 153.
[13] Mansfield, *The Collected Stories*, 118.
[14] *The Katherine Mansfield Notebooks*, II, 17.

writer Katherine Mansfield admired, placed it as an epigraph to his chapter on Winckelmann in *The Renaissance* (1873). Her brother's death triggered off the process of remembering. In the last lines of the poem dedicated to him, "To L. M. B. (1894-1915)", he becomes a mythic figure partaking of both Jesus and Osiris, and also of Hades:

> By the remembered stream my brother stands
> Waiting for me with berries in his hands ...
> 'These are my body. Sister, take and eat.'[15]

As some sort of Persephone, she is given the food of death in her dream, which she calls "Dead Man's Bread". Her brother calls for resurrection in her imagination, stories and poems. She has to convert the past into the future. Trees and flowers are the emblem of this renewal, which is the wonder. As such, they belong to the literary domain of the marvellous since they give a clear magic glimpse of the ambivalence of life, light and darkness enhancing each other in a fascinating paradoxical contrast – no duality but a strong sense of presence emerging from two significant features: reciprocity and rhythm.

"Ah, Jeanne", she writes to Jeanne Renshaw in 1921, "anyone who says to me 'do you remember' simply has my heart ... I remember everything, and perhaps the great joy of Life to me is playing just that game, going back with someone into the past."[16] The words which I would like to emphasize here are "with someone". This conversion of memory into new food for the future implies sharing with someone in an "I and you" relationship. This is the case in the pear tree episode in the *Notebooks*.[17] The ambivalence of the imagination is stressed by the alternation of the couple of third person pronouns "He" and "She", Brother and Sister (the third person means both distance and absence), and the subjective, intimate pair, "I" and "you". In this recollection, in October 1915 (her brother died on the seventh of that month), we find the original pattern of her emblem of life and the self (see also Chapter 8): a tree, the full moon, unity of being ("We were like one child"), presence and reciprocity ("I feel that too"), past and future ("Where is it now. Do you think we shall be allowed to sit in it in

---

[15] Mansfield, *Poems*, 54.
[16] *The Collected Letters of Katherine Mansfield*, IV, 294.
[17] *The Katherine Mansfield Notebooks*, II, 14-15.

Heaven."), eternity and the fleeting moment, light and darkness, and this recurrent leave-taking ("Darling goodbye – goodbye – – –") which we find in "The Wind Blows", "Psychology", and which is the subject of "The Canary" – this "sadness" in life.

In "Bliss", we come across the same pear tree "with its wide open blossoms as a symbol of her own life"[18] (see also Chapter 3). It seems to gather in one emblem her inner life, the fire burning in her heart, and her outer appearance as caught in the "cold mirror",[19] her radiance and her sense of expectation: "waiting for something... divine to happen... that she knew must happen... infallibly." The present moment of writing is a critical one – a turning-point between past and future. It culminates in an instant of communion, even delusory: two women, Miss Fulton and Bertha, gaze at the tree in blossom "like the flame of a candle"[20] under "the round silver moon". This moment is a revelation at the junction of the ephemeral and eternity. It is an instant of conversion providing a glimpse of plenitude through the feeling of fullness given by the subject's assertion of her own inner creative powers. It is a mixture of certainty and questioning (Miss Fulton's first name is Pearl, a symbol of perfection and of the Heavenly Jerusalem and, moreover, she has "moonbeam fingers"[21]), a time of full participation in the world. Katherine Mansfield remembers Wordsworth in his famous poem on the daffodils: "And she seemed to see on her eyelids the lovely pear tree ...."[22]

The aloe in "Prelude" is another such emblem. It is a ship of life, riding through space and time, in "bright moonlight",[23] and flowering. Linda feels it is coming towards her mother and herself. The experience is shared. The dream is more real than dull reality: "And I am sure I shall remember it long after I've forgotten all the other things." Memory opens the infinite beyond the circumscribed world of totality. The tree is a figure of the future in the past, a promise of survival in the imagination now – like love – and in recollection, later. Thus gaining life in the character's eyes, it might remind us of what is presented as Hermione's statue recovering life at the end of *The*

---

[18] Mansfield, *The Collected Stories*, 96.
[19] *Ibid.*, 92.
[20] *Ibid.*, 102.
[21] *Ibid.*, 105.
[22] *Ibid.*, 96.
[23] *Ibid.*, 53.

Winter's Tale. The same type of wonder, linked with the enchantment of art, is at work. The aloe is a figure of presence and transience (it is moving fast), but also of permanence through the capacity of the mind to remain attentive. Its ambivalent feature is conveyed through the rhythm that we find in the three passages referred to. In the *Notebooks*, Katherine Mansfield writes: "He puts his arm round her. They pace up and down."[24] The blossoming pear tree in "Bliss" "quivers".[25] It does not move towards them but stretches up almost "touching" the full moon. In the Notebook memory the moon is also round, therefore full, as in "Prelude".[26] The full moon means wholeness but also impending decay. It represents a moment of perfected experience, a "fullness of time". The past and the future are suspended in reciprocal balance propped by the pulsating rhythm whether iambic or trochaic. The trochaic beat we find in "Prelude" ("Now the oars fell striking quickly, quickly" or "Faster! faster!"[27]) gives an idea of the struggle between the positive and the negative leading to this surge of ecstatic desire, symbolized by vegetable life, blossoming moreover. In the Notebook episode, the season is autumn, which Katherine Mansfield describes with a Keatsian fullness in her letters (see Chapter 1). In "Bliss", the season is spring. Whether it be spring or autumn, both seasons are seasons of passage, of blossoming or fruiting – which means creation. Moreover the equinox is a balance of night and day, light and darkness. "The light and the shadow whisper together", she writes in "A Little Girl's Prayer".[28]

Therefore the vegetable emblem reveals the creative renewal of life in the mind's eye and this is best indicated by the choice of the name Kezia for the author's *alter ego* in the New Zealand stories. Kezia is Job's second daughter once he has recovered all he has lost – Job, the "man who holds a trump car such as a thunderstorm in his hand",[29] is the model for Kierkegaard's repetition (see Chapter 3). And Kezia is also the Hebrew name of an aromatic plant, some sort of cinnamon. Flowers, plants, and trees are emblems of the soul's creative power – the unknown, invisible world of life and death made flesh, as Leslie,

---

[24] *The Katherine Mansfield's Notebooks*, II, 14-15.
[25] Mansfield, *The Collected Stories*, 102.
[26] *Ibid.*, 52.
[27] *Ibid.*, 53
[28] Mansfield, *Poems*, 73.
[29] Kierkegaard, *Repetition*, in *Fear and Trembling, Repetition*, 216.

appearing in her sister's dream, invited her to grasp: "These are my body. Sister, take and eat."[30] Vegetable life is subjected to the rhythm of life and death. So is the moon, waxing and waning. In each case, Katherine Mansfield chooses the moment when life is suspended between generous splendour and impending decay.

If I shut my eyes I can see this place down to every detail – every detail ...

Through the image of the ship and the rhythm of the oars, an epic view of life is brought in. The marvellous is a distinctive feature of the epic, the Christian epic notably, in which magic is linked with otherness and a glimpse of the *unheimlich*. The ambivalent aspect of awe and ecstasy, loss and adventure, transience and comfort, is suggested in the finest way in one of Katherine Mansfield's best stories, "The Wind Blows". The wind is the symbol of the oscillating rhythm of life and death, with the *leitmotiv* throughout, iambic, "The wind, the wind",[31] and the dash that comes in-between in the second occurrence of the motif. Dashes or suspension points are used by Katherine Mansfield to disclose a break in the continuity of conscious thought. They reveal the sudden presence of some mysterious depth.

The girl, a third person, wakes up with a sense of doom: "Something dreadful has happened."[32] The impression remains vague ("Something"); the present-perfect is used. In the very first sentence, the adverb "dreadfully" – a recurrent word, and notion, in Katherine Mansfield's whole work – appears between two dashes: "Suddenly – dreadfully – she wakes up." A moment of crisis thus opens: she wakes up to a new awareness of the human plight – transience, the ephemeral, as symbolized by the violent wind but also made up for by the rhythm of music and the comfort that surrounds the piano teacher's character: "But Mr. Bullen's drawing-room is as quiet as a cave." "But" opposes the day's turmoil and its suspension in the rhythmical balance of music, as suggested by the comparison "as quiet as". The word "cave" opens a natural, mythic world. We may think of the Sibyl's cave and her oracular words and also of a Romantic setting for a Lorelei figure in the tradition of the Sublime. With Rubinstein and the description of "Solitude", we are placed in a post-Romantic

---

[30] Mansfield, *Poems*, 54.
[31] Mansfield, *The Collected Stories*, 109.
[32] *Ibid.*, 106.

world. The painting itself in its subject and description recalls the pre-Raphaelite imagination. We may think of Dante Gabriel Rossetti's portraits of women with white faces and very long hair. More precisely, it might be Frederic Leighton's *Solitude*, a work which this famous Victorian painter, close to the Pre-Raphaelites, painted in 1890. On a dark background the woman, sitting and thoughtful, is "draped in white".[33] For the young girl, life is "revolting, simply revolting",[34] but music is comforting:

> 'Life is so dreadful,' she murmurs, but she does not feel it's dreadful at all. He says something about 'waiting' and 'marking time' and 'that rare thing, a woman,' but she does not hear. It is so comfortable... for ever...[35]

The verbs "waiting" and "marking time" express the author's concern: music, or poetic rhythm, is time controlled even if it is not vanquished. It is time made art, and therefore appropriated. "The wind – the wind!": the dreadful element becomes rhythm itself, which leads to the epiphany of the future in the past made present through writing.

> *They* are on board leaning over the rail arm in arm.
> '... Who are they?'
> '... Brother and sister.'[36]

The use of the third person, in italics, is significant since it reveals the slow estrangement of the self through time, already suggested in the echo: "The wind – the wind!": "Ah, they know those two in the glass. Good-bye, dears; we shall be back soon."[37] The looking-glass, revealing the outer appearance of the characters, reveals the distance: "*those* two." And the passing of time widens the gap: "They can't see those two anymore."[38] The rhythm is iambic again: "Goodbye, goodbye." In the centre, sheltered, the childhood place is to be found, in the opposite rhythm, trochaic: "Goodbye, little island, goodbye."

---

[33] I owe this reference to one of my graduate students who found it as we were translating this short story in December 2013.
[34] *Ibid.*, 107.
[35] *Ibid.*, 109.
[36] *Ibid.*, 110 (Katherine Mansfield's emphasis).
[37] *Ibid.*, 109.
[38] *Ibid.*, 110.

The little island then is a place comparable to Mr. Bullen's cave. "Do you remember?" "Don't' forget." The process of memory is a process of creation, of *re*-creation, which makes the individual real, and this is the enchantment, the magic. The dialectics is existential. "Only through time is time conquered."[39] The present becomes the past that had been the future. Writing is a process of repetition, close to what Frances Yates called "the art of memory",[40] showing it is an attempt at arranging figures in a place, the theatre, through a rhythmical pattern of images – rhythmical in the broad sense of the word, not only the pulsation of sounds but also the syntax and the choice of words: rhythm as the resonance of being. The soul is made real through the tale. This is the wonder. "I want to be real", Katherine Mansfield wrote in 1922.[41] Memory is connected with repetition not only in "The Wind Blows" but also in "Psychology": "If I shut my eyes I can see this place down to every detail – every detail ...."[42] The male character describes a place with several things and especially the figure of the sleeping boy. And it is to be noted that memory individualizes "every detail". Through memory, the individual grasps his own moment – his own place – in time. In the same way, in "The Doll's House", the lamp is real.[43] And the reality is defined in this manner:

> They [the dolls] didn't look as though they belonged. But the lamp was perfect. It seemed to smile at Kezia, to say, 'I live here.' The lamp was real.

Being real therefore means creating oneself a place in time: the garden with the pear tree and the garden seat, near to heaven, the pear tree reaching for the full moon; the aloe transformed into a ship through an epic dream; Mr Bullen's drawing-room as a "cave"; the soul itself as a store of images and figures, the oracular soul converting the past into the future and *vice versa*.

The doll's house is such a place, endowed with an utmost energy of being:

---

[39] Eliot, "Burnt Norton", in *Collected Poems*, 192.
[40] Frances Yates, *The Art of Memory* (1966), London: Pimlico, 2000.
[41] *Letters between Katherine Mansfield and John Middleton Murry*, 401.
[42] Mansfield, *The Collected Stories*, 114.
[43] *Ibid.*, 384.

'Oh-oh!' The Burnell children sounded as though they were in despair. It was too marvellous; it was too much for them.

And this existential quest for being opens the way to the origins: "Perhaps it is the way God opens houses at the dead of night when He is taking a quiet turn with an angel ...." The present moment is linked with the eternal: "But what Kezia liked more than anything, what she liked frightfully, was the lamp." The lamp is opposed to the rest with a "But". As a flash of the eternal through the present moment, it comes as a paradox. The words connected with the symbol of reality are ambivalent: "frightfully", "despair", "marvellous". They echo "dreadfully", "dreadful", "awful", "eager", "quicker", "do you remember" and "don't forget". The place – the doll's house – has a centre – a point where the positive and the negative have achieved a dialectical, and critical, moment of balance.

Its gift is balance

A reader of Shakespeare and the Romantics, Katherine Mansfield was a Modernist not because she broke with the past but because she aimed at creating herself as an individual, through capturing figures of being in the flow of becoming, which means appropriating time as the inner pulsation of subjective achievement. She was also a reader of Proust, who shared common viewpoints with Bergson. Virginia Woolf also read Proust whose influence is obvious in *Mrs. Dalloway*, and especially in the short story sequence which was at the root of the novel: "... there is nothing to take the place of childhood. A leaf of mint brings it back: or a cup with a blue ring."[44] In the novel, Virginia Woolf aims at creating a centre amidst the elusive multiplicity of life. The party is a metaphor for the novel itself, which brings together this multiplicity without denying it: "... and she felt if only they could be brought together; so she did it. And it was an offering; to combine, to create; but to whom?"[45] Writing is at the same time a creation of the self:

---

[44] Virginia Woolf, *Mrs. Dalloway's Party. The Mrs. Dalloway Reader*, ed. Francine Prose, New York: Harcourt, 2004, 15. For more detailed a comparison between Katherine Mansfield and Virginia Woolf, see Chapter 8.
[45] Virginia Woolf, *Mrs. Dalloway* (1925), London: Penguin, 1996, 135.

> That was herself when some effort, some call on her to be herself, drew the parts together, she alone knew how different, how incompatible and composed so for the world only in one centre, one diamond, one woman who sat in her drawing-room and made a meeting-point, a radiancy no doubt in some dull lives, a refuge for the lonely to come to, perhaps.[46]

Yet this centre is no real "fullness of time" since there is another centre in the novel, an empty tomb, the cenotaph[47] in Whitehall, erected in 1919-1920 as a memorial to the Great War dead. The novel is based upon this duality, which is very different from Katherine Mansfield's ambivalent outlook, and which is symbolized by the diverging fates of Septimus and Clarissa:

> Death was defiance. Death was an attempt to communicate, people feeling the impossibility of reaching the centre which, mystically, evaded them; closeness drew apart; rapture faded; one was alone. There was an embrace in death.[48]

In this duality the marvellous has gone away through its dissociation. The sense of wonder is defeated. The subject himself is defeated in his enchanted act of creation:

> She had escaped. But that young man had killed himself.
> Somehow it was her disaster – her disgrace. It was her punishment to see sink and disappear here a man, there a woman, in this profound darkness, and she forced to stand here in her evening dress. She had schemed; she had pilfered. She was never wholly admirable.[49]

Clarissa's happiness, her success, includes sacrifice, the other's tragedy, which is what Katherine Mansfield had imagined as a consequence of her own death in "Et après", a poem written in December 1919:

> He retired
> And to the world's surprise
> Wrote those inspired, passion-fired

---

[46] *Ibid.*, 42.
[47] *Ibid.*, 57.
[48] *Ibid.*, 202.
[49] *Ibid.*, 203.

Poems of Sacrifice![50]

Sacrifice should be considered as an aesthetic view of life's drama – or at least as an interpretation of it from outside, dualistic therefore: a subject-object relationship, made of no communion but only distance, and even estrangement. Katherine Mansfield could have interpreted her brother's death as sacrifice but she never did so since death did not break the reciprocal quality of their relationship: "'These are my body. Sister, take and eat.'"[51] This is communion from subject to subject – participation therefore, and no dissociation between subject and object. With Clarissa Dalloway, the feeling of guilt tips the scales against the achievement of plenitude. Rezia's roses "were almost dead already"[52] and they "had been picked by him in the fields of Greece". From *Kezia* to *Rezia*, short for Lucrezia, the raped wife who killed herself to save her honour, something has been lost, some gift of balance, or ambivalence. Here comes to mind what Vincent O'Sullivan wrote at the beginning of his story, "Professional", describing this "gift of balance" which is writing: "It is carrying across a room a glass with the water not only to the brim, but a little above the brim, while everyone expects it to spill."[53] "Fear not, fear not", Virginia Woolf repeats throughout her novel, quoting Shakespeare's *Cymbeline*:

> Fear no more the heat o' the sun
> Nor the furious winter's rages.[54]

But throughout she dissociates the fear from the ecstasy, while Katherine Mansfield constantly manages to keep the balance. At the end of "Prelude", the calico cat topples the top of the cream jar which "flew through the air and rolled like a penny in a round on the linoleum – and did not break".[55] Even if for Kezia "it had broken the moment it flew through the air", for the writer of the story, it has not.

---

[50] Mansfield, *Poems*, 78.
[51] *Ibid.*, 54.
[52] *Ibid.*, 103.
[53] Vincent O'Sullivan, "The Professional", in *Palms and Minarets*, Wellington: Victoria University Press, 1992, 111.
[54] William Shakespeare, *Cymbeline* (1610), IV, 2, 259-60, ed. Roger Warren, Oxford: Oxford University Press, 1998, 208.
[55] Mansfield, *The Collected Stories*, 60.

The fullness of the moment has been preserved. The balance has been saved. We find the same witty miracle at the end of "Feuille d'Album": "'Excuse me Mademoiselle, you dropped this.' And he handed her an egg."[56]

The marvellous, in Katherine Mansfield's stories and poems, consists in a conversion of fear into joy. In Virginia Woolf's novel, we find the flowers, the tree of life (the "flowering tree"[57] Rezia has become just before her husband's suicide), but never this gift of yielding to the wonder of experience and becoming – this ecstasy. In the end, terror and ecstasy are vivid in Peter's mind at the thought of Clarissa, and terror comes first. Exile certainly makes a difference. Since it deprives the individual of any lazy habits or usual ties, or limits, it is an incentive to self-development through images borrowed from the outer world, and memories, coinciding with the soul's deepest desires. Exile, uprooting certainties, creates the need for this inner theatre of memory in which the figures of bygone happiness find their eternity through being remembered in their ephemeral moment of being. I think this is Katherine Mansfield's achievement: remembering the past, she does not set it in some sort of idealized eternity. This is certainly why she appeals to critics in Japan or China: she writes about the dialectics of becoming. There is always an opening in her stories and poems: to the lower social classes, as in "The Doll's House" or "The Garden-Party"; to the world, with the presence of the sea in "At the Bay", "The Wind Blows" and her strong feeling of empathy ("I felt *just* like a bird", she writes at the end of "When I Was a bird");[58] to the flow of life's experience; and her own creative soul is the theatre in which the figures of memory are kept alive. The distance of space and memory, through exile, makes the "little island" a closed, circumscribed place comparable to the biblical Creation, the Greek cosmos, or Hardy's Wessex – a stage for the human drama to be acted upon. Virginia Woolf's aim in *Mrs. Dalloway* is similar, without the distance of exile, but converges to a centre, the party, during which death is announced. The novel, abiding by the rules of the three unities, time, space and plot, remains enclosed in the limited world of tragedy, ruled by fate. Fate transcends the individual will. Necessity alienates the soul. In Kierkegaard's terms,

---

[56] *Ibid.*, 166. See Chapter 4 in the present volume.
[57] Woolf, *Mrs. Dalloway*, 163.
[58] Mansfield, *Poems*, 59.

the universal denies the particular. Septimus is the prey to the universal ("I'll give it to you", he cries before jumping out of the window[59]), represented mainly by Bradshaw, whose name recalls what Paul Ricœur,[60] using Nietzsche's phrase, calls "monumental time", that is the time of great historical events transcending individuality. Like Abraham, as described by Kierkegaard in *Fear and Trembling*, Katherine Mansfield goes beyond the universal, the ethical, the tragic. As an individual, she voices the particular and so doing, "stands in an absolute relation to the absolute".[61] Her view of life is not dual. She assumes the ambivalence of feeling and experience and takes in fear and joy in the same movement of wonder, which also means an everlasting re-formulation of the self. The negative becomes the very impulse for rebirth. Plants and flowers embody this ever-renewed surge of life while the sea is the deep breath of life radiating in the outer images of the inner soul:

> Nature spoke.
> 'I am desire' said the sea, 'I crave all, insatiably I long, untiringly I hold.'
> 'I am breath' said the wind. 'I blow over all the waste places of the earth & make them filled with my voice.'[62]

In "A Married Man's Story", the plant is rebirth and means singing:

> Through a big crack in the cement yard a poor-looking plant with dull, reddish flowers had pushed its way. I looked at the dead bird again .... And that is the first time that I remember singing – rather ... listening to a silent voice inside a little cage that was me ....[63]

Something dreadful has happened
Katherine Mansfield's setting is the Creation, that is the stage for the drama of being, not the limited political and social world, as it is for

---

[59] Woolf, *Mrs. Dalloway*, 164.
[60] Paul Ricœur, "Entre le temps mortel et le temps monumental: *Mrs. Dalloway*", in *Temps et récit: 2. La configuration dans le récit de fiction*, Paris: Seuil, 1984, 192-212.
[61] Kierkegaard, *Fear and Trembling*, in *Fear and Trembling, Repetition*, 48.
[62] *The Katherine Mansfield's Notebooks*, I, 224.
[63] Mansfield, *The Collected Stories*, 433.

Virginia Woolf. Participating in the world of things, she sets a network of correspondences which lead her to find her particular voice, or way – to use a word reminiscent of the Tao – her particular rhythm. This is her response to the dark "staring in, spying"[64] she describes in "The Canary", "her last completed story", which Vincent O'Sullivan regards as "an elegiac farewell to a caged bird that is now silent":[65] "When I found him, lying on his back, with his eye dim and his claws wrung, when I realised that never again should I hear my darling sing, something seemed to die in me." At the end of the story, she tells about the awful side of ambivalent wonder: "It is there, deep down, deep down, part of one, like one's breathing. However hard I work and tire myself I have only to stop to know it is there, waiting."[66]We move beyond the tragic through the individual's struggle to be.

Let us now come back to the present-perfect used at the beginning of "The Wind Blows". We may wonder why the future is not used, since in "The Canary" the "sadness" is "waiting". In "Bliss" also, Bertha is "waiting" for something. But in "The Wind Blows", this sense of expectation becomes the experience of the immediate past.

Katherine Mansfield's writing is the work of an individual transcending the ethical, the universal, the tragedy – what is given as our plight and can hardly be altered. Once we are alive, the dreadful thing has already happened, and it is bound to spill, or break. "There are more things in heaven and earth, Horatio, / Than are dreamt of in our philosophy", says Hamlet, in keeping with *Ecclesiastes* (VIII, 17) to his bosom friend who will keep in the end the memory of his "wounded name".[67] What we cannot control, or master, is the origin of art, the source of creation, overcoming anguish. Hence the dashes and suspension points we find throughout her work. Kierkegaard states, in *The Sickness Unto Death*: "This then is the formula which describes the state of the self when despair is completely eradicated: in relating

---

[64] *Ibid.*, 421.
[65] Vincent O'Sullivan, "Katherine Mansfield's Canary, a 'wounded bird'", *Temporel* 2: http://temporel.fr.
[66] Mansfield, *The Collected Stories*, 422.
[67] William Shakespeare, *Hamlet* (1600), I, 5, 174-75 and V, 2, 297, ed. G.R. Hibbard, Oxford: Oxford University Press, 1998, 195 and 352.

to itself and in wanting to be itself, the self is grounded transparently in the power that established it."[68]

And this is the paradox – there is no justification for the individual's particular choice: "But the one who gives up the universal in order to grasp something still higher that is not the universal, what does he do?"[69] This is exactly Katherine Mansfield's question at the end of "The Canary": "Ah, what is it? – that I heard."[70] This is essential for a poet to acknowledge this sphere of unknowing, which is infinite and makes creation possible. "The Fly" ends with what seems to be the same type of questioning but should actually be construed differently, as a void, Virginia Woolf's empty centre, only death through sacrifice remaining in utter dereliction (see Chapter 8): "What was it? It was… ."[71]

The individual goes beyond the limits of knowledge and opens the infinite. There is no empty centre therefore but profusion, abundance, a fountain of being in the breath of life. In "The Wounded Bird", the poem that should be read at the same time as "The Canary", she prays: "O my wings – lift me – lift me / I am not so dreadfully hurt …."[72] Her whole poetics is summed up in these words taken from "Vignette – 'I look out through the window'":

> The music, too is strangely restless … it is seeking something … perhaps this mystic, green plant, so faintly touched with colour ….
> …. I dream …. And there is no plant, no music – only a restless, mysterious seeking a stretching upwards to the light – and outwards – a dream like movement.
> What is it?[73]

Her whole work answers this question and puts it again at the same time. This is the wonder – time being thus renewed in a world of proclaimed subjectivity, in a transitive mind transcending the terror of otherness, a labour of love in spite of all the distance, of all the solitude.

---

[68] Søren Kierkegaard, *The Sickness Unto Death* (1849), trans. and ed. Alastair Hannay, London: Penguin, 2004, 44.
[69] Kierkegaard, *Fear and Trembling*, in *Fear and Trembling, Repetition*, 53.
[70] Mansfield, *The Collected Stories*, 422.
[71] *Ibid.*, 418.
[72] Mansfield, *Poems*, 82.
[73] *Ibid.*, 25.

CHAPTER 3

"AND GOD SAW THAT IT WAS GOOD":
KATHERINE MANSFIELD AND THE BIBLE

In her Notebooks, at the end of 1915, Katherine Mansfield wrote:

> Since I came here I have been very interested in the Bible. I have read
> the Bible for hours on end & I began to do so with just the same desire
> – I wanted to know if Lot followed close on Noah or something like
> that. But I feel so bitterly I should have known facts like this: they
> ought to be part of my breathing.[1]

Katherine Mansfield's reputation as a Modernist may blur the fact that
the Bible is a constant reference in her work. It remains unobtrusive;
the hints are scattered and, unlike D.H. Lawrence, she does not feel
she is a prophet. Yet her reading of the Bible, which partakes of what I
call the "spirit of the narrative", belongs to her strong sense of
continuity and wonder. I wish to point out the various allusions and to
consider what they add to the various stories and poems.

The centre of consciousness
The first significant element, which sets the author's outlook, is the
choice of the name Kezia for her *alter ego* in her childhood stories in
which she endeavoured to "renew"[2] all the figures of time past, in a
way which recalls Proust's endeavour[3] in *In Search of Lost Time*. As
indicated in Chapter 1, the name is taken from the Book of Job:

> He had also seven sons and three daughters. And he called the name
> of the first, Jemi'-ma; and the name of the second, Kezia; and the
> name of the third, Ker'-en-hap'-puch. And in all the land were no

---

[1] *The Katherine Mansfield Notebooks*, II, 30.
[2] "I long to renew them in writing" (*ibid.*, 32). See Chapter 1.
[3] See Chapter 4.

women found so fair as the daughters of Job; and their father gave them inheritance among their brethren.[4]

The *Jewish Study Bible* comments on these names:

> *Jemimah*, usually explained by Arabic "yumayma", "little dove". *Keziah*, usually explained as the aromatic plant cassia mentioned in Ps. 45.9. *Keren-happuch*, "a flask of blue eyeshadow", mentioned also in Jer. 4.30. The ending of the book should not be construed as a reward for Job, but simply as the end of the test begun in ch 1 and Job's restoration to his status quo ante.[5]

Psalm 45 is a love song, "commemorating a royal wedding. It mentions the name of neither king nor queen, and thus could be reused for other royal weddings".[6] Moreover, through its superscription, it is linked to the Song of Songs – "For the leader, on *shoshannim*" (45, 1): "*Shoshannim* (lilies?) predominate in the Song of Songs, and are seen as erotic (e.g. Song 5, 13); this connects to the attribute *A Love song*." The commentators insist on the fact that this Psalm is unique. Verse 9 gives a description of the "pomp and ceremonies of the wedding":[7]

> All your robes [are fragrant] with
> myrrh and aloes and cassia;
> from ivoried palaces
> lutes entertain you. (45, 9)

A reader of Katherine Mansfield's "Prelude" will notice that "cassia", linked with the name Kezia, is mentioned just after the "aloes", "The Aloe" being the story's first title.

The lilies are to be found in the Song of Songs (5, 13):

> His cheeks are like beds of spices,
> Banks of perfume
> His lips are like lilies;

---

[4] The Book of Job, 42, 13-15 (the Authorized King James Version).
[5] *The Jewish Study Bible* (1985), eds Adele Berlin and Marc Zvi Brettler, Oxford and New York: Oxford University Press, 1999, 1562.
[6] *Ibid.*, 1332.
[7] *Ibid.*, 1332-33. The translation is slightly different in the Authorized Version (45, 8): "All thy garments *smell* of myrrh, and aloes, *and* cassia, out of the ivory palaces, whereby they have made thee glad."

They drip flowing myrrh.[8]

We find the lily in Keats' *La Belle Dame Sans Merci* in Stanza 3:

> I see a lily on thy brow,
>   With anguish moist and fever dew;
> And on thy cheeks a fading rose
>   Fast withereth too.[9]

Keats, whom Katherine Mansfield was familiar with, dramatizes the disenchanted knight's viewpoint while all the biblical passages insist on the renewal of life and its sensual joy. We should add that there is an allusive hint at *The Song of Songs* in Katherine Mansfield "Psychology": "... not did she enter his [city] like a queen walking soft on petals."[10]

    We know that Kierkegaard interprets Job's fate as an instance of "repetition", which does not mean imitation of what used to be but renewal: "Job is blessed and has received everything *double*."[11] The Danish philosopher refers to Job 42, 10: "The Lord restored Job's fortunes when he prayed on behalf of his friends, and the Lord gave Job twice as he had before."[12] He insists on the power of the mind facing life's disasters, saying that Job "holds a trump card such as a thunderstorm in his hand".[13] Job, like the poet, is able to restore life through his own spiritual power. To do so, the individual has to feel in himself a radiating centre: "And the sunbeams that she had swallowed grew so big that when she started laughing they flew out – all except one, and filled the whole house."[14] Kezia provides this energy. She wants the integrity of reality to be restored. In "Prelude", first of all, she cries "Put head back! Put head back!"[15] after Pat has beheaded the

---

[8] *Ibid.*, 1573.
[9] John Keats, "La Belle Dame Sans Merci: A Ballad" (1820), in *Poetical Works*, ed. H.W. Garrod, London Oxford New York: Oxford University Press, 1976, 350.
[10] Mansfield, "Psychology", in *The Edinburgh Edition of the Collected Works of Katherine Mansfield*, II, 194; in *The Collected Stories*, 112.
[11] Kierkegaard, *Repetition*, in *Fear and Trembling, Repetition*, 212.
[12] *The Jewish Study Bible* (1985), 1562.
[13] Kierkegaard, *Repetition*, in *Fear and Trembling, Repetition*, 216.
[14] Mansfield, "The Thoughtful Child", in *The Edinburgh Edition of the Collected Works of Katherine Mansfield*, I, 127. See Chapter 1.
[15] Katherine Mansfield, "Prelude", in *The Edinburgh Edition of the Collected Works of Katherine Mansfield*, II, 82; in *The Collected Stories*, 46.

duck. Then, as we have seen, at the end of the story, the cream jar "flew through the air" but "did not break",[16] which means that something has been preserved in spite of all hindrances. Moreover Kezia is aware of the puzzling ambivalence of life; she hates "rushing animals like dogs and parrots"[17] especially when "while they are rushing, their heads swell e-enormous". Linda, her mother, echoes that sort of uneasy wonder when she feels that things are coming alive and "swell out with some mysterious important content"[18] (see Chapter 5). Through the power of vision, the rush takes an epic value: the aloe becomes "a ship with the lifted oars and the budding mast":[19] "Ah, she heard herself cry: 'Faster! Faster!' to those who were rowing." Such epiphany betrays that she "holds a trump card such as a thunderstorm" in her mind: "And I am sure I shall remember it long after I've forgotten all the other things."

Katherine Mansfield does not only remember and tell the immediate details of her past life but she raises them to the existential radiation of the epic. She goes beyond the flat account of immediacy to create a significant instant, a "moment of being", to use Virginia Woolf's phrase: "How much more real this dream was than they should go back to the house ...." With such existential accuracy, a writer resumes and renews the spirit of the narrative.

Other biblical references

Katherine Mansfield's stories are strewn with biblical references which provide a sense of continuity[20] as far as the spirit of the tale is concerned. We have mentioned (on page 7) the reference to Genesis 4, 9 : "*Am* I my brother's keeper?" in the title of the 1909 story, "His Sister's Keeper". In "Psychology" (1920), the female character thinks of the Book of Genesis while giving some cake to her boy friend:

> 'Do realize how good it is,' she implored. 'Eat it imaginatively. Roll your eyes if you can and taste in on the breath. It's not a sandwich from the hatter's bag – it's the kind of cake that might have

---

[16] *Ibid.*, 92; 60.
[17] *Ibid.*, 61; 17. See Chapter 5.
[18] *Ibid.*, 68; 27.
[19] *Ibid.*, 87; 53.
[20] See Chapter 1.

been mentioned in the Book of Genesis .... And God said: "Let there be cake. And there was cake. And God saw that it was good.""[21]

She wants the moment to be suffused with a genuine sense of being and relished as such, with the utmost reflexive consciousness. Such awareness of naked life provides a renewal of intensity and can only occur within the "I and Thou" relationship, which is at the same time, as the Song of Songs suggests, a relation with the beloved and a relation to God as the permanent inner interlocutor. In a letter to Garnet Trowell, she wrote, in October 1908: " ... since you have held and dominated my life, I feel the last veil between me and the heart of things has been swept away –."[22] Then on the 8 November 1908, she asserted: "I like always to have a great grip of Life, so that I intensify the so-called – so that truly everything is significant."[23] Such moments of intensity are new beginnings, and it is not a question of believing in God or not, but the feeling of reaching back to the origins goes with the awakening of the reflexive consciousness. One may have a feeling of sudden illumination.[24]

In "Something Childish But Very Natural" (1914), a title borrowed from S.T. Coleridge,[25] Katherine Mansfield describes two very young lovers' paradise with a suggestion of the loss of Eden through yielding to desire, at the end. The girl's name in Edna:

> She did not seem to move and yet she was leaning against Henry's shoulder; he put his arm round her – 'Are all those trees down there – apple?' she asked in a shaky voice.

---

[21] Mansfield, "Psychology", in *The Edinburgh Edition of the Collected Works of Katherine Mansfield*, II, 194; in *The Collected Stories*, 113. See also Chapter 12.
[22] To Garnet Trowell, [16 October 1908], in *The Collected Letters of Katherine Mansfield*, I, 72-73.
[23] To Garnet Trowell, [8 November 1908], in *ibid.*, 88.
[24] See Robert Misrahi, *Construction d'un château* (1981), Paris: Entrelacs, 2006, 19-20.
[25] S.T. Coleridge, "Something Childish, but Very Natural" (1799), in *Poems*, ed. John Beer, London: Everyman's Library, 1974, 226. See *The Edinburgh Edition of the Collected Works of Katherine Mansfield*, I, 388, n. 1. This poem by Coleridge also provides a source for a poem by Katherine Mansfield, "When I was a Bird" (Mansfield, *Poems*, 59). The two poets wish they were birds but it is not so easy for them or for their relatives to suspend disbelief. The same wish is expressed by Christina Rossetti in "A Wish" (1862), which starts with: "I wish I were a little bird" (Christina Rossetti, *Selected Poems*, ed. C.H. Sisson, Manchester: Carcanet, 1984, 48).

'No, darling,' said Henry. 'Some of them are full of angles and some of them are full of sugar almonds – but evening light is awfully deceptive.' She sighed. 'Henry – we mustn't stay here any longer.'[26]

Snakes appear at the end of the tale:

There's a funny present! thought Henry, staring at it. 'Perhaps it's only a make-believe one, and it's got one of those snakes inside it that fly up at you.' He laughed gently in the dream and opened it very carefully. 'It's just a folded paper.' he took it out and spread it open.

The garden became full of shadows – they span a web of darkness over the cottage and the trees and Henry and the telegram. But Henry did not move.[27]

We come across a Noah's Ark in "Marriage à la Mode" but it is missing since the house of the "new Isabel"[28] is filled with a parody of Bohemian poets and artists:

William sat down in one of the arm-chairs. Nowadays, when one felt with one hand down the sides, it wasn't to come upon a sheep with three legs or a cow that had lost one horn, or a very fat dove out of the Noah's Ark. One fished yet another little paper-covered book of smudged-looking poems ....[29]

The Noah's Ark then is the symbol of happy childhood and its sense of joy and wonder as it is in Dorothy Richardson's *Interim*:

Miriam grimaced briskly in her direction.
'Did you have a Noah's *ark*,' she asked, smiling at the fire.
'Yes; Florrie had one. Uncle George gave it to her.'
They began describing.
'Didn't you love it?' broke in Miriam presently. 'Do you remember –' and she recalled the Noah's ark as it had looked on the nursery floor, the offended stillness of the rescued family, the look of

---

[26] Katherine Mansfield, "Something Childish But Very Natural" (1914), in *The Edinburgh Edition of the Collected Works of Katherine Mansfield*, I, 386. See also Chapter 10.
[27] *Ibid.*, 388.
[28] Mansfield, "Marriage à la Mode" (1921), in *The Edinburgh Edition of the Collected Works of Katherine Mansfield*, II, 330; in *The Collected Stories*, 309. See also Chapter 5.
[29] *Ibid.*, 334-35; 316.

the elephants and giraffes and the green and yellow grasshoppers and
the red lady-bird, all standing about alive amongst the little stiff bright
green trees.[30]

We find "fields girt with Noah's Ark trees"[31] in *Notebook 8* when
Katherine Mansfield describes her trip to Paris in 1908. With her and
with Dorothy Richardson the Noah's Ark traces back to the wonders
of childhood.

If that original feeling of genuineness is betrayed with no possible
imaginative counterpart – as she manages to create in "Bliss", for
instance – the meaning of life is spoilt: "He folded his arms against
the dull, persistent gnawing, and began in his mind to write a letter to
Isabel."[32] In "The Doves' Nest", the sanctimonious Miss Anderson is
being derided:

> And then, when they had come all this way and taken the Villa Martin
> and moved in, she had turned out to be a Roman Catholic. Half her
> time, more than half, was spent wearing out the knees of her skirts in
> cold churches. It was really too ...[33]

A few lines later, the very soft atmosphere of the dove's language is
threatened by the memory of death and mourning. Katherine
Mansfield suggests the discrepancy between cool sheltering language
and existential truth through an unobtrusive hint at the Book of
Daniel: "At that Mother raised her head and gave him one of her still,
bright, exalted glances that Milly knew so well. 'I'm not in the least
hurt,' she said, as one might say it from the midst of the fiery
furnace."[34] The biblical allusion adds to the tale's humour and power
(see also Chapter 6). Here is the biblical verse: "... but if you worship
not, ye shall be cast the same hour into the midst of a burning fiery
furnace; and who *is* that God who shall deliver you out of my
hands?"[35]

---

[30] Dorothy Richardson, *Interim* (1919), in *Pilgrimage 2*, London: Virago Press, 1992,
298.
[31] *The Katherine Mansfield Notebooks*, I, 212.
[32] Mansfield, "Marriage à la Mode" (1921), in *The Edinburgh Edition of the Collected
Works of Katherine Mansfield*, II, 336; in *The Collected Stories*, 318.
[33] Katherine Mansfield, "The Doves' Nest" (1922), in *ibid.*, 449; 439. On this story
see also Chapter 5.
[34] *Ibid.*, 450; 440.
[35] The Book of Daniel, 3, 15 (the Authorized King James Version).

The story in which the biblical references are most significant is "An Indiscreet Journey",[36] in which the metaphor of the Flight into Egypt, very unobtrusively delineated, is spun for the reader to understand that Katherine Mansfield thinks of the war as a Massacre of the Innocents (see Chapter 10). In the same story, she also refers to the end of time:

> And years passed. Perhaps the war is long since over – there is no village outside at all – the streets are quiet under the grass. I have an idea this is the sort of thing one will do on the very last day of all – sit in an empty café and listen to a clock ticking until –.[37]

This feeling of an impending disaster, often connected with the wind blowing and storm raging, is recurrent in her work.

Revelations

One of Katherine Mansfield's stories bears the title, "Revelations" (1920):

> The nickel taps and jets and sprays looked somehow almost malignant. The wind rattled the window-frame; a piece of iron banged, and the young man went on changing the tongs, crouching over her. Oh, how terrifying Life was, thought Monica. How dreadful. It is the loneliness which is so appalling. We whirl along like leaves, and nobody knows – nobody cares where we fall, in what black river we float away. The tugging feeling seemed to rise in her throat. It ached, ached; she longed to cry.[38]

This sense of doom is evinced through the frequent use of such adjectives as "awful", "dreadful", "terrible" in the poems and stories. For instance, "The Wind Blows" starts with: "Suddenly – dreadfully – she wakes up. What has happened? Something dreadful has happened."[39] Brother and sister haste to the sea and exile through the storm. The only way of withstanding such violence of hurrying time is

---

[36] See Chapter 10.
[37] Mansfield, "An Indiscreet Journey" (1915), in *The Edinburgh Edition of the Collected Works of Katherine Mansfield*, I, 446; in *The Collected Stories*, 627.
[38] Katherine Mansfield, "Revelations" (1920), in *The Edinburgh Edition of the Collected Works of Katherine Mansfield*, II, 217; in *The Collected Stories*, 195.
[39] Mansfield, "The Wind Blows" (1920), in *ibid.*, 226; 106.

through rhythm, the rhythm of music, the rhythm of words (see Chapter 2). In "The Escape", the male character is threatened by sudden revelation:

> What was happening to him? Something stirred in his breast. Something dark, something unbearable and dreadful pushed in his bosom, and like a great weed it floated, rocked ... it was warm, stifling. He tried to struggle, to tear at it, and at the same moment – all was over.[40]

This sense of doom is connected to her illness then but in "At the Bay", Kezia grows suddenly aware of her own death and that of her grandmother: "This was awful."[41] In 1907, Katherine Mansfield wrote in her Notebook:

> It is the evening of Good Friday; the day of all the year surely the most significant. I always feel the nail prints in my hands, the sickening thirst in my throat, the agony of Jesus. He is surely not dead and surely all whom we love who have died are close to us – Grandmother and Jesus & all of them.
> Oh, lend me your aid – I thirst too. I hang upon the cross. Let me be crucified so that I may cry "it is finished".[42]

This passage shows a high degree of empathy with suffering. Empathy is part of the sense of the "I and You" relationship between people, which also implies continuity. However she refuses all form of parody. When "Mr Farolles, of St. John's"[43] offers "a little Communion" to Josephine and Constantia, the "Daughters of the Late Colonel" are terrified:

> But the idea of a little Communion terrified them. What! In the drawing-room by themselves – with no – no altar or anything! The piano would be much too high, thought Constantia, and Mr Farolles could not possibly lean over it with the chalice.[44]

---

[40] Katherine Mansfield, "The Escape" (1920), in *ibid.*, 221; 202.
[41] Katherine Mansfield, "At the Bay" (1921), in *ibid.*, 358; 227.
[42] *The Katherine Mansfield Notebooks*, I, 162.
[43] Katherine Mansfield, "The Daughters of the Late Colonel" (1920), in *The Edinburgh Edition of the Collected Works of Katherine Mansfield*, II, 269; in *The Collected Stories*, 267.
[44] *Ibid.*, 270; 267-68.

In "The Voyage", Fenella's grandmother bows to fate: "Grandma nodded. 'It was God's will,' said she."[45] Later in the same story, Grandma's prayers are comforting: "At last she was inside, and while she lay there panting, there sounded from above a long, soft whispering, as though someone was gently, gently rustling among tissue paper to find something. It was grandma saying her prayers ...."[46] In the same way, God, revealing the inside of houses "at the dead of night when He is taking a quiet turn with an angel"[47] in "The Doll's House" is reassuring; the revelation of life centring around an object of real perfection, which Kezia "liked *frightfully*" (my emphasis), is a real achievement. In February 1916, she wrote in her Notebook:

> When I am not writing I feel my brother calling me & he is not happy
> .... Wherever I looked there he lay I felt that God showed me to him
> like that for some express purpose & I knelt down by the bed – but I
> could not pray. I had done no work – I was not in an active state of
> grace.[48]

In "Taking the Veil", Edna – tempted into chastity as the character of the same name in "Something Childish, But Very Natural" – dreams of sacrificing her life because she had thought she was not constant in her love for Jimmy. This is a melodramatic parody of revelation:

> At that moment the future was revealed. Edna saw it all. She was
> astonished; it took her breath away at first. But, after all, what could
> be more natural? She would go into a convent .... Her father and
> mother do everything to dissuade her, in vain. As for Jimmy, his state
> of mind hardly bears thinking about. Why can't they understand? How
> can they add to her suffering like this? The world is cruel, terribly
> cruel![49]

---

[45] Katherine Mansfield, "The Voyage" (1921), in *ibid.*, 375; 325.

[46] *Ibid.*, 376-77; 327.

[47] Mansfield, "The Doll's House" (1921), in *ibid.*, 415; 384.

[48] *The Katherine Mansfield Notebooks*, II, 58.

[49] Katherine Mansfield, "Taking the Veil" (1922), in *The Edinburgh Edition of the Collected Works of Katherine Mansfield*, II, 269; in *The Collected Stories*, 410.

In her way of turning the tables on the others, Edna sounds like Anne, the female character in "Mr. and Mrs. Dove" after she has refused to marry Reginald:

> She stamped her foot at Reggie; she was crimson. "How can you be so cruel? I can't let you go until I know for certain that you are just as happy as you were before you asked me to marry you. Surely you must see that, it's so simple."
> But it did not seem at all simple to Reginald. It seemed impossibly difficult.[50]

Just before she had asked him: "Why do you mind so fearfully? Why do you look so awful?" Yet not all revelations are so awful and distressing in Katherine Mansfield's work. When she is "in an active state of grace", which means writing and creating life's existential figures, she achieves epic revelations transcending doom and gloom.

Trees of life

> Then the karaka trees would be hidden. And they were so lovely, with their broad, gleaming leaves, and their clusters of yellow fruit. They were like trees you imagine growing on a desert island, proud, solitary, lifting their leaves and fruits to the sun in a kind of silent splendour.[51]

Flowers also provide revelations of the radiating power of life in its ambivalence. Here are lilies, again:

> There, just inside the door, stood a wide, shallow tray full of pots of pink lilies. No other kind. Nothing but lilies – canna lilies, big pink flowers, wide open, radiant, almost frighteningly alive on bright crimson stems.[52]

The aloe, in "Prelude", is such tree of life, yet not standing still in Eden but launched by Linda's eager mind into life's rush, thus transcended: "Someone living ethically, however, has his mood centralized, he is not inside the mood, he is not the mood itself, he has

---

[50] Katherine Mansfield, "Mr and Mrs Dove" (1921), in *ibid.*, 306; 294.
[51] Katherine Mansfield, "The Garden-Party" (1921), in *ibid.*, 403; 247.
[52] *Ibid.*, 404; 249.

mood and has the mood in him. What he works for is continuity and that is always master over mood."[53] The pear tree in "Bliss" affirms the triumph of life over its parody; it provides the revelation of a centre. Like the lamp, it tells about belonging, about the genuine enjoyment of the fullness of life, enclosed in a personal relationship:

> And the two women stood side by side looking at the slender, flowering tree. Although it was so still it seemed, like the flame of a candle, to stretch up, to point, to quiver in the bright air, to grow taller and taller as they gazed – almost to touch the rim of the round, silver moon.
>
> How long did they stand there? Both, as it were, caught in that circle of unearthly light, understanding each other perfectly, creatures of another world, and wondering what they were to do in this one with all the blissful treasure that burned in their bosoms and dropped, in silver flowers, from their hair and hands?[54]

In spite of the disappointment and treachery, the figure of the tree remains as a token of continuity: "But the pear tree was as lovely as ever and as full of flower and as still."[55]

Katherine Mansfield resorts to biblical motifs as a way of transcending the experience of life through her imagination. "The pursuit of experience is the pursuit of the unimaginative",[56] she wrote in her Notebooks in 1907. So doing, she moves from the immediacy of the present moment and its contingency to the radiating splendour of the instant:

> ... for it is great to give up one's desire, but it is greater to hold fast to it after having given it up; it is great to lay hold of the eternal, but it is greater to hold fast of the temporal after given it up.
>
> Then came the fullness of time.[57]

---

[53] Kierkegaard, *Either... or...*, 528.

[54] Mansfield, "Bliss" (1918), in *The Edinburgh Edition of the Collected Works of Katherine Mansfield*, II, 149; in *The Collected Stories*, 102.

[55] *Ibid.*, 152; 105.

[56] *The Katherine Mansfield Notebooks*, I, 158.

[57] Kierkegaard, *Fear and Trembling*, in *Fear and Trembling, Repetition*, 18.

CHAPTER 4

"AND HE HANDED HER AN EGG": THE ART OF MEMORY IN "FEUILLE D'ALBUM", KATHERINE MANSFIELD AND PROUST

John Middleton Murry's interest in Bergson's philosophy is well-known, and Bergson's influence on Proust has become a commonplace even though its extent may still be discussed. In *Matière et mémoire* (*Matter and Memory*; 1896), the empirical philosopher distinguishes between memory acquired through practice and habit, and involuntary memory, close to the imagination and aroused by the perception we get of things in the present moment, which means recognizing, or associating some immediate perception with the images that used to be given with it.[1] From that conjunction of the past, regained through involuntary memory, and the present moment when the reminiscence is triggered off by perception, Proust deduces a sense of reality that is to him essential. He describes the process in *Le temps retrouvé* (*Time Regained*) which he started writing as early as 1909 and was published after his death, in 1927. It provides a key to the whole of the *Recherche du temps perdu* (*In Search of Lost Time*). The most famous example of that type of access to the essential is provided by the episode of the *madeleine* in *Du côté de chez Swann* (*Swann's Way*; 1913). Our past is concealed is some material object of which we have no idea. Only through sheer chance can we come across it and, if we are lucky enough to do so, the essence of our life is suddenly revealed to us, inside ourselves:

> I put down the cup and examine my own mind. It alone can discover the truth. But how? What an abyss of uncertainty, whenever the mind feels overtaken by itself; when it, the seeker, is at the same time the

"'And He Handed Her an Egg': The Art of Memory in 'Feuille d'Album', Katherine Mansfield and Proust" was published in *Katherine Mansfield Studies*, *The Journal of the Katherine Mansfield Society*, I (2009), Edinburgh: Edinburgh University Press, 35-53.
[1] Henri Bergson, *Matière et mémoire* (1896), Paris: P.U.F. Quadrige, 1982, 97.

dark region through which it must go seeking and where all its equipment will avail it nothing. Seek? More than that: create. It is face to face with something which does not yet exist, which it alone can make actual, which it alone can bring into the light of day.[2]

The last lines of this famous passage sound familiar to a reader of Kierkegaard, who defines the ethical choice: "The choice here makes two dialectical movements at once: what is chosen does not exist and comes into existence through the choice, and what is chosen exists, otherwise it would not be a choice." Moreover I have previously stressed the fact that the ethical man "now discovers that the self he chooses contains an infinite multiplicity inasmuch as it has a history".[3] The ethical choice implies that the individual is now settled within the time of becoming. Such new awareness transcends the immediacy of space and widens the present moment which becomes a moment of being through the dialectical interference of past and future. The mind's energy gives it its rhythmical shape through imagination and memory.

Katherine Mansfield and Proust

Katherine Mansfield's enthusiasm about Proust is also familiar. In a letter to J.M. Murry (1 December 1920), he is "the greatest living writer".[4] Murry and herself "lived Proust, breathed him, talked and thought of little else for two weeks"[5] in Switzerland. She calls him "fascinating" in a letter to Ottoline Morrell in December 1921.[6] Writing to Sidney Schiff in January 1922, she refers to a precise passage in Proust's *Sodome et Gomorrhe* (*Sodom and Gomorrah*; 1922): "Its just exactly the reverse of the exquisite rapture one feels in for instance that passage which ends a chapter where Proust describes the flowering apple trees in the spring rain."[7]

---

[2] Marcel Proust, *In Search of Lost Time: I. Swann's Way* (1913), trans. C.K. Scott Moncrieff and Terence Kilmartin, rev. D.J. Enright, London: Chatto and Windus, 1992, 52.

[3] Søren Kierkegaard, *Either... or...*, 517. See my Introduction, page 2.

[4] *The Collected Letters of Katherine Mansfield*, IV, 130.

[5] "To Sidney Schiff, 3 December 1921", in *ibid.*, 329.

[6] "To Ottoline Morrell", December 1921, in *ibid.*, 344.

[7] *The Collected Letters of Katherine Mansfield*, V, 12.

One recognizes a dynamic image that is central in Katherine Mansfield's work (the aloe in "Prelude", the pear tree in "Bliss", blossoming and opening the future to the individual subject). The end of Chapter 1 of *Sodome et Gomorrhe* II is: "But they [the apple trees] continued flaunting their pink flowering beauty in an icy wind beneath a shower of rain. It was a spring day."[8] The blossoming trees obviously struggle against and withstand destruction.

As Bergson had already shown, remembering means movement since: "Images shall never be anything but things, and thought is movement."[9] In Katherine Mansfield's work, images are never static but always permeated with movement – movement which means time and becoming, as in "The Wind Blows", the most perfect example of a story embodying the experience of time. In Katherine Mansfield's work, the voice wrestles with destructive time in the present moment to assert its creative power and restore the plenitude of being in spite of lost time. In "The Wind Blows", rhythm captures the past in the present moment within the iambic beat of the leitmotiv: "The wind – the wind." We shall see that "Feuille d'Album" is an allegory of writing – a movement to achieve the plenitude of time regained in the present moment, the instant. Withstanding destruction and death *now* is an existential move.

I am not going to stress the similarities with Proust's outlook only in terms of influence since I think that some writers' endeavours to assert the reality of individual life was a characteristic of the period. This move was certainly reinforced by the First World War just because the individual had been so crushed by it. For instance, Katherine Mansfield could not have been influenced by Proust's vivid description of the apple trees standing in the rain, since in 1922 *Bliss* had already been published for two years. Yet we may certainly say that Proust and Mansfield shared a common outlook. Moreover coincidences may occur such as this one: in the first chapter of *Sodome et Gomorrhe* II, the Duke of Châtellerault wants to be taken for an Englishman and keeps saying – in English and with a small *f* :

---

[8] Marcel Proust, *Sodome et Gomorrhe* (1921-1922), Paris: Gallimard Folio, 1972, 208: "Mais ceux-ci [les pommiers] continuaient à dresser leur beauté, fleurie et rose, dans le vent devenu glacial sous l'averse qui tombait: c'était une journée de printemps" (translation by Anthony Rudolf for this book).
[9] Bergson, *Matière et mémoire*, 139 (my translation).

"I do not speak french."[10] But this is only a fortuitous echo of the famous title of one of Katherine Mansfield's stories, "Je Ne Parle Pas Français", in which the main character, Raoul Duquette, was inspired by the figure of the French poet and novelist Francis Carco, Katherine Mansfield's lover in 1915.[11]

Therefore in this chapter I shall try to highlight a few elements that denote a common outlook.

Anonymous duration, tragedy and the miracle
In "Feuille d'Album", written in London in 1917,[12] the first word that strikes us, after the title, on which I shall comment later, and after "He", yet unidentified, is the adjective "impossible": "He really was an impossible person."[13] No doubt, after reading the whole story, we take the word in two senses: "intolerable" in the first part, considering the universal account which is given of the character, with "hopeless" repeated three times as a conclusion to three paragraphs, and "not possible" in the second part, which is more particular and focuses on the present moment, "now", as in "As he watched her he knew more surely than ever he must get to know her, now",[14] after being more precisely situated in time: "One evening".[15] Moreover, that word is linked with the impossible, and witty, ending:

> … he said, almost angrily: 'Excuse me, Mademoiselle, you dropped this.'
> And he handed her an egg.[16]

Presented like that, the end is a miracle, opening two directions in time. The egg, dropped and not broken, gives an example of what Kierkegaard calls "repetition" – the past being retrieved in the present moment ("now") and then opening the future, or the possibility of love here. The present moment therefore is the key moment for making up one's mind – the past suddenly leaping into the future under the

---

[10] Proust, *Sodome et Gomorrhe*, 45.
[11] Katherine Mansfield, "Je Ne Parle Pas Français", in *The Collected Stories*, 60-91.
[12] See Gerri Kimber, *Katherine Mansfield: The View from France*, Bern: Peter Lang, 2008, 236.
[13] Katherine Mansfield, "Feuille d'Album", in *The Collected Stories*, 160.
[14] *Ibid.*, 166.
[15] *Ibid.*, 163.
[16] *Ibid.*, 166.

individual subject's impulse. Memory (the imagination of the past) and the imagination (the memory of the future)[17] both play a definite role in the narrative. In the first part, "He" is the subject of a series of indefinite characters' imagination – "you", "everybody", "someone", which then becomes "she" and "a third". That is the anonymous world of featureless duration, in which everything therefore remains "hopeless". The only hope at that moment is that the main character will be given his name in a sample of friendly conversation. The only character who has a name in the story is the painter, Ian French, whose English name is French – a paradox, quite remarkable in Katherine Mansfield's case.

> "Who is he, my dear? Do you know?"
> "Yes. His name is Ian French. Painter."[18]

The narrator goes on with the enumeration started in the answer: "Someone else decided that he ought to fall in love" follows: "Someone started by giving him a mother's tender care." Although all the characters but the painter remain indefinite, he gets his name in the present moment of talk, between friends presumably. Therefore the individual is at once linked to the present moment. He gets a job too – being a painter, and is described as "Awfully clever" by another anonymous voice: "they say." Then all the most obvious commonplaces concerning man and woman relations are enumerated: "a mother's tender care", "he ought to fall in love" and "What the poor boy really wants is thoroughly rousing".[19] Those trite views belong to the universal, even if any individual can safely repeat them without thinking. He will not find hope in his absence of adequate reflection to the moment.

Considering those various indefinite universal subjects ("someone", "they"), we can speak of a chorus, as in a Greek tragedy, and of the coryphaeus for the voice giving the character a name and a job. The tragic world is the world of the universal, as opposed to the

---

[17] In Chapter Nineteen of *The White Goddess*, Robert Graves insists that that type of ubiquity in time is truly the poet's gift: "A sense of the equivocal nature of time is constantly with poets, rules out hope or anxiety about the future, concentrates interest detachedly in the present" (Robert Graves, *The White Goddess* [1948], London: Faber, 1957, 344).

[18] Mansfield, "Feuille d'Album", in *The Collected Stories*, 161.

[19] *Ibid.*, 162.

individual; moreover it is a world submitted to Necessity, which therefore leaves no room for freedom.

Imagination and memory

Then, the painter becomes the subject of the writer's imagination, following this sentence: "After heaven knows how many more attempts – for the spirit of kindness dies very hard in women – they gave him up."[20] The description of the place where he lives comes after the expression of opposition: "But –" as pronounced by one of those kind women. Therefore the narrator (or the author) sets herself in contrast to the anonymous tragic chorus and tells about the character only once "they" have given him up. The fact that Katherine Mansfield should then tackle the description of his apartment is significant, and distinctive of her art, which is an art of memory, akin to that described by Frances Yates: "This art seeks to memorize through a technique of impressing 'places' and 'images' on memory."[21] Images or figures are set in definite places in the same way as Ian French, who has been given a name, is now seen in his flat.

The place is reminiscent of Francis Carco's apartment in Paris, 13, quai aux Fleurs: "The side window looked across to another house, shabbier still and smaller, and down below there was a flower market." It is the famous flower market situated between the Hôtel-Dieu (a hospital) and the Commercial Court, on the Ile de la Cité. From there, the Ile Saint-Louis can be seen: "The two big windows faced the water; he could see the boats and the barges swinging up and down, and the fringe of an island planted with trees, like a round bouquet." The description of the place is accurate and, when you have lived in Paris some time, rouses memories: "… and where the concierge lives in a glass cage on the ground floor, wrapped up in a filthy shawl, stirring something in a saucepan and ladling out titbits to the swollen old dog lolling on a bead cushion …." Here again, through that accurate detail, the present moment is being dramatized.

The description of the flower market sounds like a quick sketch of the place, with only rough shapes drawn with a pencil:

> You could see the tops of huge umbrellas, with frills of bright flowers escaping from them, booths covered with striped awning where they

---

[20] *Ibid.*, 162.
[21] Yates, *The Art of Memory*, 11.

sold plants in boxes and clumps of wet gleaming palms in terracotta jars. Among the flowers the old women scuttled from side to side like crabs."[22]

The rhythm of the sentences calls up the gesture of the hand, quickly sketching the view and inserting a little humour in the caricature, of the concierge for instance. In both cases, the description is bathed in pleasure and humour. Yet, it is impossible to see the flower market from 13, quai aux Fleurs unless it went beyond the Hôtel-Dieu at that time, which is unlikely. Therefore Katherine Mansfield must have re-arranged the place in her memory to suit her imagination. Life is ambivalent (the place can be seen as romantic at times, remaining unromantic most of the time) but there is no trouble. That is the way it is and you should cope with it, with a little patience: "Really there was no need for him to go out. If he sat at the window until his white beard fell over the sill he still would have found something to draw ...."

The figure of an Indian saintly man is at once called up. The world therefore is at rest and duly protected. There is no doubt an exotic element in this place, repeated in what follows: "An Indian curtain that had a fringe of red leopards marching round it covered his bed by day, and on the wall beside the bed on a level with your eyes when you were lying down there was a small neatly printed notice: GET UP AT ONCE."[23] This painter, who could grow a long white beard, is thus, it is confirmed, a wise man, likely to practise some sort of asceticism – not staying long hours in bed in the morning in spite of the strong temptation to do so. And he is even able to sign solemn promises to himself. Ian French is an ethical individual.

As far as the curtain is concerned, it should be said that Katherine Mansfield often uses such "objective correlatives" as clues to her characters' predicaments. There is an "Indian curtain" in "Floryan nachdenklich", a poem written in 1913: "And the Indian curtain suddenly seems / To stir and shake with a thousand dreams."[24] The imagination and its representations commune with each other so much that the image starts to move under the influence of thought (see Bergson's remark above, on page 53). The same phenomenon occurs in "Prelude":

---

[22] Mansfield, "Feuille d'Album", in *The Collected Stories*, 162-63.
[23] *Ibid.*, 163.
[24] Mansfield, *Poems*, 38.

> In the quiet and under her tracing finger, the poppy seemed to come alive. She could feel the sticky, silky petals, the stem, hairy like a gooseberry skin, the rough leaf and the tight glazed bud. Things had a habit of coming alive like that.[25]

"Like that" recalls the way the statue of Hermione comes alive as Hermione herself at the end of *The Winter's Tale* – such power of art being a wonder. In "Bliss", the "most amusing orange coat with a procession of black monkeys round the hem and up the fronts" sounds satirical at first glance.

In "Feuille d'Album", the leopards do not come alive, fortunately, but recall the primitive rhythm of life – some sort of *élan vital* (Bergson's phrase[26]) – as the "black monkeys" do, with the author's laugh. And indeed those big cats marching round the bed by day have a beautiful effect, simply because they are out of place. Were they not described as "marching", which gives them reality through movement, they would remain decorative, and harmless. "Marching", they are active (and not so harmful after all, but ready to catch the present moment as Ian French desperately does at the end). Thinking of Proust and *Time Regained*, we can say they are "truths written with the aid of shapes".[27] Yet I think we should regard them as allusions rather than symbols. As such they suggest the primeval force of desire and, being out of place, they prepare us for the witty impossible end. As does the wise man with the long white beard.

The reference to the present moment, of waking up, which could be inferred from the description of the notice, is immediately denied at the beginning of the next paragraph: "Every day was much the same."[28] In spite of his name, his wisdom and his place, Ian Painter is still confronted to anonymous duration. He is faced with what Proust called "our inherent powerlessness to realise ourselves in material enjoyment or in effective action".[29] Only the choice in the instant, a

---

[25] Mansfield, "Prelude", in *The Collected Stories*, 27.

[26] Henri Bergson, *L'évolution créatrice* (1907), Paris: P.U.F. Quadrige, 1981, 88-98.

[27] Marcel Proust, *In Search of Lost Time: VI. Time Regained* (1927), trans. Andreas Mayor and Terence Kilmartin, rev. D.J. Enright, London: Chatto and Windus, 1992, 232.

[28] Mansfield, "Feuille d'Album", in *The Collected Stories*, 163.

[29] Proust, *Time Regained*, 231.

conjunction of the past and the future in the present ("now") can lift this dull anonymity. Proust even speaks of "resurrection":[30]

> Always, when these resurrections took place, the distant scene engendered around the common sensation had for a moment grappled, like a wrestler; with the present scene. Always the present scene had come off victorious ....[31]

He also speaks of "renewal" and "paradise lost": "... that purer air which the poets have vainly tried to situate in paradise and which could induce so profound a sensation of renewal only if it had been breathed before, since the true paradises are the paradises we have lost."[32]

Resurrection: to be REAL
Those renewed moments of intensity, Proust experiences them when memory startles him in the present moment through the means of a special object. From that resurrection of the past in the present, he deduces a feeling of reality that could be compared to a new birth. The passage is long but interesting enough in the context to be quoted:

> A moment of the past, did I say? Was it not perhaps very much more: something that, common both to the past and to the present, is much more essential than either of them? So often, in the course of my life, reality had disappointed me because at the instant when my senses perceived it my imagination, which was the only organ that I possessed for the enjoyment of beauty, could not apply itself to it, in virtue of that ineluctable law which ordains that we can only imagine what is absent. And now, suddenly, the effect of this harsh law had been neutralised, temporarily annulled, by a marvellous expedient of nature which had caused a sensation – the noise made both by the spoon and by the hammer, for instance – to be mirrored at one and the same time in the past, so that my imagination was permitted to savour it, and in the present, where the actual shock to my senses of the noise, the touch of the linen napkin, or whatever it might be, had added to the dreams of the imagination the concept of "existence" which they usually lack, and through this subterfuge had made it possible for my being to secure, to isolate, to immobilise – for a moment brief as a

---

[30] On this notion, see "So as Not to Conclude".
[31] Proust, *Time Regained*, 227.
[32] *Ibid.*, 222.

flash of lightning – what normally it never apprehends: a fragment of time in the pure state.

The passage is capital: only at the junction of memory and the imagination can reality be truly experienced, because what is real then is not the outer world itself but the joy it arouses in the individual soul. We could even say that that joy is the substance of the soul. The reality of the past moment thus re-experienced through memory gives the imagination its substance. It is an instance of existential interaction: past and present are dialectically involved in the individual's feeling of true being. Two different moments make one rebirth. There is no duality but dialogue, just as Ian French, through his ethical choice – advising himself to "GET UP AT ONCE" or "not to exceed this amount for next month" and signing the pledge – gives reality to the character faced with the tragic chorus embodying the universal. Here again there is no duality but an instance of existential dialectics. The ethical subject chooses his own rhythm.

Time, in its existential reality, is being experienced as the substance of being:

> ... and immediately the permanent and habitually concealed essence of things is liberated and our true self, which seemed – had perhaps for long years seemed – to be dead but was not altogether dead, is awakened and reanimated as it receives the celestial nourishment that is brought to it. A minute freed from the order of time has re-created in us, to feel it, the man freed from the order of time. And one can understand that this man should have confidence in his joy, even if the simple taste of a madeleine does not seem logically to contain within it the reasons for this joy, one can understand that the word "death" should have no meaning for him; situated outside time, why should he fear the future?[33]

The choice of "now"

Now, at a unique moment of time, "one evening", Ian French's imagination started working. It is springtime – a moment of renewal, and "it had been raining".[34] This new world (renewed by the gift of rain) is transfigured: "... a bright spangle hung on everything, and the

---

[33] *Ibid.*, 223-25.
[34] Mansfield, "Feuille d'Album", in *The Collected Stories*, 163.

air smelled of buds and moist earth."[35] This description leads us far from the city, into the natural element of the origins. We are entering a world of correspondences: "... and suddenly, *as if in answer to his gaze*, two wings of windows opened and a girl came out on to the tiny balcony carrying a pot of daffodils" (my emphasis) The window has "wings" and the imagination can soar. Then the girl is being imagined by the painter. This is the third step in the story: first, the character is the chorus's object, then the author/narrator's; in the end, he becomes active and handles his own story himself, still in the third person however.

Daffodils, with Katherine Mansfield, are connected with Wordsworth and memory. In "Bliss", they suggest intensity of feeling: "How strong the jonquils smelled in the warm room." (Note the word of French origin – a fragrant type of Narcissus.) And then on her eyelids when closing her eyes, Bertha feels she sees "the lovely pear tree with its wide open blossom as a symbol of her own life".[36] In a letter written in 1918, Katherine Mansfield quotes Perdita saying, after mentioning Proserpina, in *The Winter's Tale*: "Daffodils, / That come before the swallow dares, and take / The winds of March with beauty."[37] "Take" here means "affect, enchant". Autolycus had already named the daffodils at the beginning of the previous scene, announcing "the sweet o' the year" (IV, 3, 3). Writing to her husband from Bandol, Katherine Mansfield referred to this phrase: "Once the war is over all our woes are over for ever I think. Then comes in the sweet of the year for you and me."[38] In Perdita's mind, the flowers she enumerates and gives Florizel mean love and renewal of life (IV, 4, 130-32).

It is as if the two youngsters' love, placed under the sign of spring and renewal, heralded Hermione's resurrection in the next Act. The creative power of words is the same as the creative power of love – which reminds us of the Song of Songs.[39] The present moment of writing, like the revelation that memory brings, is resurrection. Therefore, in "Feuille d'Album", the daffodils, through love, open the

---

[35] *Ibid.*, 164.
[36] Mansfield, "Bliss", in *The Collected Stories*, 96.
[37] William Shakespeare, *The Winter's Tale* (1611), IV, 4, 118-20, ed. Stephen Orgel, Oxford: Oxford University Press, 1998, 174.
[38] *The Collected Letters of Katherine Mansfield*, II, 83.
[39] See Mounic, "Le Cantique des Cantiques, parabole de l'amour et du poème", in *L'Esprit du récit ou La chair du devenir: Ethique et création littéraire*, 59-84.

painter's imagination as if it were a new flower: "His heart fell out of the side window of his studio, and down to the balcony of the house opposite – buried itself in the pot of daffodils under the half-opened buds and spears of green ...."[40] Through the spring flowers, the painter enters the girl's life: "That room with the balcony was the sitting-room, and the one next door to it was the kitchen." Again this is an art of memory since the imagination sets the character in a definite place. The metonymy ("His heart") gives it an enchanted touch, reinforced by the leap (Coleridge's word speaking of the imagination): "fell out of the side window." Katherine Mansfield, like Proust, who refers to *The Arabian Nights* in *Time Regained*, betrays a great sense of wonder.

The unexpected and the unknown

In both descriptions of places, the writer's and the painter's, the imagination is at work, starting from small clues. The writer, or narrator, imagines a tidy studio: "How surprised those tender women would have been if they had managed to force the door. For he kept his studio as neat as a pin."[41] Her ironical approach of "those tender women" sets her character against the universal. Imagining Ian French as someone different from the conventional picture of the disorderly artist, she sets him, and herself as well, in a world freed from conventions. Ian French does the same when imagining the young girl, whom he sees first as "a strangely thin girl" before noticing that she does not do what ordinary girls would do: "She never sang or unbraided her hair, or held out her arms to the moon as young girls are supposed to do."[42] We feel the artistic suggestion here, and we may think of paintings by Edgar Degas (*Femme se peignant*) or Suzanne Valadon.

Then the painter, playing the part of a writer, invents the girl's biography, answering his own questions. He has already been introduced as someone relying on writing, with his solemn promises to himself. Now like Pygmalion, he creates his beloved. Therefore his life highly depends on his imagination and the process of writing, which, set in the present moment, is also dialectic – a combination of inspiration coming from the unknown and of judgement, because the

---

[40] Mansfield, "Feuille d'Album", in *The Collected Stories*, 164.
[41] *Ibid.*, 163.
[42] *Ibid.*, 164.

artist addresses someone else and must make himself understood. He situates himself at the junction of the universal and the individual. The artistic act is a grip of the present moment on eternity:

> Now when he sat down at his table he had to make an entirely new set of sworn statements .... Not to go to the side window before a certain hour: signed Ian French. Not to think about her until he had put away his paintings for the day: signed, Ian French.[43]

Through these ethical decisions, he is founding himself as a subject in time, resisting his own passions (and Katherine Mansfield considers him with a gentle irony). He also creates the girl as an *alter ego*: "She was his age, she was – well, just like him." We could say the same of Laura and Laurie in "The Garden-Party" (see "So as Not to Conclude"). And he imagines living with her, in his place, but his talent for reality is limited: "But how could he get to know her? This might go on for years ...." This remark parallels the author's on the long-bearded painter. The image is not enough and Ian French wishes to do what the male character in "Psychology" is unable to do: "They saw themselves as two little grinning puppets jigging away in nothingness."[44] The present moment is spoiled, and it hurts. Duration is empty.

Love, like the work of art, needs seizing the right moment. When the girl appears at the window, she looks as if she were a figure in a painting. When she goes out, the colours outside are unified in one single tint: "There was a lovely pink light over everything."[45] But in himself, again, we find duality: "'Here she comes,' said a voice in his head."[46] He figures out that she belongs to another world, like he does: "Her composure, her seriousness and her loneliness, the very way she walked as though she was eager to be done with this world of grown-ups, all was natural to him and so inevitable." Then he uses the pronoun "we", and some sort of a pursuit of love follows, as in the Song of Songs. He has recognized her through his intuition (the voice) and, when she puts the key into the lock, he hands her the egg, uttering the witty, impossible remark: "You dropped this." The instant

---

[43] Mansfield, "Feuille d'Album", in *The Collected Stories*, 165.
[44] Mansfield, "Psychology", in *The Collected Stories*, 116.
[45] Mansfield, "Feuille d'Album", in *The Collected Stories*, 165.
[46] *Ibid.*, 166.

is highly dramatic: it is a moment of passage from the outside to the inside, with the suggestion that something has been made up for, or mended (the loss of the egg), and even put together again. The impossible has been made real, and tangible, although fragile. This is the quality of the moment of personal decision: though vanishing and gone, it brings plenitude. The egg, moreover, is the innocent, familiar symbol of new birth. In the story, it belongs to everyday life, which makes the suggestion even more forceful. The egg is unity and plenitude made of two connected elements. Leda's egg gives birth to the Dioscuri, who are twins. We can also think of the Chinese *yin-yang*, an oval shape representing the dialectics of the Way – male and female, nothingness and existence, duration and the act of being – which should be involuntary and not come from the intellect, in the same way as Proust's moment of memory and resurrection: unity and duality, unity and multiplicity. The Tao (which means "to say" and also "Way, to go") is a dialectics of becoming with no beginning and no end.

The fullness of time

The egg, as a symbol, is also very commonly linked to the genesis of the world. In Katherine Mansfield's story, the final instant is a key to a new world – different from the "hopeless" anonymous world peopled with vague creatures ("someone", "they"). This new world looks like a children's universe, far from the grown-ups' routine. This is a world of meaningful time, achieved through the instant's opening key and paradox. Like the egg in the end, as it was dropped, it should be broken and wasted but, through personal decision, it is not: "As he watched her, he knew more surely than ever he must get to know her, now."

The work of art acutely reveals the plenitude contained in the instant:

> And this method, which seemed to me the sole method, what was it but the creation of a work of art? Already the consequences came flooding into my mind: first, whether I considered reminiscences of the kind evoked by the noise of the spoon or the taste of the madeleine, or those truths written with the aid of shapes for whose meaning I searched in my brain, where church steeples or wild grass growing in a wall they composed a magical scrawl, complex and elaborate, their essential character was that I was not free to choose

them, that such as they were they were given to me. And I realised that this must be the mark of their authenticity. I had not gone in search of the two uneven paving-stones of the courtyard upon which I had stumbled. But it was precisely the fortuitous and inevitable fashion in which this and the other sensations had been encountered that proved the trueness of the past which they brought back to life, of the images which they released, since we feel, with these sensations, the effort that they make to climb back towards the light, feel in ourselves the joy of rediscovering what is real.[47]

Between memory and the imagination, what is at stake is the feeling that life is real. We know that Katherine Mansfield wrote to her husband, on 26 December 1922, that she wanted "to be REAL",[48] and it is through growing conscious of herself with the help of those "truths written with the aid of shapes" that she gains personal substance and reality. As in "Psychology", the painter is in love with an image: "Often when I am away from here I revisit it in spirit – wander about among your red chairs, stare at the bowl of fruit on the black table – and just touch, very lightly, that marvel of a sleeping boy's head."[49] And it is that image of the "sleeping boy's head" that comes floating on the sea of their silence. Man and woman are both "hopeless" when faced to reality, as Proust said speaking of "our inherent powerlessness to realise ourselves in material enjoyment or in effective action". The image blocks the decision.

Feuille d'Album

It was a belief in the Middle Ages that love was a product of the imagination because you could only fall in love with an image. This leads us now to the title of the story, "Feuille d'Album". We think of a book of photographs, the present moment thus kept through instantaneous shots, but gone otherwise. This is the paradox of the egg. Now, this album could also be a sketchbook, and this would be appropriate for a painter. Sketching is really an act performed "to the moment". It is a decision to keep the instant alive, to perform the impossible. In addition, if, as Proust contends, the moment of revelation (memory and the imagination) is not brought about by any will, to write about it and to keep it safe in words is an act of will. In

---

[47] Proust, *Time Regained*, 232-33.
[48] *The Collected Letters of Katherine Mansfield*, V, 341.
[49] Mansfield, "Psychology", in *The Collected Stories*, 114.

Contre Sainte-Beuve (*Against Sainte-Beuve*), Proust asserts that only the intelligence can decide that the instinct should come first.[50] Writing is a dialectical process, a mixture of involuntary "inspiration" and voluntary decision.

"Feuille" also has different meanings. The word suggests lightness, frailty, and transience, whether it means a sheet of paper (*feuille* de papier) or a leaf on a tree (*feuille* d'arbre). In each case, it is something that can be cut off, or torn off – detached (a short story). It is distinct and separate as is the instant when set off against duration: "If he sat at the window until his white beard fell over the sill he still would have found something to draw …"; "But how could he get to her? This might go on for years …." In each case, the suspension points prolong the effect of extensive duration. And each time, what should be achieved is the present moment of decision: "now" – the egg that should be broken but is kept intact, and full of promises. Achieving the reality of "now", the artist, the poet, the lover, through his own act, achieves his own personal reality, through embracing both the past and the future in the present moment of creation. Proust says it means wrestling between past and present. It is true that creating means wrestling – with the angel?

And it is also the wonder. The feeling of personal reality is the enchantment as it comes both from nowhere and from a personal decision. The fact that the personal decision should be anchored in the unknown is what makes it worthwhile. As I said earlier, Proust referred to the *Arabian Nights* in *Time Regained*:

> I wiped my mouth with the napkin which he had given me; and instantly, as though I had been the character in the *Arabian Nights* who unwittingly accomplishes the very rite which can cause to appear, visible to him alone, a docile genie ready to convey him to a great distance, a new vision of azure passed before my eyes, but an azure that this time was pure and saline and swelled into blue and bosomy undulations, and so strong was this impression that the moment to which I was transported seemed to me to be the present moment.[51]

---

[50] Marcel Proust, *Contre Sainte-Beuve* (published 1954, written in 1908), Paris: Folio Gallimard, 2004, 50.
[51] Proust, *Time Regained*, 219.

The genie appears through an involuntary movement, but it is "docile". The present moment becomes "docile" to the artist who can seize it.

Another coincidence between Proust and Katherine Mansfield is to be found in *Contre Sainte-Beuve*. The introduction to such a young lady, and helping her make the transition from unknown to known, or rather making ourselves known to her, from scorned to admired, from possessed to possessor, it is *"the little hand with which we grasp the intangible future, the only one we force on it"*.[52] This is also the work of art, the miracle of telling tales and finding oneself truly alive.

The egg is not the only symbol of such wonder in Katherine Mansfield's work. In this book we have already mentioned the pear tree in "Bliss", appearing in the window (a figure in a frame: an art of memory) and the aloe in "Prelude": "And I am sure I shall remember it long after I've forgotten all the other things."[53] Through the present moment, the past catches up with the future, and, at the end of "Prelude", incidentally, the top of cream jar that should break does not: "And the top of the cream jar flew through the air and rolled like a penny in a round on the linoleum – and did not break."[54] However, the head of the duck cannot be put back, as Kezia screamed Pat should do: "'Put head back! Put head back!' she screamed."[55] The story itself, when told like a tale of the *Arabian Nights* is such a paradox: "The wind carries their voices – away fly the sentences like little narrow ribbons."[56] But the impression of the wind remains in the rhythm of the words once uttered, and then written: "The wind – the wind."

"The pleasure of that madness"

The art of memory which consists in placing figures in special settings in order to be able to remember them, is an art of the imagination, and it is dramatic too since it combines the living creature, the "I" of the present moment, with its *alter ego*, the "You" of the past. This is an instance of reflexive consciousness on the background of the unknown, which tallies with Kierkegaard's definition of the individual

---

[52] Proust, *Contre Sainte-Beuve*, 108-109 (translation by Anthony Rudolf for this book; my emphases).
[53] Mansfield, "Prelude", in *The Collected Stories*, 53.
[54] *Ibid.*, 60.
[55] *Ibid.*, 46.
[56] Mansfield, "The Wind Blows", in *The Collected Stories*, 110.

subject: "This then is the formula which describes the state of the self when despair is completely eradicated: in relation to itself and in wanting to be itself, the self is grounded transparently in the power that established it."[57] Moreover as we have already indicated in Chapter 3 Kezia is the name of Job's daughter when he has recovered everything.

Job is the model from which Kierkegaard deduces his notion of repetition:

> *Now* they come to him and eat bread with him and are sorry for him and console him; his brothers and sisters, each one of them, give him a farthing and a gold ring – Job is blessed and has received everything *double*. – This is called a *repetition*.[58]

The notion is explained in temporal terms in *Fear and Trembling* (1843).[59] As quoted earlier Kierkegaard defines what he calls the ethical choice in *Either... or...* (1843) and claims that being created is not enough: to be free I must choose myself. Kierkegaard strongly reacted to German idealism as represented by Hegel, whose main concern was to consider the universal. Before his ethical choice, "now", the painter, in the universal world of the tragic chorus, remains "hopeless". When he hands her an egg, he has gripped reality and himself in the present moment of the individual, as Proust said in *Contre Sainte-Beuve*. In the "I" and "You" relationship, he comes back to the essential and opens the future as the girl is ready to open the door with her key. This individual apprehension of time is opposed to the transcendent time of history, which was imposed upon the individuals, and especially the soldiers, during the war. In *Mrs. Dalloway*, Virginia Woolf contrasted monumental time and individual duration in keeping with Bergson's view. Proust wrote, in *Contre Sainte-Beuve*: "For me reality is individual."[60] Katherine Mansfield likens the artist's world with the child's. The grown-ups live in a world of linear duration, of routine and anonymity. The artist and the child, having faith in the impossible, like Abraham, as described by Kierkegaard in *Fear and Trembling*, are able to seize the present

---

[57] Kierkegaard, *The Sickness unto Death*, 44.

[58] Kierkegaard, *Repetition*, in *Fear and Trembling*, *Repetition*, 212 (Kierkegaard's emphases).

[59] Kierkegaard, *Fear and Trembling*, in *ibid.*, 18. See epigraph and Introduction (2-3).

[60] Proust, *Contre Sainte-Beuve*, 94.

moment in all its intensity: "And he handed her an egg." Therefore, several notions are closely linked: the individual's life becomes "REAL" in the present moment of the ethical choice and this reality is conveyed through such impressionistic details as the observation of the concierge, the flower market, the leopards, or the daffodils. The whole pattern is highly consistent. The multiplicity of details and the instants they belong to is intended to suggest the essential. Proust writes:

> To his contemplation of the essence of things I had decided therefore that in future I must attach myself, so as somehow to immobilise it. But how, by what means, was I to do this?[61]

"And he handed her an egg." This is childish but this is art. Life is seen in its nakedness: and one only cares about the essential. And, for Proust, one of the most famous instances of such resurrecting reminiscence is the episode of the madeleine, leading him back to the delights of his own childhood – delights of plenitude: "Then came the fullness of time." The lamp, in "The Doll's House", is such an instance of an individual presence so well belonging to its place that it becomes a figure of plenitude:

> But the lamp was perfect. It seemed to smile at Kezia, to say, 'I live here.' The lamp was real.[62]

This capacity to achieve plenitude in the present moment (the fullness of time) creates a world of correspondences, as described in "A Married Man's Story":

> I saw it all, but not as I had seen before .... Everything lived, everything. But that was not all. I was equally alive and – it's the only way I can express it – the barriers were down between us – I had come into my own world![63]

Such renewal is deduced from a questioning of the past: "Who am I, in fact, as I sit here at this table, but my own past? If I deny that, I am

---

[61] Proust, *Time Regained*, 229.
[62] Mansfield, "The Doll's House", in *The Collected Stories*, 384.
[63] Mansfield, "A Married Man's Story", in *The Collected Stories*, 437. See also "So as Not to Conclude".

nothing."[64] It means reconciliation in time and space – a reconciliation which is brought about by an inner impulse:

> I looked at the dead bird again .... And that is the first time that I remember singing – rather... listening to a silent voice inside a little cage that was me.[65]

The voice is the emanation of the original silence, to be listened to and translated into words: "But how, by what means, was I to do this?" Proust wonders. There is no universal answer – only the work of the individual artist, "now", for the world and the self to be renewed in the present moment of creation, which is an ethical choice, founding the free individual subject. This is why the work of art, which is no sheer object, but rather a subjective object, can come to life again, like the poppy under Linda's finger – and the whole world becomes subjective then:

> But the strangest part of this coming alive of things was what they did. They listened, they seemed to swell out with some mysterious important content, and when they were full she felt that they smiled. But it was not for her, only, their sly secret smile; they were members of a secret society and they smiled among themselves.[66]

The metamorphosis of things is endowed with all the ambivalence of childish visions; the wonder is tainted with fear, and, to a certain extent, in a world devoted to the universal, the individual attempt is clumsy: "In a moment he was out again, and following her past his house across the flower market, dodging among the huge umbrellas and treading on the fallen flowers and the round marks where the pots had stood ...."[67] In the universal, the individual is a funambulist.

Hermione's metamorphosis in *The Winter's Tale* (V, 3, 98-111)[68] is seen with ambivalence: "If this be magic, let it be an art / Lawful as eating", says Leontes. The statue is being resurrected by the music: "Music; awake her – strike!" Paulina's voice and the rhythm of Shakespeare's verse call her back to life:

---

[64] *Ibid.*, 434.
[65] *Ibid.*, 433.
[66] Mansfield, "Prelude", in *The Collected Stories*, 27.
[67] Mansfield, "Feuille d'Album", in *The Collected Stories*, 166.
[68] Shakespeare, *The Winter's Tale*, 229.

> 'Tis time; descend; be stone no more; approach;
> Strike all that look upon with marvel – come,
> I'll fill your grave up.

This resurrection of the past, although madly impossible, is real delight:

> No settled senses of the world can match
> The pleasure of that madness.
>
> (V, 3, 72-73)[69]

Life can only be saved in the present moment. The unbroken egg at the end of "Feuille d'Album" is the fullness of time thus regained through the work of art, which is open to endless reading and therefore endless renewal, in a world of correspondences, of "truths written with the aid of shapes" – the egg, the pear tree, the aloe, Pygmalion's Galatea coming to life through the work of his imagination, Hermione and the past coming back to life, through the art of memory and the present moment becoming absolutely REAL: "You dropped this."

---

[69] *Ibid.*, 227.

CHAPTER 5

BIRDS ... SWELLING AND DYING,
IN KATHERINE MANSFIELD'S STORIES AND POEMS –
THE SADNESS OF IT, THE VOICE

As there are a lot of flowers, trees and insects in Katherine Mansfield's work, there are also a lot of birds. They appear here and there on wallpaper, in the garden, or in similes. As such they animate the storyteller's prose or the poet's verse and also partake of its metamorphic aspect. They can also become emblems of a fault, as in "Mr. Reginald Peacock's Day", or help to highlight the humorous, and sad, features of a particular scene, and predicament, as in "Mr. and Mrs. Dove" and "The Doves' Nest". As existential emblems, they are all the more linked with the sadness that the author of "The Canary" mentions at the end of the story. We shall see how they embody Katherine Mansfield's perception of life in its ambivalence, as expressed in "At the Bay", for instance:

> And lying in her cane chair, Linda felt so light; she felt like a leaf.
> Along came Life like a wind and she was seized and shaken; she had
> to go. Oh dear, would it always be so? Was there no escape?[1]

Birds embody the author's philosophy of life and tell us a lot about her understanding of the poetical voice. This essay will help us to go deeper into the author's thought and to measure Schopenhauer's influence on her through Hardy and Proust, especially. As a reader of Nietzsche, she was indirectly aware of Schopenhauer's pessimist outlook, an influence on the philosopher of the eternal return and

---

"Birds... swelling and dying, in Katherine Mansfield's stories and poems – the sadness of it, the voice" was written for the Menton Conference in September 2009. A French version, "Ces oiseaux qui enflent et qui meurent" was published in *Europe*, 1003-1004 (November-December 2012), 88-103.

[1] Mansfield, *The Collected Stories*, 221. In the notes for this chapter, I do not mention the story each time since I refer to a large number of them.

amor fati. Talking of "The Canary", we shall consider Keats' "Ode to a Nightingale", and appreciate the differences between the two views, which will help us to assess the quality of Katherine Mansfield's symbolism.

A world alive with birds

We find a constant set of correspondences between Nature, the human world and language itself in Katherine Mansfield's work. In "Prelude", "some tiny owls"[2] are to be found in the garden. Then, when morning comes, the birds wake up, "the goldfinches and linnets and fan-tails" as well as "a lovely kingfisher".[3] In "At the Bay", the same situation is described, at sunrise: "Myriads of birds were singing. A goldfinch flew over the shepherd's head and, perching on the tiptop of a spray, it turned to the sun, ruffling its small breast feathers."[4] In each case the birds give evidence of life through their song and swiftness – the verb "flicked" is used in "Prelude".

Katherine Mansfield likes owls. We find them not only in "Prelude" but also in "Her First Ball", as "baby owls"[5] which Leila wants to listen to. They mean being at home and having a rest after her spoilt beginning:

> It sounded terribly true. Was this first ball only the beginning of her last ball, after all? At that the music seemed to change; it sounded sad, sad; it rose upon a great sigh. Oh, how quickly things changed![6]

The fat man's voice is the voice of Fate and necessity, which Schopenhauer revived, calling it the "Will", insisting on the ancient[7]

---

[2] *Ibid.*, 23.

[3] *Ibid.*, 24.

[4] *Ibid.*, 207.

[5] *Ibid.*, 343.

[6] *Ibid.*, 342.

[7] "Whence things have their origin, / Thence also their destruction happens, / As is the order of things". This principle, which Léon Chestov attacks in *Sur la balance de Job* since it denies the legitimacy of individual life, is expressed in a fragment attributed to Anaximander (*c.* 610-546 BCE). Léon Chestov also criticizes the way of reasoning, based upon a retrospective look, instead of looking ahead – considering the past, a principle of death, instead of considering the future, and therefore choosing life. See *Internet Encyclopedia of Philosophy:* http://www.iep.utm.edu/anaximan/. See also Léon Chestov, "A propos de la philosophie de l'histoire", in *Sur la balance de Job* (1929), Paris: Flammarion, 1971, 250.

notion that all that is born is doomed to die. Although a comfort, birds do not belong to an ideal world. For instance, the larks, at the beginning of "The Woman at the Store" do not share the ethereal joy of Shelley's skylark: "Hundreds of larks shrilled; the sky was slate colour, and the sound of the larks reminded me of slate pencils scraping over its surface."[8] There is something jarring in this epiphany.

Those real birds have replicas in the world of man-made objects. In "Prelude", the "tiny owls" mentioned, in section IV, re-appear in section VI as jewels at Mrs Fairfield's throat: "a silver crescent moon with five little owls seated on it",[9] which might be taken as some sort of compromise between Athena and Artemis. The correspondence between the natural and the human worlds goes the other way round with the parrot wall paper as seen by Kezia: "Through a square hall filled with bales and hundreds of parrots (but the parrots were only on the wall-paper) down a narrow passage where the parrots persisted in flying past Kezia with her lamp."[10] The mythic suggestion has been prepared just before, when the little girl was shown as saying: "I hate rushing animals like dogs and parrots."[11] We guess that this is an ordeal for Kezia and, with the light and the narrow passage, the scene takes the appearance of an initiation. It is in keeping with the fact that the family is moving to a new house. Initiation means new birth, and this is what Linda is suggesting later in the story when, associating her husband with a Newfoundland dog, she says that sexual love is killing her. And she uses Kezia's verb, "to rush": "He was too strong for her; she had always hated things that rush at her, from a child."[12] She also says that at such moments she finds her husband "frightening", as if Life herself, like the wind, were rushing at her. And she calls him a "thing". What is frightening is the irrepressible *élan vital* that gives birth and kills in the same movement (see note 7): Leila's "first ball" is also the beginning of her last one, as she remarked for herself. Later, in "At the Bay", Linda thinks: "She was broken, made weak, her courage was gone, through child-bearing. And what made it

---

[8] Mansfield, *The Collected Stories*, 550.
[9] *Ibid.*, 29.
[10] *Ibid.*, 18.
[11] *Ibid.*, 17.
[12] *Ibid.*, 54.

doubly hard to bear was, she did not love her children."[13] The tale itself, however, assembles all those sundry aspects of reality. It humbly transcends necessity.

The doves cooing at appropriate times in "Mr. and Mrs. Dove" also have their correspondences in the world of man-made objects, the "very fat dove out of the Noah's Ark",[14] as William longingly recalls in "Marriage à la Mode". It is a symbol of resurrection, and a new covenant, both dismissed in this story. His wife Isabel is no longer what she used to be and he is tormented by "the dull, persistent gnawing in his breast".[15] Isabel's "new way"[16] is her husband's death through lack of love and subsequent neglect.

In "The Voyage", a title suggesting initiation, the swan's head means fleeting time: "As well as her luggage strapped into a neat sausage, Fenella carried clasped to her her grandma's umbrella, and the handle, which was a swan's head, kept giving her shoulder a sharp little peck as if it too wanted her to hurry...." The poor girl has to take this voyage because her mother is dead. We think of Kezia telling her grandmother in "At the Bay":

> '... You couldn't leave me. You couldn't not be there.' This was awful. 'Promise me you won't ever do it, grandma,' pleaded Kezia.[17]

We shall come back on this double negation: "You couldn't not be there." "The Voyage" ends with this quatrain, written by the grandmother:

> Lost! One Golden Hour
> Set with Sixty Diamond Minutes.
> *No* Reward is Offered
> For It Is Gone For Ever![18]

"Was there no escape?" wondered Linda in "At the Bay".

The swan is also Lohengrin's in "Mr. Reginald Peacock's Day", in connection with the artist's voice, a tenor, in Wagner's opera, in

---

[13] *Ibid.*, 223.
[14] *Ibid.*, 316.
[15] *Ibid.*, 311.
[16] *Ibid.*, 310.
[17] *Ibid.*, 227.
[18] *Ibid.*, 330.

which Lohengrin may be seen as a figure of the artist. Thus we get into the world of language. The birds are the subject of Beryl's song in "Prelude":

> '... birds I see That sing aloud from every tree ...' But when she reached the dining-room she stopped singing, her face changed; it became gloomy and sullen.
> 'One may as well rot here as anywhere else,' she muttered savagely, digging the stiff brass safety-pins into the red serge curtains.[19]

"But" is the important word here: in Katherine Mansfield's work birds are not only the joy and will to live (from a standard idealistic viewpoint) but also life as an irrepressible self-destroying force. This is to be found in "Prelude":

> She made a cup of her hands and caught the tiny bird and stroked its head with her finger. It was quite tame. But a funny thing happened. As she spoke it began to swell, it ruffled and pouched, it grew bigger and bigger and its round eyes seemed to smile knowingly at her. Now her arms were hardly wide enough to hold it and she dropped it into her apron. It had become a baby with a big naked head and a gaping bird-mouth, opening and shutting.[20]

All things, not only birds, swell in the same way:

> 'I dreamed about birds last night,' thought Linda. What was it? She had forgotten. But the strangest part of this coming alive of things was what they did. They listened, they seemed to swell out with some mysterious important content, and when they were full she felt that they smiled. But it was not for her, only, their sly secret smile; they were members of a secret society and they smiled among themselves.[21]

This independence of things, suggesting an ironic self-contained gesturing of reality, definitely reminds us of Schopenhauer's Will, this ineluctable instinct to live and propagate life, which is fatal – the only consolation being art, and, more particularly, music. This casts an

---

[19] *Ibid.*, 31.
[20] *Ibid.*, 24.
[21] *Ibid.*, 27.

interesting light on Katherine Mansfield's resorting to rhythm, in "The Wind Blows" most conspicuously, as a way to structure her narrative resistance to the anguish of destructive time. Schopenhauer held that music provided an access to the Will, or the origin of being. The German philosopher had a strong influence on nineteenth-century literature, on "dear old Hardy"[22] especially, as Katherine Mansfield calls him in a letter to Dorothy Brett (11 November 1921) and then on Proust[23] who through the combination of the imagination and involuntary memory, said he reached the intuition of the essence of life. Baudelaire, who had written a poem called, in English, "Anywhere out of the World",[24] imagines, in "La chambre double", that the seconds, coming out of the clock, say: "Je suis la Vie, l'insupportable, l'implacable Vie ! / I am Life, the unbearable, unremitting Life."[25] ("Was there no escape?" Linda wondered.)

Although he defended himself against it, Chekhov had the reputation of a pessimistic writer. The short story which inspired Katherine Mansfield in "The Child Who Was Tired", "Let Me Sleep" (1888), is the story of an infanticide. A young servant keeps feeling sleepy and cannot go to sleep because she must look after her masters' baby. As a maid of all work, she is not well treated. She feels the baby is her enemy since he prevents her from falling asleep. In her story, Katherine Mansfield, in the line of what she was to develop later with the character of Linda, insists on the number of children – three other sharing the maid's bed, the baby, and another to come: "Another baby! Hasn't she finished having them *yet*? thought the Child."[26] And the "Frau" feels that her "insides are all twisted up with having children too quickly".[27] The Child, a "free-born one", is compared to an "owl"[28] and the cruelty of life is strongly stressed. When she smothers the baby, the Child thinks of "a duck with its head off, wriggling".[29] Therefore she used Chekhov's idea but adapted it to her

---

[22] *The Collected Letters of Katherine Mansfield*, IV, 316.
[23] On this issue, see Anne Henry, *La tentation de Marcel Proust*, Paris: P.U.F., 2000.
[24] Charles Baudelaire, *Le Spleen de Paris* (1863), Paris : Le Livre de Poche, 1969, 137.
[25] *Ibid.*, 22.
[26] Mansfield, *The Collected Stories*, 746.
[27] *Ibid.*, 750.
[28] *Ibid.*, 751.
[29] *Ibid.*, 752.

own world, already using motifs to be developed later in "Prelude" and other tales.

In some of Chekhov's stories, although the Russian writer displayed a vivid sense of tragedy, we find an attack on pessimism and the nihilistic attitude it brings about. In "Ward 6" (1892), Doctor Raguine expatiates on the idea that life is a trap, and even more, a dead end, which only the mind can transcend. The same pessimistic outlook pervades "Rothschild's Violin" (1894). However, in "Lights" (1888), through the character of Nikolaï Ananiev, Chekhov criticizes the pessimistic views of his time and the lack of moral judgement it induces. In "The Fiancée" (1903), he advocates individual assertion and freedom. And in "The Student" (1894), he links what we may call the spirit of the narrative to a feeling of continuity and happiness. He took this story as an argument against those who accused him of pessimism.[30] And Chekhov set great store by music, especially in the way he composed his tales.

In some of her letters in 1920, Katherine Mansfield seems to take Chekhov as a model: "Tchekhov felt just like that",[31] she wrote in December 1920. In "Bliss", she writes, spelling the name in her own way, that Bertha's guests "reminded her of a play by Tchekof!".[32] In "Three Years" (1895), Chekhov describes the two girls, Sasha and Lida, who have just been bereaved of their mother, as "huddling together like animals when they are cold".[33] Katherine Mansfield's way of describing little girls recalls such sensitive Chekhovian notation – Lottie being compared to "a bird falling out of the nest"[34] in "Prelude", and Jose to a "butterfly"[35] in "The Garden-Party"; "our Else" in "The Doll's House", is likened to "a little white owl";[36] when they follow Kezia through the courtyard, the Kelveys are said to be "two little stray cats"[37] and, through Beryl's viewpoint, they become

---

[30] My remarks on Chekhov are based upon the following editions in French: Anton Tchékhov, *Œuvres*, I, II, and III, Paris: Gallimard Pléiade, 1970, and *Le duel, Ma vie, Lueurs, Une banale histoire, La fiancée*, Paris: Le Livre de Poche, 1971.

[31] *The Collected Letters of Katherine Mansfield*, IV, 148.

[32] Mansfield, "Bliss", in *The Collected Stories*, 100.

[33] Anton Chekhov, "Three Years", *The Literature Network*, http://www.online-literature.com/o_henry/1277/

[34] Mansfield, *The Collected Stories*, 18.

[35] *Ibid.*, 246.

[36] *Ibid.*, 386.

[37] *Ibid.*, 390.

"little rats"; Kezia is compared to "a little brown owl"[38] by her father, in "The Little Girl" as the Child is in her Chekhovian tale. Such comparison to rather small animals stresses the children's vulnerable frailty. Katherine Mansfield displays the same concern for the lower classes and the pain of hard work as Chekhov in such stories as "Three Years" (already mentioned), "Murder" (1895), "The House with the Mezzanine" (1896), or "Peasants" (1897), for instance. Her way of describing the working class district in "The Garden-Party"[39] may recall Chekhov's brief description of the workers' houses in "A Case History" (1898), a story which William Carlos Williams may have remembered in "The Use of Force" (1933). Chekhov is a permanent reference for storytellers.

Another comparable feature that Katherine Mansfield may be said to have learned from Chekhov is the way the elements are treated, for instance in such stories as "On Official Duty" (1899) and in "In the Hollow" (1900). In the former tale, the tempest and its sounds are rendered through onomatopoeias, which is a way of making them share in language. They are becoming audible figures in the human drama. Katherine Mansfield does the same in "The Escape", in which the sea says "Hish, hish".[40] In her Notebooks, when she refers to the power of the sea, the latter becomes a real personified figure since it is able to talk: "'I am desire' said the sea, 'I crave all, insatiably I long, untiringly I hold.'"[41] We have noticed how she keeps animating motionless motifs. In "In the Hollow", Chekhov lends language to the frogs, which are supposed to reveal the uniqueness of the present moment. Katherine Mansfield's epiphanic figures belong to the same type of concern – exemplifying the unique quality of the human drama.

Thus converting immediate experience into art means challenging necessity and enhancing the possibilities of the mind. Language, simply, means possibility, even if the awareness it implies, through being able to embrace past, present, and future within the mind, may

---

[38] *Ibid.*, 568.
[39] *Ibid.*, 259.
[40] *Ibid.*, 201. See Chapter 6.
[41] *The Katherine Mansfield Notebooks*, I, 224. See Chapter 7.

be dreadful, awful, terrible. The Open is a conversion of the abyss, as Baudelaire also understood in such a poem as "La vie antérieure".[42]

In Chapter 36 of The *World as Will and Representation*, Schopenhauer claims that art provides an intuitive knowledge of the "intimate essence of all life and existence", or a representation of the will, this "natural, blind force" (I, 21). In Katherine Mansfield's poem, "Floryan nachdenklich", written in 1913, birds as motifs in traditional craft give an idea of the will through its representation:

> And the Indian curtain suddenly seems
> To stir and shake with a thousand dreams.
> ...
> On the great brown boughs of the Indian tree
> Little birds sing and preen their wings.[43]

Katherine Mansfield uses many similes involving birds, as in "A Dill Pickle", a story in which memory and the imagination are closely linked. A man and a woman meet again after six years and recall a few moments spent together. He tells her about his trip to Russia, which they had wished to make together but did not and she sees everything: "... although she was not certain what a dill pickle was, she saw the greenish glass jar with a red chilli like a parrot's beak glimmering through."[44] She can even taste the mysterious dill pickle. These similes reveal the metamorphic power of the imagination, as it is obvious in dreams. In "Prelude", the "round flowers" are "like red and white birds".[45] In "The Garden-Party", the guests are "like bright birds that had alighted in the Sheridans' garden for this one afternoon, on their way to – where?".[46] These migrating birds are also nomads in time as we have seen. The comparison can be sarcastic, as in "Miss Brill": "He scraped with his foot and flapped his arms like a rooster about to crow."[47] It can be endearing as "our Else" is described in

---

[42] Charles Baudelaire, *Les Fleurs du Mal* (1857), Paris: Le Livre de Poche, 1967, 28. See Mounic, "Joujou du pauvre et Maison de poupée: De Baudelaire à Katherine Mansfield", in *L'Esprit du récit ou La chair du devenir: Ethique et création littéraire*, 428-29.

[43] Mansfield, *Poems*, 38.

[44] Mansfield, *The Collected Stories*, 171.

[45] *Ibid.*, 55.

[46] *Ibid.*, 257.

[47] *Ibid.*, 331.

"The Doll's House": "She was a tiny wishbone of a child, with cropped hair and enormous solemn eyes – a little white owl."[48] The metaphor is twofold – the wishbone and the owl. Kezia is compared to "a little brown owl" in "The Little Girl" (see above). In "Father and the Girls", Ernestine is likened to "a bright bird".[49] The metamorphosis is obvious in "At the Bay": "The manuka tree, bent by the southerly winds, was like a bird on one leg stretching out a wing."[50] Metamorphosis means that the process of becoming animates the work itself.

Now, birds have wings and a voice, and this gives matter to similes. Music could give wings to objects, in "Honeymoon": "… and it played so gaily that Fanny felt if she wasn't careful even the cups and saucers might grow little wings and fly away."[51] In "The Singing Lesson", "a voice like a bird cried, 'Muriel'".[52] In those instances, birds are on the side of joy and the consolation of art. Katherine Mansfield parodies Romanticism and its idealism in "The Sister of the Baroness": "Did the spirit of romance spread her rose wings only over aristocratic Germany?"[53] In "Bliss", we come across the legendary birds of resurrection through fire: "The fire had died down in the drawing-room to a red, flickering 'nest of baby phoenixes,' said Face."[54] The imagination, and especially children's imagination, has such a power of metamorphosis and resurrection; in "Prelude", Kezia finds "a pill box black and shiny outside and red in, holding a blob of cotton wool. 'I could keep a bird's egg in that,' she decided."[55] In the same way, in "Feuille d'Album", the painter Ian French decides that he should make the acquaintance of the young girl he sees through the window: "'Excuse me, Mademoiselle, you dropped this.' And he handed her an egg."[56] The decisive quality of the present moment is contained in this witty ending.

Through the alliance of memory and the imagination, a process Proust described in *Time Regained*, the present moment gets a new

---

[48] *Ibid.*, 386.
[49] *Ibid.*, 467.
[50] *Ibid.*, 242.
[51] *Ibid.*, 396.
[52] *Ibid.*, 344.
[53] *Ibid.*, 694.
[54] *Ibid.*, 101.
[55] *Ibid.*, 14.
[56] *Ibid.*, 166.

resonance and depth (see Chapter 4). What should be broken, scattered, and forgotten is given new unexpected unity. This is the consolation of art. Yet it is derived from an inescapable something (sadness?) as Miss Brill feels: "And what they played was warm, sunny, yet there was just a faint chill – a something, what was it? – not sadness – no, not sadness – a something that made you want to sing."[57] This is the mystery, expressed by a vague word, "something", which goes with the knowledge of the essence of life as Schopenhauer says in Book II, 18.

Before pondering over this feeling of sadness in "The Canary" especially, I would like to go through the stories in which the bird is used as the emblem of a moral fault, or of a situation, for humorous purposes.

Birds as emblems

The peacock is an emblem of vanity and Katherine Mansfield, in "Mr. Reginald Peacock's Day", satirizes an artist's conceit. What is at stake is the idealized, and heroic, view of the artist, as represented by Lohengrin, Parsifal's son, whose genius is jeopardized by the temporal chains of marriage, as if the ethereal artist's soul had condescended to suffer the vicissitudes of incarnation, which, from a Platonic and Christian viewpoint, means imprisonment in the cage of the body: "It seemed that she took a malicious delight in making life more difficult for him than – Heaven knows – it was, by denying him the right as an artist, by trying to drag him to her level."[58] The metaphor of the wings, then, is Romantic: "Well – she had done her best to clip his wings."[59] Katherine Mansfield gently mocks him: "... he began to do his exercises – deep breathing, bending forward and back, squatting like a frog and shooting out his legs."[60] The mirror is a test – in Mansfield's work mirrors are generally harmful, breaking the inner unity of the self: "... the sight of himself gave him a thrill of purely artistic satisfaction." The so-called artist proves to be a social climber, and his very name, "Peacock", has to be taken as an almost

---

[57] *Ibid.*, 334.
[58] *Ibid.*, 144.
[59] *Ibid.*, 145.
[60] *Ibid.*, 146.

heraldic emblem of vanity: "Vanity, that bright bird, lifted its wings again, lifted them until he felt his breast would break."[61]

The connection between the wings and the breast is significant in Katherine Mansfield's work, considering her illness and the many references to it in the stories. In her last poem, "The Wounded Bird", written in July 1922, she beseeches:

> O my wings – lift me – lift me
> I am not so dreadfully hurt...[62]

This implies that her style is humour rather than irony since her personal suffering involves her, so to speak, in universal suffering. Even for Reginald Peacock, as an artist, she can feel some sort of empathy. She is never sovereign, hence her liking for small birds and animals and her identifying with them: "... the strange beast in her bosom began to purr...."[63]

Therefore, in "Mr. and Mrs. Dove", the humour is mitigated with the pain. In the title, the problem word is "and". It reminds me of what Veronica Forrest-Thomson says about the hyphen, which links and severs at the same time. In the story, the male character, also called Reginald, finds the link much too loose while the female character, Anne, is afraid of its hopeless routine quality – another way to say that she does not love him. And eventually she turns the tables on him and reproaches him for being cruel and unhappy: "But it did not seem so simple to Reginald. It seemed impossibly difficult."[64] The doves, which usually are a symbol of blind devoted love, become an emblem of mechanical unrequited devotion: "'Away she runs, and after her,' cried Anne, and she sat back on her heels, 'comes poor Mr. Dove, bowing and bowing ... and that's their whole life. They never do anything else, you know.'"[65] Their mechanical cooing accompanies, at appropriate moments, Reginald's lovemaking. The comic is derived, as in "Mr. Reginald Peacock's Day", from mechanical behaviour, in keeping with Bergson's analysis of it. According to Bergson, one of

---

[61] *Ibid.*, 148.
[62] Mansfield, *Poems*, 82.
[63] Katherine Mansfield, "A Dill Pickle", in *The Collected Stories*, 173.
[64] *Ibid.*, 294.
[65] *Ibid.*, 291.

the sources of the comic is the mechanical impression a series of acts and events may give.[66]

In "The Doves' Nest", Katherine Mansfield satirizes the character of the widowed mother, living on the Riviera with her daughter and a friend, a Roman Catholic, Miss Anderson, of whom she says: "Half her time, more than half, was spent wearing out the knees of her skirts in cold churches."[67] And she welcomes a stranger who wanted to meet her husband, inviting him for lunch – a man in the middle of the "doves' nest": "'Florence so damp,' cooed Mother."[68] Being a dove, then, means keeping the surface of things unharmed, preening the outer appearances so that no one looks hurt nor embarrassed. To achieve such deed, the conversation should not drop, whatever everybody says:

> You must rock it, nurse it, keep it on the move if you want to keep on smiling. What could be simpler? But even Father… Mother winced away from memories that were not as sweet as memories ought to be.[69]

Katherine Mansfield denounces what Graves later called "the cool web of language",[70] or the power of "volubility" to conceal the cruelty of the human predicament. The mother's expertise in taking only the smooth and dismissing the rough does not work so well with her daughter: "At that Mother raised her head and gave him one of her still, exalted glances that Milly knew so well. 'I'm not in the least hurt,' she said, as one might say it from the midst of the fiery furnace."[71]

The oblique reference to Daniel, 3, 14-25 and Nebuchadnezar's fiery furnace in which the three men denouncing idolatry are not burnt, gives resonance to the story (see also Chapter 3). All this social preservation of the smooth is actually a way of concealing, and even

---

[66] "Est comique tout arrangement d'actes et d'événements qui nous donne, insérées l'une dans l'autre, l'illusion de la vie et la sensation nette d'un agencement mécanique" (Henri Bergson, *Le rire* [1900], Paris: P.U.F. Quadrige, 1981, 53).
[67] Mansfield, *The Collected Stories*, 439.
[68] *Ibid.*, 441.
[69] *Ibid.*, 453.
[70] See Anne Mounic, *Counting the Beats: Robert Graves' Poetry of Unrest*, Amsterdam: Rodopi, 2012, 179.
[71] Mansfield, *The Collected Stories*, 440.

more, of denying the inner truth – the very essence of man's plight. Arranging the flowers in a dish on the dining-room table, Marie, the servant, calls her arrangements of fresh bunches "tombs". This imprisonment in the "doves' nest" arouses a reaction with the young girl: "Milly felt a yearning – what was it? – it was like a yearning to fly."[72] The reality of life is to be found deeper than the sheltering from it. This awareness of the "sadness" is the price to pay to be "real" as Katherine Mansfield claimed she wanted to be in a letter to her husband on 26 December 1922,[73] but birds have wings, to fly away. We shall see that they are the emblem of the dialectics of existence. Using this term, I am referring to Kierkegaard.

The sadness and the voice
In her unfinished story, "A Married Man's Story", the narrator describes a dead bird his schoolmates have left in his overcoat pocket: "… that terribly soft, cold little body, with the legs thin as pins and the claws wrung", and says that he "didn't feel sorry for it – no!". We remember (see also Chapter 2, on p. 35) that the man who has depicted himself as a boy as "a plant in a cupboard" finally admits:

> Through a big crack in the cement yard a poor-looking plant with dull, reddish flowers had pushed its way. I looked at the dead bird again .... And that is the very first time that I remember singing – rather… listening to a silent voice inside a little cage that was me.[74]

Genuine knowledge, says Schopenhauer, can only come from ourselves, from the subjective viewpoint, from our inner immediate experience of the Will. But the world, as a represented object, gives the will the mirror in which it gets to know itself (I, 54). Through this conjunction of the objective image (which is not an "objective correlative" because it is not allegorical but triggers off the unexpected knowledge) and the subjective impulse, a step has been made towards the apprehension of the existential plight – and it is dialectic. The dead bird and the growing plant are two sides of the same reality: life, and the intimate truth of it – the "silent voice inside a little cage".

---

[72] *Ibid.*, 444.
[73] *The Collected Letters of Katherine Mansfield*, V, 341.
[74] Mansfield, *The Collected Stories*, 433.

Such consolation can be achieved through art only. The inner voice, as the source for the song, or the narrative, keeps wrestling against necessity, thus opening the future in spite of the retrospective outlook, disheartening and negative. Yet, with Katherine Mansfield, the power of rhythm reveals the origin of being as the core of individuality, and we should say it is the poet's task to convert that irrepressible impulse of living into an existential achievement. Proust performed the same task in *In Search of Lost Time* – gathering all those scattered moments of being into a unifying subjective perspective. As he said, reality is individual. Such art is not psychological, but highly existential, and Kierkegaard tells us a lot about such conversion of the immediate into the instant set in what he calls Eternity. In "Prelude", Kezia screams: "Put head back! Put head back!" and the cry becomes mechanical and meaningless: "until it sounded like a loud strange hiccup"[75] – and therefore ridiculous, since "The white duck did not look as if it had ever had a head when Alice placed it in front of Stanley Burnell that night".[76] Here is another instance of the "cool web", or the "doves' nest" of smoothing sociability. The author of the story does not use that type of language to make up for the loss and the suffering, without the lie. With the metamorphic power of her art, she can repair the intense pain that she has described, and awakened: at the end, the cream jar "did not break".[77] The story puts every bit of memory together – "And he handed her an egg" (see Chapter 4).

In "The Canary", we find the same dead bird as in "A Married Man's Story". The narrator, a middle-aged woman who rents rooms for indifferent young men in her house, insists on the fact that birds are truly "company":[78]

> ... Have you kept birds? If you haven't all this must sound, perhaps, exaggerated. People have the idea that birds are heartless, cold little creatures, not like dogs or cats.

The question is then: how different are birds from cats and dogs? From the episode that the narrator recounts just afterwards, in the

---

[75] *Ibid.*, 46.
[76] *Ibid.*, 50.
[77] *Ibid.*, 60.
[78] *Ibid.*, 420.

same paragraph, we understand that her bird could communicate with her, and comfort her, as she was faced with the tragedy, or the nightmare, of life:

> It was a winter night and raining hard. I suppose I was still half asleep, but through the kitchen window, that hadn't a blind, it seemed to me the dark was staring in, spying. And suddenly I felt it was unbearable that I had no one to whom I could say "I've had such a dreadful dream," or – or "Hide me from the dark." I even covered my face for a minute. And there came a little "Sweet! Sweet!" ... that was so beautifully comforting that I nearly cried.[79]

The canary is a small, harmless creature, capable of empathy through identification with it: "When I Was a Bird",[80] Katherine Mansfield wrote around 1916 or 1917:

> I climbed up the karaka tree
> Into a nest made of leaves
> But soft as feathers
> I made up a song that went on singing by itself

The bird is associated with a protective home and a song, with softness as well. Is presence makes the whole world itself a peaceful shelter:

> The sky was like a blue nest with white feathers
> And the sun was the mother bird keeping it warm.
> That's what my song said; though it hadn't any words.

Reading those lines I think of Gerard Manley Hopkins' "God's Grandeur":

> Oh, morning, at the brown brink eastwards, springs –
> Because the Holy Ghost over the bent
> World broods with warm breast and with ah! bright wings.[81]

---

[79] *Ibid.*, 421.
[80] Mansfield, *Poems*, 59.
[81] Gerard Manley Hopkins, "God's Grandeur" (1877), in *The Major Works*, ed. Catherine Phillips, Oxford: Oxford University Press, 2002, 128.

From a different viewpoint, Hopkins builds the same type of comforting shelter through giving bodily reality to a spiritual symbol. Katherine Mansfield almost does the contrary since she spiritualizes her immediate impulse for comfort and empathy. However we may see an analogy between the two moves, both stemming from a desire to say that life can be renewed in spite of the evidence of death. The song induces and results in this very experience of renewal.

The canary's death puts an end to an "I and You" relationship, which is exactly the relationship that the narrator sets up with us, the readers, from the very beginning: "You see that big nail to the right of the front door?"[82] "You" is the first subject of this solitary "I" now that the canary, through his death, has become a third person: "... I loved him. How I loved him!"[83] She used to tell him: "You're a regular little actor", or "Now that's quite enough. You're only showing off", with the same softness as Katherine Mansfield mocked Mr. Reginald Peacock. Through this "I and You" exchange, the bird is a presence to her while she is only a third person for her lodgers: "the Scarecrow", made to frighten birds, then. And the bird's death means absence within her own self: "... something seemed to die in me. My heart felt hollow, as if it was his cage."[84] This remark has to be placed in parallel with the married man's: "... listening to a silent voice inside a little cage that was me."

The bird is a voice. It is time to consider Keats' "Ode to a Nightingale",[85] written in 1819, when he was aware of his illness, the same as Katherine Mansfield and which used to be called "consumption". The nightingale is a universal, and ancient,[86] symbol of the poet's voice. In his poem, Keats addresses the bird, which means happiness and lightness as compared to the poet's pain and melancholy drowsiness. The eight stanzas are an alternation of elevation and despair (rising and falling, as in Virginia Woolf's *Mrs Dalloway*: see Chapter 8): "Away! away! for I will fly to thee ... / ...

---

[82] Mansfield, *The Collected Stories*, 418.

[83] *Ibid.*, 419.

[84] *Ibid.*, 421-22.

[85] John Keats, "Ode to a Nightingale", in *Poetical Works*, 207.

[86] In his Third Ode, Bacchylides, Pindar's rival, called himself "the Cean nightingale" (Wikipedia: http://en.wikipedia.org/wiki/Bacchylides). The nightingale appears in medieval Bestiaries. Pierre de Beauvais mentions it as the bird who dies by dint of singing. Françoise Armengaud et Daniel Poirion, "Bestiaires", *Encyclopédie Universalis*, 2009.

on the viewless wings of Poesy." Yet death remains a temptation: "Now more than ever seems it rich to die, / To cease upon the midnight with no pain." The poet discards it: "Still wouldst thou sing, and I have ears in vain – / To thy high requiem become a sod." Although Keats's idealistic view of death as slumber and oblivion ("I've been half in love with easeful Death") prevents him from screaming like Kezia, faced with its reality in the poultry yard, his nightingale is not as ethereal as Shelley's skylark. His song is incarnate, with the famous effect of synaesthesia in the fifth stanza and the intimate unity of feelings reached in the dark of the night. Moreover the idea of the bird's immortality does not prevent him from feeling forlorn in the end of the poem when "thy plaintive anthem fades / Past the near meadows". Although Keats' perception of the human plight, in spite of the third stanza describing "The weariness, the fever, and the fret" of suffering men, is still wrapped in what Graves called the "cool web of language", which had not yet been stripped of the "doves' nest" by Nietzsche's defiance of its idealizing power, the poem ends with questioning after the word "adieu" has been repeated three times:

> Was it a vision, or a waking dream?
> Fled is that music: – Do I wake or sleep?

Katherine Mansfield's last completed story also ends with questions: "But isn't it extraordinary that under his sweet, joyful little singing it was just this – sadness? – Ah, what is it? – that I heard."[87] In each case, the mystery of the occurrence is stressed. Keats questions his subjectivity. Indeed, with the nightingale as a symbol of the poet's voice, he has borrowed from ancestral symbolism: "The voice I hear this passing night was heard / In ancient days by emperor and clown." The present moment bears no distinction in the universal; hence the passage from "mid-May" to "summer eves" in the fifth stanza.

The canary, owned by this very ordinary woman, is also a very ordinary pet. T.S. Eliot would see an instance of debasement in that passage from the noble ancient bird to the modern demotic voice only capable of uttering "sweet! sweet!",[88] as an echo of the poem quoted

---

[87] Mansfield, *The Collected Stories*, 422.
[88] We find a prelude to this type of passage from collective symbolism to a personal emblem in Flaubert's "Un cœur simple". For the plain Felicité, her parrot becomes an

above on p. 88, "When I Was a Bird": "Then when he was quite near I said: 'sweet – sweet.'"[89] It is only that in Katherine Mansfield's case, what counts above all is the present moment and the individual. Here again I am taking Kierkegaard's viewpoint, the existential viewpoint. Therefore the beautiful and the universal have to be ruled out. What remains is the question about the essential – the sadness: "What is it? – that I heard." And this does not mean, as has been said by the French Structuralists, that there is no author, but that the author does not claim absolute sovereignty. She is no model; she tells no universal truth. She only wants to give meaning to the present moment. Katherine Mansfield's symbols remain familiar – the egg just bought at the dairy in "Feuille d'Album", for instance. Except for the peacock and the swan, her birds are tiny ones, or poultry. Yet it does not mean that she is a realistic writer. From the account of everyday life, she moves to a sense of wonder, and this is because the question we find at the end of "The Canary" pervades her whole work. What is individual in its origins may be shared by all.

Vincent O'Sullivan says that that story should be read at the same time as "The Wounded Bird"[90] and claims: "As one reads Katherine Mansfield's correspondence and notebooks for 1922, it becomes even more clear than in the preceding few years that her dominant concern was not simply to recover her health, but how to evaluate experience, how satisfactorily to define her own reality." And I would say, considering the last question she asks in "The Canary", that aiming at defining her own reality, she also wonders about the reality of life and its terrible ambivalence. Her tone, in the poem, is closer to Keats' although she is at the same time the suffering poet and the bird with liberating wings – an aspect of the ambivalence:

> At night – in the wide bed
> With the leaves and flowers
> Gently weaving in the darkness
> She is like a wounded bird at rest on a pool.
> Timidly, timidly she lifts her head from her wing.
> In the sky there are two stars

---

emblem of the Holy Spirit (Gustave Flaubert, *Trois contes* [1877], Paris: Garnier-Flammarion, 2001, 43-78).
[89] Mansfield, *Poems*, 59.
[90] O'Sullivan, "Katherine Mansfield's 'Canary', a 'Wounded Bird'", *Temporel* n° 2 – La cage. http://temporel.fr/Katherine-Mansfield-s-Canary-a

> Floating – shining –
> O waters – do not cover me!
> I would look long and long at those beautiful stars!
> O my wings – lift me – lift me
> I am not so dreadfully hurt ...[91]

It is night, as in the "Ode to a Nightingale" and the setting is Nature. A pattern of repetition is at work involving two elements each time: "Timidly, timidly", "two stars", "long and long", "lift me – lift me". It is implicit that the bird has two wings and some words are coupled two by two: "leaves and flowers", "Floating – shining." The last line is a partial negation. She does not pretend not to be hurt, but simply "not so dreadfully". She fears drowning, the loss of contact with the air, the impossibility of breathing. It recalls the fly, whose courage the boss, contemplating her wrestling to remain alive, admired. It had drowned in the inkpot and now cleans the ink from its wings: "Now one could imagine that the little front legs rubbed against each other lightly, joyfully. The horrible danger was over; it had escaped; it was ready for life again."[92] It is counting without the perversity of the boss, who wonders, at the end, after the insect's death: "... he fell to wondering what it was he had been thinking about before. What was it? It was ...."[93] And the same sense of mystery looms between the suspension points. Like the hyphen which links and severs at the same time, the dots reveal a mystery and veil it at the same time. At the end of "The Fly", the dash suggests the boss' oblivion, due to this ethical irresponsibility. The dead bird says "something different" – not "the sorrow that we all know, like illness and poverty and death":

> It is there, deep down, deep down, part of one, like one's breathing. However hard I work and tire myself I have only to stop to know it is there, waiting. I often wonder if everybody feels the same. One can never know. But isn't it extraordinary that under his sweet, joyful singing it was just this – sadness? – Ah, what is it? – that I heard.[94]

---

[91] Mansfield, "The Wounded Bird" (1922), in Mansfield, *Poems*, 82.
[92] Mansfield, *The Collected Stories*, 417.
[93] *Ibid.*, 418.
[94] *Ibid.*, 421.

We should now try to analyse the complete final passage. The indeterminate element the narrator seeks to express has nothing to do with the pain we can put a name on. It lies beyond language and is as necessary and involuntary as breathing. To "know it is there", you have to "stop", which means that with a special attention, or concentration, you can apprehend it. It is an individual feeling, which could be shared. It lies under the frail joy of living. It is difficult not to see here the origin of life, what the Taoists called the "principle" and what Schopenhauer called the "Will". The bird's voice, then, is like the dots, or dashes, which punctuate Katherine Mansfield's work. As they only suggest the mystery, the terrible silence beneath, they enable the reader to breathe and they guarantee the genuine quality of the voice – the will as the individual subject can experience it in his inner self. And this will, becoming a voice, also means an instance of one's personal creative power: "My heart felt hollow, as if it was his cage. I shall get over it. Of course. I must." How could we explain that she "must" "get over it" if it is not through the impulse of the will to live – that eventually, and blindly, leads to death? But memory and the imagination fill the gap. This is what Proust experienced, and thus overcame Schopenhauer's pessimism. This is also Katherine Mansfield's philosophy. Art gives an understanding and helps transcending what Lautréamont called the "cage of Time".[95] We find another cage in Henry James' story, "In the Cage" (1898), which symbolizes the main character's inner life and her capacity to create out of "the rhythm of the larger life",[96] which she perceives in "the little post-and-telegraph-office".[97] Although Katherine Mansfield did not really like Henry James, her symbol of the cage as the creative self might have been inspired by this story, especially if we consider this sentence (her canary uttering a "sweet! sweet!" when singing): "... and after he had gone she was in possession of no name, of no address, of no meaning, of nothing but a vague, *sweet sound and an immense impression*."[98] The young telegraphist could also wonder: "Ah, what is it? – that I heard."

---

[95] Isidore Ducasse, Comte de Lautréamont, *Les Chants de Maldoror* (1869), Paris: Poésie Gallimard, 1988, 97.

[96] Henry James, *Selected Tales*, eds Peter Messent and Tom Paulin, London: Everyman, 1982, 122.

[97] *Ibid.*, 119-20.

[98] *Ibid.*, 129 (my emphasis).

At the end of the story, we hear the bird's song and the silence of the deep sadness. The bird is life in its ambivalence, the prisoner of a cage out of which his song (his voice, or the poet's) and his wings are the escape – which answers Linda's question in "At the Bay": "Was there no escape?" The short story called "The Wind Blows" says there is no escape except in rhythm, in art – a use of the blind will as individual creative potency, or it means madness, as described by Jonathan in "At the Bay":

> But as it is, I'm like an insect that's flown into a room of its own accord. I dash against the walls, dash against the windows, flop against the ceiling, do everything on God's earth, in fact, except fly out again. And all the while I'm thinking, like that moth, or that butterfly, or whatever it is, 'The shortness of life: the shortness of life!' I've only one night and one day, and there's this vast dangerous garden, waiting out there, undiscovered, unexplored.[99]

The unknown, waiting, as the sadness is waiting at the end of "The Canary", arouses curiosity: being "unexplored", it wants to be explored; being "undiscovered", it wants to be discovered, so that art, being at the same time the dead bird and the singing voice with wings, says, like Kezia to her grandma in "At the Bay": "You couldn't leave me. You couldn't not be there." The double negation calls for unremitting presence, in the memory and the imagination. "I like that aloe", Linda tells her mother as they are going into the garden at night: "I like it more than anything here. And I am sure I shall remember it long after I've forgotten all the other things."[100] Art places all those present moments of subjective choice in eternity – like stars.

Counting less on the universal, the modern author relies much more on his own power of vision. He is more of an author than the idealist poet if we consider that the original meaning of the Latin word *auctor* is "creator, initiator, founder". Considering the symbol of the bird, Katherine Mansfield uses the traditional emblem: a bird means elevation, freedom and full breathing, the spiritual being. But she also sees in it the earthly creature involved in the present moment of being – thus swelling and dying. With her, the symbol is incarnate, fully embodied, and therefore highly resonant; moreover it has the power of

---

[99] Mansfield, *The Collected Stories*, 237.
[100] *Ibid.*, 53.

revealing the essence of existential dialectics – necessity (the will, the rush) and potency (the voice), joy (the song) and sadness (the deep silence of life), the hollow (death and the cage) and plenitude ("my wings" and the stars). Here "and" means "impossible to dissociate".

We could even say that Katherine Mansfield does not say, like Keats, in his dualistic outlook, "Away! Away!", thus wishing to chase melancholy, but, in the unity of being she derives from her bold awareness of the "sadness", "let's listen carefully" to find the genuine tuning in to the reality of life. "I felt *just* like a bird", she writes in "When I Was a Bird". The question at the end of "The Canary": "Ah, what is it? – that I heard" is an invitation for the reader to "stop to know it is there, waiting". It opens the infinite within the finite – not above it. And it is no transgression but an individual choice. Proust said (see Chapter 4) in *Contre Sainte-Beuve*: "For me reality is individual."[101]

---

[101] Proust, *Contre Sainte-Beuve*, 94.

CHAPTER 6

REVELATIONS ON THE TRAIN
AND OTHER MEANS OF METAMORPHOSIS AND RHYTHM
IN KATHERINE MANSFIELD'S WORK

It was a virtue not to stay
To go our headstrong and heroic way[1]

Means of transportation – means of metamorphosis – have a particular significance in Katherine Mansfield's work. I think of the train in "An Indiscreet Journey", "Something Childish But Very Natural", or "The Little Governess", of the ship at the end of "The Wind Blows",[2] when the story's hurried rhythm culminates in the exile from the "little island",[3] some sort of passage through the looking-glass, and of the epic image of the aloe, "a ship with the oars lifted"[4] in "Prelude". Those few instances suggest a strong connection between the dimensions of revelation, travelling, metamorphosis, and rhythm. That is what I would like to explore in this chapter, and we shall see how the movement of exile and uprooting may induce an epic view of life and of its ambivalence. We may also connect the torment of illness and the feeling of not belonging. Yet the experience of otherness is both a source of delight and awe, which can be connected with Mansfield's childhood in New Zealand. In "The Woman at the Store", she speaks of "the savage spirit of the country"[5] (see Chapter 11). But, in "How Pearl Button Was Kidnapped", "Pearl had never been happy like this before".[6] The softness of one of the "two dark women"[7] and

---

[1] Robert Graves, "The White Goddess", ll. 7-8, in *Poems and Satires 1951*, in *Collected Poems*, eds Beryl Graves and Dunstan Ward, Manchester: Carcanet, 1997, 179.
[2] Mansfield, *The Collected Stories*, 617, 596, 174, 106. In the notes for this chapter, I do not mention the story each time since I refer to a large number of them.
[3] *Ibid.*, 110.
[4] *Ibid.*, 53.
[5] *Ibid.*, 554.
[6] *Ibid.*, 522.

their way of living proves an antidote to the routine of the "House of Boxes".[8]

Train journeys: a rough initiation to life

The narrator of "Je Ne Parle Pas Français", waiting for his English friend at the Gare Saint-Lazare in Paris, describes the little bunch of people waiting for the travellers on the arriving train as "some kind of many-headed monster and Paris behind us nothing but a great trap we had set to catch these sleepy innocents".[9] The image is quite forceful and the narrator goes on: "Into the trap they walked and were snatched and taken off to be devoured. Where was my prey?" We think of Dedalus' maze in Crete with the Minotaur at the core, devouring his lot of young men, with the notion of ruthless sacrifice. At the beginning of "The Little Governess", the instructions of the "lady at the Governess Bureau"[10] arouse fear at once: "You haven't been abroad before, have you?" This question suggests a rough initiation to come: "Well, I always tell my girls that it's better to mistrust people at first rather than trust them, and it's safer to suspect people of evil intentions rather than good ones ...."[11] The whole story is comprised within this contrast between confidence and mistrust since the "perfect grandfather"[12] she meets on the train turns into a "horrible" old man who kisses her "on the mouth". Suddenly, his face – lips and eyes – looks devilish: "He pushed his face forward, his lips smiling broadly; and how his little blue eyes gleamed behind the spectacles!"[13] The sketch suggests a devouring demon in hell, definitely opening the eyes of the girl with the "grateful baby heart" which "glowed with love for the fairy grandfather"[14] – once again, a rough initiation: "It sounds rather hard but we've got to be women of the world, haven't we?"[15] said the lady at the beginning of the tale, which can be read as a fairy tale turning sour. Moreover, to seduce her the old man gives her strawberries. Like the Tempter's fruit in Eden, the juicy berries are the

---

[7] *Ibid.*, 520.
[8] *Ibid.*, 519.
[9] *Ibid.*, 77.
[10] *Ibid.*, 174.
[11] *Ibid.*, 175.
[12] *Ibid.*, 183.
[13] *Ibid.*, 188.
[14] *Ibid.*, 187.
[15] *Ibid.*, 175.

prelude to her fall as was heralded before with the use of the adjective "tragic" and the comparison of her hair with flowers and fruit: "Alas! how tragic for a little governess to possess hair that made one think of tangerines and marigolds, of apricots and tortoiseshell cats and champagne!"[16] The connection between feeding, devouring, and seducing is now quite clear.

We find the train again in "The Escape": "It was his fault, wholly and solely his fault, that they had missed the train."[17] And the fault lies simply in some sort of kind-hearted innocence, her husband's "exquisite belief in human nature", which causes the female character to be exposed to the rushing crowd, and particularly the faces of "those hideous children waving from the windows". Later the faces of children encountered on the road are "impish":[18] "Horrid little monkeys!" Beryl's naming the poor Kelvey girls "little rats" in "The Doll's House" comes to mind. It opposes the author's favourable comparison: "Like two little stray cats." [19] We also think of Linda's despair about having children and her feeling that there is no escape, in "At the Bay". Her sincere words, "I don't like babies",[20] do not shake her baby boy's confidence in her, but even this apparent state of innocence is questioned:

> Something pink, something soft waved in front of him .... This time he determined to catch it. He made a tremendous effort and rolled right over.[21]

The meaning of the word, considering its Latin root (*nocere*, to harm), "innocent" or "innocuous", is denied for the sake of the prelapsarian idea of not knowing about evil, the first meaning given in the *OED*. Childish innocence is viewed as a state of primitive barbarity, a rushing impulse to live; it is no angelic harmlessness. The experience of origins is ambivalent. The need for a sheltering peacefulness is accompanied with a demand for truth. Language must be true to life in its diversity.

---

[16] *Ibid.*, 180.
[17] *Ibid.*, 196.
[18] *Ibid.*, 197.
[19] *Ibid.*, 390.
[20] *Ibid.*, 223.
[21] *Ibid.*, 224.

In her 1903 poems, the young Katherine Mansfield writes about night, about wild life against decorum ("The Chief's Bombay Tiger"[22]) and even uses Maori language in "In the Darkness".[23] The experience of origins is an experience of otherness. "Since leaving New Zealand / I grieve to say / A great Bombay tiger / Has come to stay."[24] Those lines were written on the ship to London in 1903. Travelling triggers off a realization of otherness, which may resort to the use of another language, the language of the natives of the "little island"[25] indeed. The woman, in "How Pearl Button Was Kidnapped", is "warm as a cat".[26] In "Something Childish But Very Natural", the young couple's Rousseauist dream of an unspoilt life on earth peters out. The story is some sort of counterpoint to Keats' "Ode on a Grecian Urn": such timeless suspension of fulfilment ("I have a feeling often and often that it's dangerous to wait for things"[27]) and therefore of initiation into life as it is, leads to darkness and absence. Here again the rush of the train arouses personal initiation: "Henry's heart began to thump and beat to the beat of the train."[28] But Edna shrinks from another kind of darkness, the darkness of deep desire, and we think of D.H. Lawrence's work and world, with his insistence on the sense of touch (see Chapter 7):

> "We'll be in that loathsome tunnel again in a minute," said Henry. "Edna! can I – just touch your hair?"
> She drew back quickly. "Oh no, please don't," and as they were going into the dark she moved a little away from him.[29]

In "The Escape", the female character is the devouring one, or at least so is she perceived by her gentle husband:

> The little bag, with its shiny, silvery jaws open, lay on her lap. He could see her powder-puff, her *rouge stick*, a bundle of letters, a *phial*

---

[22] *The Katherine Mansfield Notebooks*, I, 23.
[23] *Ibid.*, 25.
[24] *Ibid.*, 23.
[25] Mansfield, *The Collected Stories*, 110.
[26] *Ibid.*, 521.
[27] *Ibid.*, 610.
[28] *Ibid.*, 599.
[29] *Ibid.*, 604.

of tiny black pills like seeds, a broken *cigarette*, a mirror, white ivory *tablets* with lists on them that had been heavily scored through.[30]

In the list of objects, most are connected with the mouth. A few lines before, the bag was said to have a "little maw".[31] They both wish to find an escape from each other. What makes the situation more oppressive and unbearable is the wind, the dust – like ash – a mirror, the children's begging ("Poor little mice!"[32]) and the hissing sound of the sea ("Hish, hish."[33]). His escape comes to the man when he sees a tree inside a garden gate and the white shape of what should be a house, when he hears the silence, and a woman's voice. This final epiphany recalls similar figures in Katherine Mansfield's tales, like the pear tree in "Bliss" or the aloe in "Prelude", which can be construed as the epic conversion of the original fright as regards devouring time and becoming (see Chapters 2 and 4). Those figures are the fruit of the writer's own initiation to her art. Speaking of the magazine *Rhythm*, founded by John Middleton Murry and the Scottish painter J.D. Fergusson in the summer 1911, Frederick Goodyear (see Chapter 1) referred to "the neo-barbarians, men and women who to the timid and unimaginative seem merely perverse and atavistic, that must familiarize us with our outcast selves".[34] "Idiotic"[35] civilization prevents the access to the deeper genuine self whose discovery, nonetheless, is not harmless although it is essential to the truth of art.

A writer's initiation to her art
In "The Little Governess", the train is endowed with subjective feelings: "The train seemed glad to have left the station. With a long leap it sprang into the dark."[36] We think of a wildcat – or the "Bombay tiger" mentioned earlier:

---

[30] *Ibid.*, 198 (my emphases).
[31] *Ibid.*, 197.
[32] *Ibid.*, 199.
[33] *Ibid.*, 201.
[34] Angela Smith, "Paris Is Simply a Place of Freedom", *Temporel* n° 7, May 2009, http://temporel.fr/Rhythm-par-Angela-Smith.
[35] Mansfield, *The Collected Stories*, 92, 95.
[36] *Ibid.*, 179.

> The train shattered on, baring its dark, flaming breast to the hills and
> to the valleys. It was warm in the carriage. She seemed to lean against
> the dark rushing and to be carried away and away.[37]

The train displays an animal's energy, like the tram-car in Lawrence's
"Tickets, Please":

> To ride on these cars is always an adventure. Since we are in war-
> time, the drivers are men unfit for active service: cripples and
> hunchbacks. So they have the spirit of the devil in them.[38]

We have already noticed that the verb "rush" is significant in
Mansfield's tales: "I hate rushing animals like dogs and parrots", says
Kezia in "Prelude", and she adds: "I often dream that animals rush at
me – even camels – and while they are rushing their heads swell e-
enormous."[39] Linda, her mother, is disturbed by the same
phenomenon: "He [her husband, compared to a Newfoundland dog]
was too strong for her; she had always hated things that rush at her,
from a child."[40] And she dreams of birds swelling, thus giving a figure
to what Schopenhauer called the Will (see Chapter 5), that is the
irresistible unknowable self-destroying energy of life, the dark reality
that pervades Mansfield's work:

> What was happening to him? Something stirred in his breast.
> Something dark, something unbearable and dreadful pushed in his
> bosom, and like a great weed it floated, rocked ... it was warm,
> stifling. He tried to struggle to tear at it, and at the same moment – all
> was over.[41]

In "The Escape", the male character finds relief from this awful
feeling in the vision of the tree and the muted sound of the voice in the
silence. The barbarity of such dark life may be at the same time
captured and converted into existential truth through art, if the poem
or the painting identifies with life. Baudelaire also yearned for "un

---

[37] *Ibid.*, 181.
[38] D.H. Lawrence, "Tickets, Please!", in *England, My England* (1922), London:
Penguin, 1960, 41.
[39] Mansfield, *The Collected Stories*, 17.
[40] *Ibid.*, 54.
[41] *Ibid.*, 202.

chef-d'œuvre d'art vivant"[42] ("a living masterpiece of art"). Katherine Mansfield wanted to "*be REAL*"[43] (see Chapter 10).

William, in "Marriage à la Mode" feels the same sort of anguish within, which puts an end to the peaceful memories of childhood:

> The exquisite freshness of Isabel! When he *had been* a little boy, it was his delight to run into the garden after a shower of rain and shake the rose-bush over him. Isabel was that rose-bush, petal-soft, sparkling and cool. And he *was still* that little boy. *But* there was no running into the garden now, no laughing and shaking. The dull, persistent gnawing in his breast started again.[44]

The use of the past-perfect stresses the distance in time, contradicted through the association of happiness and memory, which set a continuity in time ("was still"), immediately snapped off by the presence of pain. William is then confronted with Isabel's "new way";[45] and he feels a stranger in his own house, a "new house"[46] in which he is but a visitor, coming at the weekend by train. Isabel's new friend, who wants to "rescue" her from her "selfish"[47] husband is called Moira, recalling the Greek name of the Fates, *Moira*, or Fate personified (see "So as Not to Conclude"), which also means, as a common name, "lot", "portion", or "destiny". Isabel, whom Moira calls Titania, thus belongs to a deceiving fairy world, as deceiving as the fairy grandfather in "The Little Governess".

There is such a thing as original innocence and shelter – symbolized by the "Noah's Ark",[48] saving the world from its end – but it can also be counterfeited so as to bewilder real innocence. In "Her First Ball", the "fat man" although he "squeezed her closer still" while dancing with the young girl does not deceive her but cools her enthusiasm with his pessimistic view of destructive time (see also Chapter 5):

---

[42] Charles Baudelaire, "Une mort héroïque", in *Le Spleen de Paris*, 83.
[43] *The Collected Letters of Katherine Mansfield, 1922-1923*, V, 341.
[44] Mansfield, *The Collected Stories*, 311-12 (my emphases).
[45] *Ibid.*, 310.
[46] *Ibid.*, 312.
[47] *Ibid.*, 313.
[48] *Ibid.*, 316.

> Oh, how quickly things changed! Why didn't happiness last for ever?
> For ever wasn't a bit too long.[49]

At least it is not too long for Orlando, in *As You Like It* (1600), who promises he will love Rosalind "For ever and a day",[50] thus associating, long before Kierkegaard, the present moment and eternity, which gives love an absolute existential status. Katherine Mansfield must have pondered over this famous cue. In "The Journey to Bruges", a story written in France, the sea voyage is associated with timelessness:

> In the shortest sea voyage there is no sense of time. You have been down in the cabin for hours or days or years. Nobody knows or cares. You know all the people to the point of indifference. You do not belong in dry land any more – you are caught in the pendulum itself, and left there, idly swinging.[51]

In her Notebooks, the name of Poe is mentioned in the list of the books she has read;[52] we may therefore associate the pendulum with the pit. Not belonging to dry land any longer implies the extraordinary experience of emancipation and freedom, with a particular sensitivity to what Baudelaire called "le gouffre",[53] "the abyss".

Katherine Mansfield does not wish to hide the awful reality of life behind the idealistic mask. She mocks German idealism in "The Sister of the Baroness": "Did the spirit of romance spread her rose wings only over aristocratic Germany?"[54] She has Henry say, in "Something Childish But Very Natural": "We ought to be building nests instead of houses, I always think."[55] But she depicts "The Doves' Nest" and Mrs Fawcett's soft language as stifling for Milly who feels "a yearning to fly".[56] She also suggests that such suavity is a lie: "At that Mother

---

[49] *Ibid.*, 342.
[50] William Shakespeare, *As You Like It* (1600), IV, 1, 132, ed. Alan Brissenden, Oxford: Oxford University Press, 1993, 192.
[51] Mansfield, *The Collected Stories*, 528.
[52] *The Katherine Mansfield Notebooks*, I, 32.
[53] Baudelaire, "Une mort héroïque", in *Le Spleen de Paris*, 83: "... l'ivresse de l'Art est plus apte que toute autre à voiler les terreurs du gouffre" (" ... the ecstasy of Art is more capable than any other to veil the terrors of the abyss").
[54] Mansfield, *The Collected Stories*, 695.
[55] *Ibid.*, 603.
[56] *Ibid.*, 444.

raised her head and gave him one of her still, bright, exalted glances that Milly knew well. 'I'm not in the least hurt,' she said, as one might say it from the midst of the fiery furnace."[57]

The allusion might go unnoticed but gives a clue to the mood of the story and to the writer's outlook (see Chapter 3). The "fiery furnace" is Nebuchadnezzar's punishment for the three young men who refused to worship the King's image of gold (Daniel, 3, 14-25). It suggests cruelty, sacrifice, and devouring energy. Yet, as in Blake's poetry, life's energy is not rejected in Katherine Mansfield's work. Although Kezia and Linda mistrust rushing creatures and their barbarity, nothing is ever presented as static in her tales and poems. In "Bliss", Mrs Norman Knight wears a "most amusing orange coat with a procession of black monkeys round the hem and up the fronts";[58] through the use of the word "procession", instead of "motif" or "design", she insists on movement. The effect is even more obvious with the "Indian curtain" in "Feuille d'Album" (see Chapter 4) since it "had a fringe of red leopards marching round it".[59] We find another animated "Indian curtain" in "Floryan nachdenklich", a poem written in 1913: "And the great tree grows and moves and spreads / Through the silent room"[60]. In "Prelude", Linda sees the poppy "come alive": "Things had a habit of coming alive like that. Not only large substantial things like furniture but curtains and the patterns of stuffs and the fringes of quilts and cushions."[61] Through becoming alive, things become personal and subjective. When starting, the train becomes personal and subjective. In "An Indiscreet Journey", when it begins to move, it is on the narrator's side,[62] and then, in the "smaller, shabbier train", the "sea-gull" on top of the "ordinary little"[63] woman's hat echoes and increases her own fear at the same time. The bird's presence in this situation and context is as inappropriate as the narrator's: "She had won, she had won. I was terrified."[64] But the terror is the thrill of her flight too.

---

[57] *Ibid.*, 440.
[58] *Ibid.*, 97.
[59] *Ibid.*, 163.
[60] Mansfield, *Poems*, 38.
[61] Mansfield, *The Collected Stories*, 27.
[62] *Ibid.*, 618.
[63] *Ibid.*, 622.
[64] *Ibid.*, 623.

In "The Little Governess" or "Something Childish But Very Natural", the movement of the train is quite as "rushing" as it is at the end of *La Bête humaine* (1890) by Emile Zola when the engine, no longer under human control, and crowded with soldiers going to the Front (1870), destroys everything with prodigious, irresistible strength. In her Notebooks, Katherine Mansfield wrote: "Zola defines Art as nature seen through a temperament (drives in a victoria to see the peasants)."[65] In "An Indiscreet Journey", the train's movement manifests this "temperament" which not only sees what happens but also records it. The war is revealed to the reader through the movement of the train: "And now there were soldiers everywhere working on the railway line, leaning against trucks or standing hands on hips, eyes fixed on the train as though they expected at least one camera at every window."[66] The train windows are more than simply eyes; they are recording eyes, cameras, which is quite paradoxical since a photograph means fixity. What is to be found is a language revealing this vital energy without stifling it: "O my wings – lift me – lift me."[67] In "The Fly", the insect also strives hard to escape from the boss' badgering.

"An Indiscreet Journey" is presented as initiation through an insistence on movement, comparison and resonance, and a pattern of images and figures derived from the Scriptures. With St Anne, God I and God II, the "heavy Egyptian cigarette",[68] and a few other hints, the narrator suggests a judgment on war as the Massacre of the Innocents, which caused the Flight into Egypt (see Chapter 10 for a more detailed analysis). (Therefore it is no mere chance that Raoul Duquette, who is derived from the character of Francis Carco, should think of this episode in "Je Ne Parle Pas Français": "One would not have been surprised if the door had opened and the Virgin Mary had come in, riding upon an ass, her meek hands folded over her big belly ...."[69]) Reality becomes figurative without losing its immediacy. It thus gains further resonance and significance. The writer presents everything through her own subjective movement, and the figures are submitted to metamorphosis.

---

[65] *The Katherine Mansfield Notebooks*, I, 165.
[66] Mansfield, *The Collected Stories*, 619.
[67] Mansfield, *Poems*, 82.
[68] Mansfield, *The Collected Stories*, 623.
[69] *Ibid.*, 63.

Through the looking-glass, the escape

In the movement which opens "At the Bay", from the expectation induced by the blurring mist to the appearance of the "pattering" sheep, the shepherd and the dog, the sounds take the significance of slow revelation and awakening to renewed subjective consciousness: "... and then such a silence that it seemed someone was listening."[70] Then the sheep seem to open the world to the new day, the flock spreading "out like a fan"[71] and penetrating children's dreams, as if the world were newly created. In the same way, at the beginning of "Prelude", the Burnells move into a new house, and the change is made under the sign of the wind and darkness: "With the dark crept the wind snuffling and howling."[72] Kezia thinks she could turn a pillbox found in her parents' room into some sort of nest ("'I could keep a bird's egg in that,' she decided."[73]) and we learn that she "liked to stand so before the window".[74]

Windows are also quite significant in "Feuille d'Album": they give a frame and a vista to the artist's vision but they are also a means of communicating, at least in the painter's imagination. In "The Wind Blows", Matilda perceives the storm outside through its sounds first and then looking out of the window: "And she begins to plait her hair with shaking fingers, not daring to look in the glass."[75] The window is an opening on to something else, some kind of otherness, while the mirror offers a sorry duplication of the self. It is no harmless object. In "Prelude", it is associated with discontented Beryl: "What had that creature in the glass to do with her, and why was she staring?"[76] Her reflection in the mirror reveals a "false self"[77] to her, which is playfully derided by Kezia in the end of the story when she "stuck the top of the cream jar over [the calico cat's] ear". The cat reacts like a clumsy clown and "the top of the cream jar flew through the air" but "did not break". [78] Yet in spite of all Kezia feels the need to make her escape.

---

[70] *Ibid.*, 205.
[71] *Ibid.*, 207.
[72] *Ibid.*, 15.
[73] *Ibid.*, 14.
[74] *Ibid.*, 15.
[75] *Ibid.*, 106.
[76] *Ibid.*, 58.
[77] *Ibid.*, 59.
[78] *Ibid.*, 60.

In "Pictures", the mirror appears in the same paragraph as "a high, cold wind":

> And then she sat down on one of the benches to powder her nose. But the person in the pocket mirror made a hideous face at her, and that was too much for Miss Moss; she had a good cry. It cheered her wonderfully.[79]

The outer self the looking glass reveals produces an estrangement and a split in the personality. In "The Man Without a Temperament", a story written in Ospedaletti in January 1920, the female character, who is ill, seems to see her illness reflected in her husband's behaviour ("Robert, the awful thing is – I suppose it's my illness"[80]). The motif of the "signet ring" he turns on "his little finger" time and again suggests his minding "awfully being out here with [her]".[67] Her illness means that estrangement is looming. It is some sort of motionless exile.

In "The Wind Blows", the duality suggested by the repetition of "The wind, the wind"[81] widens through movement and time, and even more in the evocation of exile. Then the third person, the person of absence, is used: "... Who are they?"[82] The water becomes an abyss of darkness. But: "They cannot walk fast enough." They seek to escape from the oppressive nest of childhood as if it could only be loved from a distance: "Does Mother imagine for one moment that she is going to darn all those stockings knotted up on the quilt like a coil of snakes?"[83] Yet in the same way as the rushing train is ambivalent (a revealing energy only for someone who has overgrown original innocence, or ignorance), voyages also mean initiation. We have seen how her first sea voyage quickened her awareness of the wild strangeness of life.

Ships and voyages

> They could see the lighthouse shining on Quarantine Island, and the green lights on the old coal hulks.

---

[79] *Ibid.*, 127.
[80] *Ibid.*, 143.
[81] *Ibid.*, 109.
[82] *Ibid.*, 110.
[83] *Ibid.*, 109.

> "There comes the Picton boat," said the storeman, pointing to a little steamer all hung with bright beads.[84]

The boat sailing from the South to the North, from Picton to Wellington, a 92 km voyage, says the advertising of the ferry company, aroused Katherine Mansfield's sense of wonder with its lights and its intimation of a world beyond the setting of everyday life. It is an appeal, like the "little yacht"[85] (a hat belonging to a "very stout gentleman"), a perfect instance of metamorphosis, and an opening, at the end of "Pictures": "And she sailed after the little yacht out of the café." In "Prelude", the Picton boat is mentioned during the removal. In "The Voyage", although the occasion is sad since Fenella has lost her mother and is about to leave her father, nevertheless the boat is endowed with enchanting mystery: "Lying beside the dark wharf, all strung, all beaded with round golden lights, the Picton boat looked as if she was more ready to sail among stars than out into the cold sea."[86]

The ferry has something celestial about it and should be associated with the lamp that we find at least in two stories, first in "Prelude", as Kezia gets into the new house, and then in "The Doll's House". In the latter story, it is said to be "real".[87] Its perfection is linked to the feeling of living somewhere, of belonging. The doll's house itself is described as marvellous and associated with God and the angels. It is an imitation of a house, and as such it is delighting, but the lamp, although it is only *like* a lamp ("But there was something inside that *looked like* oil and moved when you shook it"; my emphases) is endowed with a subjective quality: "It seemed to smile at Kezia, to say, 'I live here.' The lamp was real." The sense of reality is conveyed by the feeling of presence, of some sort of subjective response to be found in the outer world, cut off from its ordinariness and swinging like a pendulum in timelessness. The voyage breaks with ordinary linear time, and resembles a surge of wonder, a leap into the unknown.

Kezia's lamp, in "Prelude", is associated to the act of breathing: "The old woman bent down and gave the bright breathing thing into her hands and then she caught up drunken Lottie."[88] The fact that it

---

[84] *Ibid.*, 16.
[85] *Ibid.*, 128.
[86] *Ibid.*, 322.
[87] *Ibid.*, 384.
[88] *Ibid.*, 18.

should have been handed to Kezia by her grandmother is also significant because of the love the girl feels for her, which is expressed, later, in "At the Bay", with the double negative which we have already commented upon (see Chapter 5): "You couldn't not be there", following a meditation on death:

> Kezia lay still thinking this over. She didn't want to die. It meant she would have to leave here, leave everywhere, for ever, leave, – leave her grandma.[89]

The fact of "leaving" is therefore ambivalent: the Picton boat, with all its lights, stands out against darkness. It gives a familiar intimation of otherness. In "Psychology", the two protagonists meet in the woman's studio, among her familiar things ("She wanted time in which to free herself from all these familiar things with which she lived so vividly"[90]), but they are prevented from yielding to their mutual desire though a sense of otherness, thus figured (see also "So as Not to Conclude"):

> That silence could be contained in the circle of warm, delightful fire and lamplight. How many times hadn't they flung something into it just for the fun of watching the ripples break on the easy shores. But into this unfamiliar pool the head of the little boy sleeping dropped – and the ripples flowed away, away – boundlessly far – into deep glittering darkness.[91]

The same interweaving of light and darkness, of the familiar world and the world beyond, in time and in space, is to be found in "The Wind Blows". The desire for escape is linked with the feeling of something strange: "Bogey's voice is breaking." The musical coherence of the familiar world is threatened: "The wind carries their voices – away fly the sentences like little narrow ribbons."[92] Throughout the story, the world is shaken by wild forces: the familiar world is blown apart by the strong wind, by the two teenagers' haste to leave the house, and their strong desire to escape until their final leap into the far future, and exile. Yet, at the same time, within the

---

[89] *Ibid.*, 227.
[90] *Ibid.*, 112.
[91] *Ibid.*, 114.
[92] *Ibid.*, 110.

story itself, everything is being pieced together through rhythm – not simply the musical beats ("the little drums"[93] of Beethoven's minor movement) – but the rhythm of the existential dialectics at work in the tale, and which is figured in the end through the contrast of light and darkness: "It's the light that makes her look so *awfully beautiful* and mysterious ...."[94] Through what is almost an oxymoron, "awfully beautiful", Katherine Mansfield evinces her sense of beauty: something throbbing with tremendous energy, rooted in tragic darkness (the pit), but radiating with light, something breathing and endowed with wings, and a voice. Such figures, most of the time, are the emblems of a conversion of tragedy (the sense of the past and its irrevocable necessity – an abrupt obstacle, a ravine, as Plato suggests in *Cratylus*, 420 e) into epic wonder (the sense of the future, of looking ahead and living) through the power of the mind. In "Bliss", we understand how Bertha had been impressed by Wordsworth's famous poem on the daffodils, and the poetic power of memory:

> How strong the jonquils smelled in the warm room. Too strong? Oh, no. And yet, as though overcome, she flung down on a couch and pressed her hands to her eyes.
> "I'm too happy – too happy!" she murmured.
> And she seemed to see on her eyelids the lovely pear tree with its wide open blossoms as a symbol of her own life.[95]

Memory comes as a paradox in the rushing flow of becoming:

> Now the dark stretches a wing over the tumbling water. They can't see those two any more. Good-bye, good-bye. Don't forget ... But the ship is gone, now.[96]

The end contradicts the remark made earlier when the main character looks at herself in the mirror: "Ah, they know those two in the glass. Good-bye, dears; we shall be back soon."[97] It gives the feeling that the tale, through the active energy of memory, transcends the simple down-to-earth reflection in the mirror, and, embracing darkness, also

---

[93] *Ibid.*, 108.
[94] *Ibid.*, 110 (my emphasis).
[95] *Ibid.*, 96.
[96] *Ibid.*, 110.
[97] *Ibid.*, 109.

leaps through the looking-glass to confront otherness in all its dimensions.

The words "awful", "awfully", "dreadful", "dreadfully" are used time and again by Katherine Mansfield but they are intensifiers of her desire for reality. The word "awful"[98] is used in "The Voyage" when grandma says goodbye to Fenella's father but it does not cancel the marvellous aspect of the Picton boat. Her figures of the epic of life convert the tragedy, the gnawing darkness at the core of being, into radiating energy. Yet the sea voyage should connect two shores, although they may remain alien to each other. In "In the Darkness", a poem she probably wrote on board the S.S. Niwaru in 1903, she writes: "I am sitting in the darkness / And the whole house is still / But I feel I need your presence / Since I've been ill."[99] When such presence is denied, the voyage is threatened.

In "The Man Without a Temperament", the two beds in the dark are likened to "two ships".[100] The comparison is spun two pages further: "The moon – the room is painted white with moonlight. The light trembles in the mirrors; the two beds seem to float." The mirrors seem to shake the fullness of light, making it "tremble". But, more significant, just before came this reflection: "There are a great many stars; an enormous white moon hangs over the garden. Far away lightning flutters – flutters like a wing – flutters like a broken bird that tries to fly and sinks again and again struggles."[101] "... the ecstasy of Art is more capable than any other to veil [and unveil] the terrors of the abyss", we might say, borrowing from Baudelaire (see n.53 above). Pearl Button, in her happiness at being kidnapped, associates the sense of touch, the smell, the softness of a bed, darkness, and breathing: "She was softer than a bed and she had a nice smell – a smell that made you bury your head and breathe and breathe it ...."[102]

The epic achievement
At the end of "The Escape", the male character sees "the tree", a paradox of light and darkness ("a great arc of copper leaves that gave back the light and yet were sombre"), against an indefinite

---

[98] *Ibid.*, 323.
[99] *The Katherine Mansfield Notebooks*, I, 25.
[100] Mansfield, *The Collected Stories*, 140.
[101] *Ibid.*, 142.
[102] *Ibid.*, 520.

background ("a whiteness, a softness, an opaque mass, half hidden – with delicate pillars"). Then comes a deep silence and a "woman's voice", singing but not breaking the silence. The moment is an escape; the moment is marvellous but the following description, "As he looked at the tree he felt his breathing die away and he became part of the silence", sounds ambivalent when we read what follows:

> Suddenly, as the voice rose, soft, dreaming, gentle, he knew that it would come floating to him from the hidden leaves and his peace was shattered. What was happening to him? Something stirred in his breast. Something dark, something unbearable and dreadful pushed in his bosom, and like a great weed it floated, rocked ... it was warm, stifling. He tried to struggle to tear at it, and at the same moment – all was over.[103]

The epic figure of the tree and the peaceful silence it brings forth transcends the narrow relationship to oneself, as in the looking-glass, and the unhappiness of life locked within the limits of what is usual and familiar. Katherine Mansfield wanted to sail abroad: her exile was voluntary. Yet her illness was the element of strangeness – the exile within – she had to convert into a strengthened sense of being. "The Fly" gives an account of this struggle to be in spite of all. The darkness in her bosom ("The familiar dull gnawing in his breast"[104] in "Marriage à la Mode") is transcended to a wider existential reality at the end of "The Canary":

> ... All the same, without being morbid, and giving way to – to memories and so on, I must confess that there does seem to me something sad in life. It is hard to say what it is. I don't mean the sorrow that we all know, like illness and poverty and death. No, it is something different. It is there, deep down, deep down, deep down, part of one, like one's breathing.[105]

It is what a writer's initiation amounts to: tackling life's personal experience (the immediate) and moving beyond the simple autobiographical report (the simple reflection in the looking-glass) to achieve a more than personal but highly personal epic of life – the

---

[103] *Ibid.*, 201-202.
[104] *Ibid.*, 320.
[105] *Ibid.*, 422.

instant thus magnified within the awful rush of becoming. It amounts to an ethical conversion of contingency, what Rudolf Kassner called a return to oneself in the infinite, a movement of freedom.

The pear tree, in "Bliss", provides such a conversion of unhappiness and despair into some strong radiating reality, "a circle of unearthly light",[106] which is not dismissed at the end of the story in spite of the new pain. It contrasts with Raoul Duquette's bitterness "against Life",[107] his satisfaction at seeing himself in the mirror, his conceit, and his trite art, as suggested by his titles: *Wrong Doors, Left Umbrellas*. Katherine Mansfield aims the same kind of attack in "Marriage à la Mode" when she describes Isabel's new artist friends' greedy manners (see "So as Not to Conclude").

Her art transcends the ordinary, which means escape, but it cannot be described as escapism since she penetrates the dark reality of life, yet does not indulge in tragedy. Her view is epic and Linda's aloe in "Prelude" looks like Argo, the Argonauts' ship built with the oracular beam from Dodona. Linda "heard herself cry: 'Faster! Faster!' to those who were rowing".[108] This repeated comparative echoes "Quicker! Quicker!"[109] in "The Wind Blows". The epic figure provides a synthesis in time since it projects itself in the future as memory of the past: "And I am sure I shall remember it long after I've forgotten all the other things."[110] The modern individual epic transcends finite space with its intuition of the infinity of becoming. The traditional epic voyage makes life's journey through time visible. "How much more real this dream was than that they should go back to the house where the sleeping children lay and where Stanley and Beryl played cribbage": Beryl is the unhappy character who cannot transcend her disappointment with her reflection in the mirror. Exile, "quicker! quicker!", brings the aura of mystery which helps to enhance life's marvellous depth – the flame leaping out of darkness through the looking-glass. The reflection in the mirror is transcended by the rushing power of becoming. "Faster! Faster!" Katherine Mansfield's writing is characterized by movement and metamorphosis. The very structure of her tales is a metamorphic

---

[106] *Ibid.*, 102.
[107] *Ibid.*, 62.
[108] *Ibid.*, 53.
[109] *Ibid.*, 110.
[110] *Ibid.*, 53.

rendering of becoming, and provides a paradoxical restitution through art of what should have been lost forever. Such rhythm also transcends the "idiotic"[111] feature of civilization: "Why be given a body if you have to keep it shut up in a case like a rare, rare fiddle?"[112] Bergson, who influenced Murry's views when he founded the magazine *Rhythm*, to which Mansfield significantly contributed, thought that we were free when our whole personality was involved in what we did. He also thought that life is movement and energy.[113]

Identifying with life like Baudelaire celebrating the "living masterpiece of art", Katherine Mansfield embraces its movement and withstands anything that might lock her in, whether "idiotic" civilization, the "House of Boxes", or acquiescence to tragedy. One thinks of a poet who was nearly her contemporary, though thirteen years older, R.M. Rilke (1875-1926): "Atmen, du unsichtbares Gedicht!"[114] We may say that Katherine Mansfield is a writer of "the Open" – "das Offene" (see "So as Not to Conclude"): "Mit allen Augen sieht die Kreatur / das Offene." The "Open" is the vision without any hindrances or limitations, of which the "free animal" is capable: "und wenn es geht, so gehts / in Ewigkeit, so wie die Brunnen gehen."[115] It implies acquiescing to the infinity of becoming; it implies unhampered movement, the emancipated movement of being, counteracting the obstacle of necessity on behalf of freedom. This wish is symbolized by the wings, in Katherine Mansfield's tales and poems, and the symbol is ambivalent. The mystery of being is the "wing" of the "dark" which "stretches over the tumbling water",[116] in "The Wind Blows". Darkness may be frightening, and "awful", but it can also be a source of pleasure, as in "How Pearl Button Was Kidnapped":

---

[111] *Ibid.*, 92, 95.

[112] *Ibid.*, 92.

[113] Henri Bergson, *Essai sur les données immédiates de la conscience* (1888), Paris : P.U.F., 2001, 129, 98-99.

[114] R.M. Rilke, *Les Sonnets à Orphée* (1922), in *Les Elégies de Duino, Les Sonnets à Orphée*, bilingual edition, Paris: Seuil Points, 1974, 144.

[115] R.M. Rilke, "Die achte Elegie", *Les Elégies de Duino* (1912-1922), in *Les Elégies de Duino, Les Sonnets à Orphée*, 74. "With all eyes does the creature see / the open". "and when it moves, it moves / in eternity, as the fountains do."

[116] Mansfield, *The Collected Stories*, 110.

Pearl tried to look through them but it was quite dark. Birds were singing. She nestled closer in the big lap. The woman was warm as a cat, and she moved up and down when she breathed, just like purring.[117]

The wings are also the whole being's vital energy wrestling with its denial to secure its access to the "Open":

Oh, waters – do not cover me!
I would look long and long at those beautiful stars!
O my wings – lift me – lift me
I am not so dreadfully hurt ...[118]

In 1908, Mansfield wrote about the "singular charm and barrenness" of Wellington, "with climatic effects – wind, rain, spring, night, the sea, the cloud pageantry", and about her desire to "leave the place and go to Europe, to live there a dual existence". She mentions disillusionment but nevertheless expresses the wish to "return to London" and "to live there an existence so full & so strange that Life itself seemed to greet her".[119] She thinks of illness and death but imagines that her character returns to Wellington to die there. The voyage back home is also an epic motif, the topic of the *Odyssey*, for instance. In her native place, she experienced the first intuition of the "Open", the awful appeal of leaving, the rushing impulse. Thinking in terms of the centre and its periphery, if Europe, before the Great War, imposed itself as a centre of civilization, annexing its satellites and exerting a particular cultural attraction, we may say that Katherine Mansfield's awareness of the dark rushing impulse to live, through her confrontation to otherness in her native place, brought to the core what had been ruled out in the arrogant triumph of identity (the dissatisfying mirror). The move to the "heart of darkness" is an indiscreet journey and the First World War unveiled the abyss at the heart of European "idiotic" civilization. But the realization of otherness leads to plenitude, and no longer to the empty centre which the denial of existential reality and the lack of a temperament leave gaping. "'Rot!' he whispers."[120]

---

[117] *Ibid.*, 521.

[118] Mansfield, *Poems*, 82.

[119] *The Katherine Mansfield Notebooks*, I, 111-12.

[120] Mansfield, "The Man Without a Temperament", in *The Collected Stories*, 143.

CHAPTER 7

"PALPABLE DARKNESS" – "O MY WINGS!":
KATHERINE MANSFIELD AND D.H. LAWRENCE

> Or one of those apricots that feels
> warm as a hand when you take
>
> it up from the table on the veranda.
> It says 'afternoon' any time of night
>
> or day.[1]

Katherine Mansfield's views as regards Lawrence are very ambivalent. She writes: "Wasn't Lawrence awfully nice that night. Ah, one must always *love* Lawrence for his 'being'."[2] Yet she also speaks of his "pride"[3] and, after the release of *Women in Love* in 1920-21, says:

> It seems to me there is something hopelessly wrong with Lawrence now, & don't you feel, too theres a kind of devilish exasperation & even as he would say PURE stupidity, It makes me groan. I wish I could find a really good book for a change.[4]

D.H. Lawrence does not mince his words when he writes about *Bliss and Other Stories*, published in 1920: "The *Nation* said K[atherine]'s book was the best short story book that could be or had been written. Spit on her for me when you see her, she's a liar out and out."[5] Later,

---

[1] Vincent O'Sullivan, "Before You Go", in *Cette voûte de si pur respire/That Vault of Such Pure Breath*, Poems, Bilingual edition, trans. Anne Mounic, Paris: Inventaire, 2006, 52.
[2] To S.S. Koteliansky, [*c*. 20 December 1921], in *The Collected Letters of Katherine Mansfield*, IV, 343.
[3] To J.M. Murry, [24 November 1922], in *ibid.*, V, 326.
[4] To Sylvia Lynd, [early September 1921], in *ibid.*, IV, 274.
[5] *The Selected Letters of D.H. Lawrence*, ed. James T. Boulton, Cambridge: Cambridge University Press, 1997, 185.

in 1923, when *The Dove's Nest and Other Stories* was published after Katherine Mansfield's death, he remarked: "I think it's a downright cheek to ask the public to buy that waste-paper basket."[6] He compares Turgenev to her, saying she is "very critical"[7] but wrote to the Murrys in 1916: "I believe in you, and there's the end of it."[8] A few weeks after her brother's death, he said to her: "Do not be sad. It is one life which is passing away from us, one 'I' is dying; but there is another coming into being, which is the happy, creative you."[9] In that letter he voices all his ideas concerning the necessary death of the narrow self that he developed in *Women in Love*, which he was writing at the period, and in "The Horse Dealer's Daughter", a short story he started in 1916 and resumed in 1921. And to Murry he wrote, in February 1923, after Katherine's death:

> Yes, I always knew a bond in my heart. Feel a fear where the bond is broken now. Feel as if the old moorings were breaking all. What is going to happen to us all?[10]

And Katherine's description of Lawrence's behaviour in Cornwall in 1916 is famous:

> He simply *raves*, roars, beats the table, abuses every body .... I hate games where people lose their tempers in this way – Its so witless. In fact they are not my kind at all.[11]

Yet in her notebooks, in September 1918, she admits:

> My fits of temper are really terrifying .... Strangely enough these fits are Lawrence and Frieda over again. I am more like L. than anybody. We are <u>unthinkably</u> alike, in fact.[12]

---

[6] *Ibid.*, 260.
[7] *Ibid.*, 146.
[8] *Ibid.*, 122.
[9] *Ibid.*, 112.
[10] *Ibid.*, 251.
[11] To Beatrice Campbell, [4 May 1916], in *The Collected Letters of Katherine Mansfield*, I, 261.
[12] *The Katherine Mansfield Notebooks*, II, 143.

In August 1921, still thinking he was "wrong", she noticed: "What makes Lawrence a *real* writer is his passion. Without passion one writes in the air or on the sands of the seashore."[13]

A mutual exasperation
At first sight we should think that it is not reasonable to compare D.H. Lawrence's and Katherine Mansfield's work: an accumulation of long novels, some essays and travel books, several collections of vehement verse, partly influenced by Whitman, and several collections of short stories, quite different from Mansfield's; but from her three collections of stories published in her lifetime, and a few poems as well as a fair number of book reviews; from both, a huge number of letters. Lawrence was only three years older than Katherine Mansfield and, affected by the same illness, lived seven years after her. We could say that she was spared such works as *Kangaroo*, his Australian novel (1923), or *The Plumed Serpent* (1926), a novel which can be associated with such a terrible short story as "The Woman Who Rode Away", written when Lawrence lived in Taos, and first published in 1925. One could argue that there is a huge difference of scope between Lawrence the prophet and the little voice of the New Zealand exile. Moreover Lawrence's views on "the subject of *maleness*"[14] exasperated Mansfield while his portrait of her as Gudrun in *Women in Love* is rather critical of "her perfect *sang-froid*", her "look of diffidence and confidence",[15] the "body of cold power in her".[16] Gerald saw her as "a dangerous, hostile spirit": "There was a diabolic coldness in her, too much to bear."[17] In her "completeness"[18] and isolation, she seems to be distant and unattainable – a sibyl rather than a prophet.

Darkness palpable
For D.H. Lawrence, the sense of touch is decisive. A stroke of the hand sets a link, or rather a bondage, between the outer world and the depth of the invisible being: "But the soft, straying tenderness of her

---

[13] *The Collected Letters of Katherine Mansfield*, IV, 270.
[14] *Ibid.*, 330.
[15] D.H. Lawrence, *Women in Love* (1920), London: Penguin, 1974, 8.
[16] *Ibid.*, 135.
[17] *Ibid.*, 498.
[18] *Ibid.*, 501.

hand on his face startled something out of his soul."[19] And Hadrian, in "You Touched Me", then feels he is bound to Matilda as she is to him. In "The Horse Dealer's Daughter", Mabel's touching Fergusson, her hands "drawing him down to her", together with her "murmur of deep rhapsodic assurance",[20] is revolting to him: "And yet – and yet – he had not the power to break away." It is almost certain that Lawrence never read Maine de Biran (1766-1824) but it is difficult here not to think of what the French philosopher called "the immediate touch of the sensitive soul" and which is the inner apprehension of our most intimate, and fleeting, sensations, which "vanish at the very moment when the self wants to go deeper, like Eurydice, sent back among the shades of Hades at a single glance".[21]

Maine de Biran's views differ from Freud's since he admits that what cannot be represented can nevertheless be felt and exist without necessarily being shamefully suppressed. It is Lawrence's "palpable darkness".[22] In "The Blind Man", the sense of touch reveals Maurice's inner power of knowing the deeper being beyond appearances: "He seemed to take him, in the soft, travelling grasp."[23] In this paragraph, describing how Maurice passed his "naked hand" on Bertie's head, shoulder and hand, the word "grasp", noun or verb, is repeated four times. The use of the adjective "naked" is also significant since the hand gets to the knowledge of the naked being, and its single original essence – exactly what Bertie is reluctant to apprehend. When Maurice, asking him to touch his scarred eyes, "pressed the fingers of the other man upon his disfigured sockets, trembling in every fibre", Bertie "stood as if in a swoon, unconscious, imprisoned".

Katherine Mansfield seems to be more aloof and her outlook sounds more spiritual, if we consider, for instance "The New Zealander" in the *Notebooks*, around 1908:

---

[19] Lawrence, "You Touched Me", in *England, My England*, 116.

[20] *Ibid.*, 170.

[21] Maine de Biran, *Rapports du physique et du moral de l'homme*, Paris: Vrin, 1984, 128 (my translation). On the analogy between Maine de Biran's and Lawrence's views, see Anne Mounic, "D.H. Lawrence: Darkness visible, ténèbres palpables, ou le puits de l'être. *Temporel*, n° 5, http://temporel.fr/D-H-Lawrence-Tenebres-palpables. Also: Anne Mounic, *Jacob ou l'être du possible*, Paris: Caractères, 2009, 192-210.

[22] D.H. Lawrence, *The Rainbow* (1915), London: Penguin, 1987, 230.

[23] Lawrence, *England, My England*, 73.

> "I am desire" said the sea, "I crave all, insatiably I long, untiringly I hold."
> "I am breath" said the wind. "I blow over all the waste places of the earth & make them filled with my voice."

Reading those lines, however, we may feel that there is no obstacle in her to the expression of her inner creative power: the sea's desire, her desire, combining with the breath of the wind penetrating the world with its voice call for the presence of love:

> Rewa stood upright, stretched out her arms. Darkness shrouded the world. Through the storm she heard footsteps behind her, wheeled round sharply, her terror distorting her face. But he came forward & caught her in his arms. "You" she said, "you".[24]

Between the young woman and the Creation, filled with the breath of the wind, there is absolute empathy, as there seems to be in the love scene between Rupert and Ursula in "Excurse", Chapter 23 of *Women in Love*:

> There were faint sounds from the wood, but no disturbance, no possible disturbance, the world was under a strange ban, a new mystery had supervened. They threw off their clothes, and he gathered her to him, and found her, found the pure lambent reality of her for ever invisible flesh.[25]

Yet Rupert, Lawrence's *alter ego*, wants no "fusion"[26] but "the way of freedom".[27] With Ursula, he wishes to achieve "this star-equilibrium which alone is freedom".[28] The "palpable darkness" in which Maurice lives induces the new knowledge of otherness in the other and in himself, the apprehension of the "pure lambent reality of her for ever invisible flesh":

> Quenched, inhuman, his fingers upon her unrevealed nudity were the fingers of silence upon silence, the body of mysterious night upon the body of mysterious night, the night masculine and feminine, never to

---

[24] *The Katherine Mansfield Notebooks*, I, 224.
[25] Lawrence, *Women in Love*, 360-61.
[26] *Ibid.*, 248.
[27] *Ibid.*, 287.
[28] *Ibid.*, 360.

be seen with the eyes, or known with the mind, only known as a palpable revelation of living otherness.[29]

This knowledge is a new birth, reflexive and reciprocal:

> And then within the night where nothing is,
> And I am only next to nothingness,
> Touch me, oh touch me, give me destinies
> By touch, and a new nakedness.[30]

This new birth is made possible through these two movements of the mind – reflexivity and reciprocity – as revealed in language by repetition and coordination. The reflexive consciousness, which induces this feeling of being newly born, is stirred through the reciprocal intercourse of two subjectivities: "For she was to him what he was to her, the immemorial magnificence of mystic, palpable, real otherness."[31]

Rhapsodic, in two ways

With her allusive, impressionistic style, Katherine Mansfield sounds very different from Lawrence, who, as Ursula says about Birkin, might be considered as "the Sunday school teacher", a "preacher".[32] He says things, again and again, discusses them through his characters. And the biblical knowledge he has acquired, with his mother mainly, in childhood, permeates his work. We could think he is dogmatic and only wishes to develop his one idea. In *Apocalypse*, an essay completed in January 1930, he writes:

> So that today, although I have 'forgotten' my Bible, I need only begin to read a chapter to realize that I 'know' it with an almost nauseating fixity. And I must confess, my first reaction is one of dislike, repulsion, and even resentment. My very instincts *resent* the Bible.[33]

---

[29] *Ibid.*, 361.
[30] D.H. Lawrence, *Complete Poems*, eds Vivian de Sola Pinto and Warren Roberts, London: Penguin Books, 1993, 738.
[31] Lawrence, *Women in Love*, 361.
[32] *Ibid.*, 283.
[33] D.H. Lawrence, *Apocalypse* (1931), London: Penguin, 1981, 3 (Lawrence's emphasis).

However, despite his dislike of the Puritan reading of the Bible, he refers to the Scriptures in his whole work.[34] In *The Rainbow*, Anna feels she is standing on the Pisgah mountain,[35] like Moses contemplating the Promised Land he will never reach. The title of the book itself refers to God's covenant after the Flood, directly mentioned in Chapter 11, "First Love",[36] and criticized by Ursula. Yet Lawrence clings to the idea of a new covenant: "She saw in the rainbow the earth's new architecture, the old, brittle corruption of houses and factories swept away, the world built up in a living fabric of Truth, fitting to the over-arching heaven."[37] This is the end of the novel, in which Moses was also present in the reference to the Burning Bush, now powerless and sterile: "God burned no more in that bush. It was dead matter lying there."[38]

But Lawrence the prophet wants to instigate a new beginning. After he had written *The Rainbow*, in 1915, he had the idea of founding a small community called *Rananim* (Psalms 33, 1), a Hebrew plural meaning "green, fresh or flourishing";[39] he wished to gather "some twenty righteous or at least like-minded people dedicated to fostering 'new shoots of life' within themselves, and subsequently to seeding the sterile ruins of Western civilisation". Bertrand Russell, who had been approached on that project, compared Lawrence to "Ezekiel or some Old Testament prophet, prophesying. Of course, the blood of his nonconformist preaching ancestors is strong in him, but he sees everything and is always right."[40] Murry too had been considered a possible recruit.

Therefore, Lawrence's critical apprehension of the Bible does not erase the values he owes to his biblical education and, moreover, the fact that he should be so tempted to prophesy does not turn his writings into sheer allegory – which he severely condemns in Chapter Ten of *Apocalypse*: "Symbols mean something: yet they mean something different to every man. Fix the meaning of a symbol, and

---

[34] See T.R. Wright, *D.H. Lawrence and the Bible*, Cambridge: Cambridge University Press, 2000.

[35] Lawrence, *The Rainbow*, 185.

[36] *Ibid.*, 325.

[37] *Ibid.*, 496.

[38] *Ibid.*, 203.

[39] Keith Sagar, *The Life of D.H. Lawrence*, London: Methuen, 1982, 75.

[40] *Ibid.*, 83.

you have fallen into the common place of allegory."[41] And it is true that, in spite of his desire to express his ideas, Lawrence also gives vent to the complexities and contradictions of life. In his Foreword to *Fantasia of the Unconscious*, he presents himself as a genuine poet, deducing his thought from the experience of writing, which is a quest for knowledge of what is yet unknown:

> This pseudo-philosophy of mine – 'pollyanalytics', as one of my respected critics might say – is deduced from the novels and poems, not the reverse. *The novels and poems come unwatched out of one's pen ....* The novels and poems are pure passionate experience. These 'pollyanalytics' are inferences made afterwards, from the experience.[42]

His concern is not the finite world of dogmatic belief, but the probing of experience.

This desire to delve into the unknown in the deep soul in order to find the roots of "the inner, unknown drama"[43] and write "the epic of the soul of mankind" is the reason for Lawrence's rhapsodic style. He uses the word himself to characterize Mabel's way of speaking in "The Horse-Dealer's Daughter": "'You love me,' she repeated, in a murmur of deep rhapsodic assurance. 'You love me.'"[44] Hermione, a character inspired by Lady Ottoline Morrell, is compared to a rhapsodist – a singing epic poet in ancient Greece, whom Socrates criticises in *Ion*, one of Plato's early dialogues, "sewing songs together" – in Chapter 8 of *Women in Love*, "Breadalby".[45] Gudrun "sang in strange, rhapsodic tones"[46] in Chapter 20, "Snowed Up", asking Gerald to leave her alone since she is being carried away by the beauty of the mountains. And Lawrence uses this rhapsodic style of repetition and metamorphosis:

> She traced with her hands the line of his loins and thighs, at the back, and a living fire ran through her, from him, darkly. It was a dark flood of electric passion she released from him, drew into herself. She had

---

[41] Lawrence, *Apocalypse*, 60.
[42] *Ibid.*, 15 (my emphasis).
[43] Lawrence, *The Rainbow*, 280.
[44] Lawrence, *England, My England*, 170.
[45] Lawrence, *Women in Love*, 94: "Hermione, lifting the face of a rhapsodist."
[46] *Ibid.*, 503.

established a rich new circuit, a new current of passional electric energy, between the two of them, released from the darkest poles of the body and established in perfect circuit. It was a dark fire of electricity that rushed from him to her, and flooded them both with rich peace, satisfaction.[47]

From the repeated words and the polyptotons, the deep meaning emerges: "fire, darkly, dark, flood, electric, passion, release, establish, rich, new, circuit, passional, darkest, electricity." We can also spot chains of meanings: "fire, passion, energy"; the "circuit" is transformed into a "current", which goes with the "flood" of electricity. And the "living fire" at the beginning is transformed into "a dark fire", which is an oxymoron, recalling courtly love and Petrarchan poetry, while the metaphor of electric energy traces back to German Romanticism and *Naturphilosophy*.[48] We find such influence, and reference to Galvani, in Poe's stories as well. At the beginning, the "flood" was "dark" and "of electric passion". It becomes "a new current of passional electricity": "passional", used as an adjective, rather than "passioned" or "passionate", is significant. The *OUP* only gives a substantive: "A book containing accounts of the suffering of saints and martyrs, for reading on their festival days." It seems that here, as an adjective, it refers to the essence of passion rather than to its manifestation, which tallies with the meaning of the passage, and of its rhapsodic style.

Ursula's hand, drawing an invisible line on Rupert's "loins and thighs" triggers off a surge of indomitable inner power that transcends the hitherto established limits of the self – what Lawrence calls death and resurrection on the model of the "man who died",[49] and his Passion. He describes such metamorphosis in "The Thorn in the Flesh" (another biblical title, referring to Paul's, 2 Corinthians, 12, 7), a story written in June 1913: "Warm, with a glow in their hearts and faces, they rose again, modest, but transfigured with happiness."[50] The motif of the Transfiguration (Matthew, 17, 1-8), in the context, implies a metamorphosis of darkness into radiance, and a revelation coming from an invisible voice, presenting Jesus as the Son of God,

---

[47] *Ibid.*, 353.
[48] See Georges Gusdorf, *Le savoir romantique de la nature*, Paris: Payot, 1985.
[49] D.H. Lawrence, *The Man Who Died* (1929), in *Love Among the Haystacks* (1960), Harmondsworth: Penguin, 1986.
[50] Lawrence, *The Prussian Officer and Other Stories*, 42.

His Incarnation therefore: "And Jesus came and *touched* them, and said: 'Arise, and be not afraid'" (Matthew, 17, 7 – my italics). God made flesh "touches" his disciples after the revelation of His essence. The sense of touch reveals the dark energy of being and Lawrence's metamorphic style follows what Maine de Biran called the "immediate touch of the sensitive soul". The verbs used are verbs of movement – "ran through", "rushed", and "flooded" – or suggesting new freedom – "released" – but also determination and permanence – "established".

The passage is truly poetic since its meaning cannot only be deduced from the plain meaning of the words but also from their arrangement. It is significant that the "rich new circuit" should become a "perfect circuit" and that "rich" should also qualify the "peace" thus obtained in the end. The prepositions are also essential for the meaning: "through her, from him"; "she released from him, drew into herself"; "between the two of them"; "from him to her". They all denote passage from one to the other, and reciprocity until the final unity of being, "flooded them both":

> 'My love,' she cried, lifting her face to him, her eyes, her mouth open in transport.
> 'My love,' he answered, bending and kissing her, always kissing her.

Through repetition and metamorphosis, the words seem to brush against this unknown reality of the flesh, the essence of being, and to force it outwards as a snake charmer will have the dark animal undulate before our eyes. And now Schopenhauer should be summoned for two reasons: first, Hermione, the "rhapsodist", is submitted to "the unfailing mechanism of her will",[51] which recalls Schopenhauer will to live, an indomitable process which we can only know through intuition because it is also at work in our individual bodies. However the will, according to Maine de Biran, is also the conscious power which aims at controlling the fluid Eurydice, the mute life of the flesh at the depth of being. The will, controlling the self, is essential for Stoic philosophers. Rupert tells Ursula, in Chapter 19, "Moony": "I want you to drop your assertive *will*, your frightened apprehensive self-insistence, that is what I want. I want you to trust

---

[51] Lawrence, *Women in Love*, 111.

yourself so implicitly that you can let yourself go."[52] Yet, Schopenhauer must have been right to insist upon the fatalistic character of the will, or Lawrence could never have written such a paradoxical sentence: "I *want* you to *drop* your assertive *will*." Inspired by Indian mysticism, the German philosopher advocates the annihilation of the will through the extinction of selfhood, which Thomas Hardy exemplified at the end of *Tess of the d'Urbervilles*. The second reason for recalling Schopenhauer is that he considers the arts as a means of revealing the essence of being, that is the will, and especially music, which is an accurate copy of the will.[53] Music reveals the intimate essence of the world. So does language, we may infer, when it becomes "rhapsodic". In "Snowed Up", Gerald leaves Gudrun in her ecstatic state: "He stood back a little, and left her standing there, statue-like, transported into the mystic glowing east."[54] We shall see Lawrence is critical of such dualistic viewpoint but let us come back to Katherine Mansfield.

In "Psychology", published in 1921, there is absolutely no "fusion" between the two lovers: "Passion would have ruined everything; they quite saw that."[55] They find it difficult to break the silence between them, and never touch each other. Instead, the male character says that when he is not in her studio, he imagines the place: "I revisit it in spirit – wander about among your red chairs, stare at the bowl of fruit on the black table – and just *touch*, very lightly, that marvel of a sleeping boy's head."[56] But when in the presence of the object, he just looks at it. Their relationship remains distant, through the distance of memory, or the distance of what D.W. Winnicott[57] calls the "potential space" between the individuals:

> That silence could be contained in the circle of warm, delightful fire and lamplight. How many times hadn't they flung something into it for just the fun of watching the ripples break on the easy shores. But

---

[52] *Ibid.*, 283 (Lawrence's emphasis).
[53] Arthur Schopenhauer, *The World as Will and Representation*, I, §52. *Le monde comme volonté et comme représentation* (1819-1851), Paris: P.U.F. Quadrige, 2004, 335.
[54] Lawrence, *Women in Love*, 503.
[55] Mansfield, *The Collected Stories*, 113.
[56] *Ibid.*, 114 (my emphasis). On this story, see also Chapter 6 and "So as Not to Conclude".
[57] See D.W. Winnicott, *Playing and Reality*, London: Tavistock, 1971, Chapter 7.

into this familiar pool the head of the little boy sleeping his timeless sleep dropped – and the ripples flowed away, away – boundlessly far – into deep glittering darkness.

If we compare this passage to those quoted from Lawrence's work, we might say it is exactly the reverse: "Why didn't they just give way to it – yield – and see what will happen then?"[58] The characters brush against fulfilment but avoid it: "All was over. What was over? Oh – something was."[59] The intuition of the "deep, glittering darkness" remains indefinite: "something", and the present moment, devoid of realization, is left hanging in timelessness, as in Keats' "Ode on a Grecian Urn":

> Bold lover, never, never canst thou kiss,
> Though winning near the goal – yet, do not grieve.[60]

It is only at the end, when she has embraced her female friend who came to bring her violets, that she feels joy, "as if she had woken up out of a childish sleep. Even the act of breathing was a joy ...."[61] Yet the violets are "a little dead bunch", like Ophelia's withered violets:[62] Violets are for faithfulness. We may feel some bitterness here.

Yet, in spite of her different existential stand, I think we can say that Katherine Mansfield develops her own rhapsodic style. We find instances of repetition in "Psychology": "... they had had their experiences, and very rich and varied they had been, but now was the time for harvest – harvest."[63] The male character says: "If I shut my eyes I can see this place down to every detail – every detail ...."[64] Each time, the repetition is split by a dash, as if it was echoed through "this unfamiliar pool". We find the same kind of thing in "The Wind Blows", another story published in 1921 in *Bliss*.

The story starts with a pattern of repetition and metamorphosis:

---

[58] Mansfield, *The Collected Stories*, 115.
[59] *Ibid.*, 117.
[60] Keats, *Poetical Works*, 210.
[61] Mansfield, *The Collected Stories*, 118.
[62] Shakespeare, *Hamlet*, IV, 5, 184-85, 308.
[63] Mansfield, *The Collected Stories*, 113.
[64] *Ibid.*, 114.

> Suddenly – dreadfully – she wakes up. What has just happened? Something dreadful has happened. No nothing has happened.[65]

The notion of suddenness is transformed into dreadfulness. A question follows, which gets an indefinite answer, "Something dreadful", which is immediately negated: "nothing has happened." "Happened" is repeated three times, which means that the present moment is being questioned – the present moment of awakening, of coming back to consciousness: "What has just happened?" The question, therefore, refers to the unknown world of darkness that can only be apprehended through the "immediate touch of the sensitive soul". And it receives an echo in the outer world: "It is only the wind shaking the house." The wind then becomes the symbol of what separates in time; the self is split: "Ah, they know those two in the glass."[66] The mirror brings about the first dissociation of the self. Then time completes the divorce: "The wind carries their voices – away fly the sentence like little narrow ribbons."[67] The characters project themselves into the future: "*They* are on board leaning over the rail arm in arm." But the future is also the past:

> Now the dark stretches a wing over the tumbling water. They can't see those two any more. Goodbye, goodbye. Don't forget …. But the ship is gone, now.
>
> The wind – the wind.

Throughout the story, "the wind – the wind" is repeated, most of the time with the dash in-between. "Goodbye, goodbye", with the same iambic rhythm, parallels the repetition of "the wind". We find other repetitions: "Come on! Come on!", or "Quicker! Quicker!" – the haste being aptly expressed through the trochaic rhythm, and showing the reversed movement, as in "Good**bye**, **li**ttle **isl**and, good**bye** …." The stressed syllables, in bold, reveal two opposite rhythms in the tetrameter, iambic at the beginning and at the end, and trochaic at the core, where home is – with the inner voice of creation. The dashes, and all the blanks in Katherine Mansfield's rhythm could well reveal the loss of her native country, her exile, reinforcing the feeling of the

---

[65] *Ibid.*, 106.

[66] *Ibid.*, 109.

[67] *Ibid.*, 110.

passage of time. The pool in "Psychology" was called "unfamiliar". It is the indefinite darkness of the sibyl's inspiration, and voice.

The wind opens the world of memory – the lost familiar world revisited "in spirit" as the male character in "Psychology" says. In that story, the Book of Genesis is mentioned (see Chapter 3) and I see an allusion to the Creation in this sentence: "Now the dark stretches a wing over the tumbling water." This is Genesis, 1, 2: "… and darkness was upon the face of the deep. And the spirit of God moved upon the face of the waters" (Authorized Version). Katherine Mansfield writes in 1921: "I've been reading the book of Job! There are times when I turn on the bible. It is marvellous!"[68] For her, creation is re-creation of the past in the present moment. After her brother's death, she writes in her Notebooks:

> I hear his voice in trees and flowers, in scents and light and shadow. Have people, apart from those far away people, ever existed for me? …. I feel I have a duty to perform to the lovely time when we were both alive. I want to write about it and he wanted me to. We talked it over in my little top room in London. I said: I will just put on the front page: To my brother – Leslie Heron Beauchamp. Very well: it shall be done.[69]

And on 19 November 1915, in a letter to S.S. Koteliansky, who was also a friend of Lawrence's (he inspired the name of his community, *Rananim*), she says: "To tell you the truth these things that I have heard about him blind me to all that is happening here – All this is like a long uneasy ripple – nothing else – and below – in the still pool there is my little brother."[70]

The image of the pool and the ripples, which we find in "Psychology", suggests that Katherine Mansfield's work, from *Bliss* onwards, is based upon the experience of absence. In a poem written in 1919, "Covering Wings", she exclaims:

> Love! Love! Your tenderness,
> Your beautiful, watchful ways
> Grasp me, fold me, cover me;
> I lie in a kind of daze,

---

[68] *The Collected Letters of Katherine Mansfield*, IV, 303.
[69] *The Katherine Mansfield Notebooks*, II, 16.
[70] *The Collected Letters of Katherine Mansfield*, I, 200.

> Neither asleep nor yet awake,
> Neither a bud nor flower.[71]

And she ends with:

> Love! Love! grief of my heart!
> As a tree droops over a stream
> You hush me, lull me, darken me,
> The shadow hiding the gleam.
> Your drooping and tragical boughs of grace
> Are heavy as though with rain.
> Run! Run!
> Into the sun!
> Let us be children again.

The sense of touch is being spiritualized in the poems, the hands becoming wings as she identifies herself with birds, a "wounded bird" in her last poem, written, like "The Canary", in July 1922, as Vincent O'Sullivan notes in "Katherine Mansfield's Canary, a 'wounded bird'":[72]

> O my wings – lift me – lift me
> I am not so dreadfully hurt.[73]

The metamorphosis of the hand into a wing might have been suggested to her by the reading of Mallarmé's "Démon de l'analogie".[74] And the flowers seem to be what D.W. Winnicott calls "transitional objects";[75] in the last quotation especially, the figure of Persephone emerges:

> Here's moss. How the smell of it lingers

---

[71] Mansfield, *Poems*, 70.

[72] See *Temporel* n° 2: http://temporel.fr/Katherine-Mansfield-s-Canary-a.

[73] Mansfield, *Poems*, 82.

[74] In this prose poem, whose title ("The Imp of Analogy") betrays Poe's influence on Mallarmé, a wing is metamorphosed into a hand "making the gesture of a stroke descending on something, the voice itself" (" faisant le geste d'une caresse descendant sur quelque chose, la voix même"). Stéphane Mallarmé, "Le Démon de l'analogie" (1874), in *Œuvres complètes*, ed. Bertrand Marchal, Paris: Gallimard Pléiade, 1998, I, 417.

[75] See Winnicott, *Playing and Reality*, Chapter 1.

On my cold fingers.[76]

Ah, darling mine!
Find them, gather them for me one by one.[77]

And I stood holding my dead bouquet
In a dead world.[78]

In "Sunset", she identifies with a "beam of light" resembling "a creature condemned to die" and endeavouring to shelter herself:

But her white arms lift to cover her shining head
And she presses close to the waves to make herself small.
On their listless knees the beam of light lies dead
And the bird of shadow falls.[79]

Whether she be light, or light as a bird, her illness cuts her off from emotional security and deepens the feeling of frailty and sadness she expresses in "The Canary". Her words are a glitter of light, or a brushing of wings on the "still pool" of darkness and absence – which is also the pain in her breast. After leaving Isabel, William, in "Marriage à la Mode", "folded his arms against the dull, persistent gnawing",[80] and, like the female character at the end of "Psychology", started writing a letter to his wife. In both cases, love is apprehended in the distance of writing, which is akin to the distance of memory.

This feature should be contrasted with what Lawrence says of the sense of touch in *Fantasia of the Unconscious*:

From the cardiac plexus the child goes forth in bliss. It seeks the revelation of the unknown. It wonderingly seeks the mother. It opens its small hands and spreads its small fingers to touch her. And bliss, bliss, bliss, it meets the wonder in mid-air and in mid-space it finds the loveliness of the mother's face.[81]

---

[76] "Sorrowing Love", in *Poems*, 72.
[77] "Secret Flowers", in *ibid.*, 74.
[78] "Old-Fashioned Widow's Song", in *ibid.*, 76.
[79] *Ibid.*, 75.
[80] Mansfield, *The Collected Stories*, 318.
[81] D.H. Lawrence, *Fantasia of the Unconscious* (1922), London: Penguin, 1986, 39.

From this perspective, the loss is intensified, but Katherine Mansfield writes, in "The Wind Blows", not only "She won't. She hates Mother"[82] but also: "No, Mother. I do not see why I should ...."[83] The question of individuality is at stake which implies a necessary distance between mother and daughter.

The past revived into the future

"Ah, Jeanne, anyone who says to me 'do you remember' simply has my heart .... I remember everything and perhaps the great joy of Life to me is in playing that game, going back *with someone* into the past."[84]Against the dark unknown and the indefinite essence of being, Katherine Mansfield develops an art of memory, defined by Frances Yates[85] as dramatic since it consists in placing figures in definite places, and rhythmical because the places are set in a definite pattern. Rhythm is a significant element for Mansfield – who was one of the founders of the magazine *Rhythm* – and we have seen how metamorphic her writing is. In "Prelude", her first New Zealand story, the "spirit of place"[86] is emphasized by the fact they the Burnells are moving to a new house. Place is immediately linked to movement, and to passage, or ephemerality: "With the dark crept the wind snuffling and howling."[87]

Images of creation as well as destruction are transformed throughout the story. The metamorphoses in the narrative correspond to the metamorphoses in life. Kezia is linked with renewal and resurrection. Writing means gathering the scattered moments of life in one particular instant of creation; it is a conversion of chaotic darkness into powerful light, the Romantic "soleil noir" ("dark sun"), and it creates epic symbols of individual existence like the aloe, a ship in "bright moonlight",[88] responding to Linda's voice: "Faster! Faster!" The rhythm is trochaic and echoes "quickly, quickly" in the narrative a few lines before, preluding to "Quicker! Quicker!" in "The Wind Blows". The individual voice is the expression of the creative power

---

[82] Mansfield, *The Collected Stories*, 107.
[83] *Ibid.*, 109.
[84] *The Collected Letters of Katherine Mansfield*, IV, 294 (my emphasis).
[85] Yates, *The Art of Memory*. See also Chapter 4.
[86] D.H. Lawrence, "The Spirit of Place", in *Studies in Classic American Literature*, London: Penguin, 1977, 7-14.
[87] Mansfield, *The Collected Stories*, 15.
[88] *Ibid.*, 53.

that resides in the depth of being[89] and is ever renewed in duration. It creates dynamic images resulting from a double movement, both reflexive and reciprocal; the "I" addresses a "You", and the third person is the mystery of existence, creative, or destructive:

> Let us go into the garden, mother. I like that aloe. I like it more than anything here. And I am sure I shall remember it long after I've forgotten all the other things.

Facing destructive time and converting it, through memory and imagination, into visions of wonder set in dear places: "… the high grassy bank on which the aloe rested rose up like a wave",[90] the individual subject faces the negative and tames it through a dialectic view of becoming. This process differs from Schopenhauer's mystic renunciation of the self. The individual decision counters the fatalistic view of life – nevertheless, not the tragedy – but the power of the narrative spirit is enhanced. There is no escape, except in the spiritual wrestling with negation, on the model of Jacob wrestling with the angel – a night scene, an embrace and a dialogue with destruction, leading to a new name at dawn – a new birth.

One of the stories in the "waste-paper basket" is "The Doll's House". The place in miniature, a suitable setting for the drama of existence since it is intended as a toy to mimic the larger life, is as open as the naked being, "the way God opens houses at the dead of night".[91] And the lamp, which is the imitation of a lamp – "But there was something inside that *looked like* oil" (my emphasis) – "was perfect". Its absolute adequacy to the place makes it "real". It is the appropriate figure in the art of memory. It is the appropriate voice, the creative moment, and the story, or poem, itself, apt enough to give a notion of the reality of life – life as we feel it through the drama of existence. The lamp, "in the middle of the dining-room table" – the place where the family gathers in mutual exchange (what I call reciprocity) – is an existential centre and provides a reflection of existence and a mutual acknowledgement of it: "I seen the lamp", says "our Else" at the end of the story, although Kezia did not utter the monosyllabic revelation when showing the doll's house to the

---

[89] See Anne Mounic, *Jacob ou l'être du possible*, 288-92.
[90] Mansfield, *The Collected Stories*, 52-53.
[91] *Ibid.*, 384. On "The Doll's House", see also Chapter 4.

Kelveys: "and that's the – ." We find here a perfect instance of what Kierkegaard calls "interiority" – when the words said belong to the person who receives them as if they were his own, and truly they are his own.[92] The doll's house is the place of nowhere, a creation of the spirit, revealing the essence of existence.

Such revelation fits the "dead of night". "*I love* the night", the "married man" says: "*I love* to feel the tide of darkness rising *slowly and slowly* washing, turning *over and over*, lifting, floating, *all that lies* strewn upon the dark beach, *all that lies* hid in rock hollows. *I love, I love* this strange feeling of drifting – whither?"[93] I stress the effects of repetition to show how reflexive this process is. And it leads to the unknown, to what can only be submitted to our questioning.[94] It is the Romantic contention that there is a knowledge of the self to be acquired beyond the visible world and the phenomena perceptible to reason – beyond the finite world, lies the infinite. Novalis says so in his *Hymnen an die Nacht* written in 1800 and Keats, in 1819, likening the poet to a nightingale – a traditional simile – shows him as not seeing but guessing. What such Modernist writers as Katherine Mansfield or D.H. Lawrence brought to that contention is the individual viewpoint, or Blake's "minute Particulars".[95] "Every man himself, and therefore, a surpassing singleness of mankind", D.H. Lawrence writes during the Great War in his "Manifesto".[96] And just before, in the last section of the poem, he writes a line which recalls Katherine Mansfield's ontological epiphanies: "Every human being will then be like a flower, untrammelled."[97]

In 1920-22, D.H. Lawrence does not follow Schopenhauer advocating the renunciation of individuality. His "star-equilibrium" is a rhythmical combination of the single life and its yielding to

---

[92] Søren Kierkegaard, *Post-scriptum aux Miettes philosophiques*, Paris: Gallimard Tel, 2001, 173.

[93] Mansfield, *The Collected Stories*, 435 (my emphases).

[94] It is interesting to note that the word in Hebrew, *sheol*, for the invisible world beyond – what the Greeks called Hades – comes from a strong verb, *lichol*, meaning "to question, to demand an answer". It is the verb used in the episode of Jacob wrestling with the angel, when he grasps and asks the angel what His name is (Genesis, 32, 30).

[95] William Blake, *Jerusalem* (1804-1820), in *Complete Writings*, ed. Geoffrey Keynes, Oxford: Oxford University Press, 1989, 673.

[96] D.H. Lawrence, "Manifesto", in *Look! We Have Come Through!* (1917), in *Complete Poems*, 268.

[97] *Ibid.*, 267.

otherness, but Rupert insists on his will to keep his freedom. Although his settings are much larger than the small doll's house (he travelled a lot, voluntarily), in an essay mentioned earlier he emphasizes the importance of the "spirit of place", stressing the paradox of freedom. His viewpoint is biblical:

> Men are free when they are in a living homeland, not when they are straying and breaking away. Men are free when they are obeying some deep, *inward voice* of religious belief. Obeying from within. Men are free when they belong to a living, organic, *believing* community, active in fulfilling some unfulfilled, perhaps unrealized purpose.[98]

Moses saw the Promised Land from the mountain of Nebo before he died, but the "inward voice", in the biblical tradition, is embodied in the figure of Jacob (Genesis, 27, 22): "The voice is Jacob's voice, but the hands *are* the hands of Esau." Esau limits himself to the finite world while Jacob is both past and future, life's experience and the words to tell about it. He is the creative being – the fountain, the well (Lawrence's "well of darkness"[99]).

Both Katherine Mansfield and D.H. Lawrence dislike mirrors, which only reveal an appearance of being. When "catching sight of her reflection in the mirror",[100] Isabel becomes the conventional maternal figure, "and for a moment her grey eyes looked amused and *wicked, a little sardonic*, out of her transfigured Madonna face".[101] In the distance of the eyesight, the "inward voice" is suppressed and almost disfigured into a stereotype. In the mirror, the personality is cleft, as it is by time in "The Wind Blows": "What had that creature in the glass to do with her, and why was she staring?" wonders Beryl in "Prelude".[102] The "inward voice" means transcendence within immanence while the eye in the mirror is the pitiless eye of outward transcendence barring the soul from its immediate power of sensitive touch.

---

[98] Lawrence, "The Spirit of Place", in *Studies in Classic American Literature*, 12 (my emphasis).

[99] D.H. Lawrence, "The Blind Man", in *England, My England*, 61.

[100] *Ibid.*, 59.

[101] *Ibid.*, 60.

[102] Mansfield, *The Collected Stories*, 58.

The "star-equilibrium"

In this world of freedom obtained through reflexive knowledge and reciprocal acknowledgement, each will develop his or her own voice. So if we come to think of the value of each work, we may say, like the boy asked by his grandmother if he likes her best, in Vincent O'Sullivan's "The Professional": "Oh, you don't have to say you like one thing more just because you like something else as well, do you Gran?"[103] So perhaps Lawrence should have adapted his "star-equilibrium" outlook to his appreciation of Katherine Mansfield's work. She sounds much less assertive, but sometimes truly exasperated. Yet, not knowing either of them personally, we may go beyond the immediate irritations of the sensitive soul in the present moment and learn from the way both poets managed to come to terms with them – "with passion". After all, sibyls and prophets sit side by side on Michelangelo's Sistine Chapel frescoes. What is common to them both is the ever-renewed questioning of the mystery of being: "– Ah, what is it? – that I heard."

---

[103] O'Sullivan, *Palms and Minarets*, 113.

CHAPTER 8

"'I AM DESIRE' SAID THE SEA" – "THE KISS OF A WAVE": KATHERINE MANSFIELD AND VIRGINIA WOOLF

This chapter is designed to show in what ways Virginia Woolf is indebted to Katherine Mansfield in her novel situated in 1923, the year of Mansfield's death in Avon near Fontainebleau, in France, and how different their viewpoints are. Many elements found in *Mrs. Dalloway*, such as the great insistence on the flowers and trees – trees of life – are essential to Katherine Mansfield's poetics. She herself knew how she was indebted to Oscar Wilde, who makes great use of trees and blossoms in his work, and especially in *The Picture of Dorian Gray*. With her early awareness that art "is absolutely self development",[1] she had a strong sense of how to transcend all immediate impressions to create a work of art magnifying the present moment of being, which I call converting the immediate into the existential instant set in timelessness.[2] "Eternity is in love with the productions of time",[3] William Blake wrote in *The Marriage of Heaven and Hell*. For Kierkegaard, the ethical choice enables the subject to go beyond the aesthetic phase into the ethical and the religious, which is the ultimate assertion of individuality. It is paradoxical since the apparent isolation it creates is accompanied with the individual's strong connection with his own history, in which "he stands in relation to other individuals of the race and to the race as a whole".[4] Such metamorphosis, which is immediate and spontaneous for Katherine Mansfield, comes up against the duality of Virginia Woolf's tragic outlook in *Mrs. Dalloway*. Such different viewpoints are also dependent on how the writer contemplates the relationship between time and space.

---

[1] *The Katherine Mansfield Notebooks*, I, 110. See Chapter 1.
[2] See Mounic, Chapter 3, in *L'inerte ou l'exquis: Pensée poétique, pensée du singulier*.
[3] William Blake, *The Marriage of Heaven and Hell*, in *Complete Writings*, 151.
[4] Kierkegaard, *Either... or...*, 518. See Chapter 1.

The empty centre

From the first lines of *Mrs. Dalloway*, the reader feels a strong connection with Katherine Mansfield's world. At the beginning of the novel the sense of an impending dreadful event is stressed: "... feeling as she did, standing there at the open window, that something awful was about to happen."[5] We later learn that it refers to the break of her relationship with Peter Walsh. What was Paradise turns into Hell; the same adjective is later used from Peter Walsh's point of view: "It was an awful evening!"[6] A few lines before, the adjective had been found, qualifying the visit of "the man who had married his housemaid":[7] "an awful visit it had been. She was absurdly overdressed, 'like a cockatoo', Clarissa had said, imitating her, and she never stopped talking." The bird points out social impropriety while Kezia's fear of parrots is a fear of life's surge. What appears as "the devilish part"[8] of Clarissa corresponds to Peter's own lack of ability to react – his new helplessness: "And he couldn't see her, couldn't explain to her; couldn't have it out." The threefold repetition of "couldn't" recalls the time (*The Hours* being the novel's initial title) – three o'clock, the time when Richard goes back home with his bunch of roses, his feeling of happiness ("Happiness is this, he thought"[9]) and his unfulfilled desire to tell Clarissa he loves her. He could not say so however:

> He must be off, he said, getting up. But he stood for a moment as if he was about to say something; and he wondered what? Why? There were the roses.[10]

This sudden oblivious state of what he really wished to say recalls the boss' hesitation at the end of Mansfield's "The Fly":

> And while the old dog padded away he fell to wondering what it was he had been thinking about before. What was it? It was .... He took out

---

[5] Virginia Woolf, *Mrs. Dalloway* (1925), Oxford: Oxford University Press, 2000, 3.
[6] *Ibid.*, 51.
[7] *Ibid.*, 50.
[8] *Ibid.*, 51.
[9] *Ibid.*, 99.
[10] *Ibid.*, 101.

his handkerchief and passed it inside his collar. For the life of him he could not remember.[11]

In both cases the situation is different. Yet at the end of "The Fly" Katherine Mansfield discloses what Virginia Woolf calls the "empty centre" in *Mrs. Dalloway*, first talking of the cenotaph, the "empty tomb",[12] and then, during her party, meditating about Septimus' suicide:

> Death was defiance. Death was an attempt to communicate, people feeling the impossibility of reaching the centre which, mystically, evaded them; closeness drew apart; rapture faded; one was alone. There was an embrace in death.[13]

Septimus' wish to die is also called "awful"[14] in the novel. This conception of an elusive centre recalls negative theology, God being what cannot be known. The novel transcends this impossibility, Clarissa providing a centre of gravity for multiplicity to be at least gathered:

> That was her self – pointed; dart-like; definite. that was her self when some effort, some call on her to be her self, drew the pars together, she alone knew how different, how incompatible and composed so for the world only into one centre, one diamond, one woman who sat in her drawing-room and made a meeting-point, a radiancy no doubt in some dull lives, a refuge for the lonely to come to, perhaps.[15]

The party stands for the novel, which transcends its own elusiveness through its quest for a centre:

> But to go deeper, beneath what people said (and these judgements, how superficial, how fragmentary they are!) in her own mind now, what did it mean to her, this thing called life? Oh, it was very queer. Here So-en-So in South Kensington; someone up in Bayswater; and somebody else, say, in Mayfair. And she felt quite continuously a

---

[11] Mansfield, *The Edinburgh Edition of the Collected Works of Katherine Mansfield*, II, 480; *The Collected Stories*, 418.
[12] Woolf, *Mrs. Dalloway*, 43.
[13] *Ibid.*, 156.
[14] *Ibid.*, 13.
[15] *Ibid.*, 32.

> sense of their existence; and she felt what a waste, and he felt what a
> pity; and she felt if only they could be brought together; so she did it.
> And it was an offering; to combine, to create; but to whom?[16]

The novel overcomes the various failures to communicate,
Richard's inability to tell Clarissa he loves her; Peter's helplessness at
Bourton when they were young; Septimus' inability to feel, so
incapacitated is he by the war trauma: "For now that it was all over,
truce signed, and the dead buried, he had, especially in the evening,
these sudden thunder-claps of fear. He could not feel."[17] The sentence
is repeated: "... that he could not feel."[18] Then the idea is resumed
with variation: "But he felt nothing."[19] And again, on the same page,
associated with death: "That he did not feel." This has to be placed in
a parallel with the expression Peter repeats: "The death of the soul."[20]
Then it becomes: "... the death of her soul."

The double movement of "rising and falling"[21] which is a feature
of the novel is a movement of death (Septimus facing the fatal tyranny
of authority and falling on "Mrs. Filmer's area railings"[22]) and
resurrection: Clarissa lives a new life through gathering the people she
loves and the past moments of her life. Such renewed relationship
means continuity of life. In the end, Clarissa's presence is given
evidence of through Peter's words:

> It is Clarissa, he said.
> For there she was.[23]

Elusiveness

The whole novel is placed under the double sign of movement and
number, in a vision which recalls Lucretius' *De Rerum Natura* and is
especially indebted to Bergson's view of duration as the substance of
the world and of the inner life. This genuine reality is to be perceived
through intuition. Clock time is opposed to this continuous duration in

---

[16] *Ibid.*, 103.
[17] *Ibid.*, 74.
[18] *Ibid.*, 75.
[19] *Ibid.*, 77.
[20] *Ibid.*, 50.
[21] *Ibid.*, 19.
[22] *Ibid.*, 127.
[23] *Ibid.*, 165.

which the past survives. In *Mrs. Dalloway*, the characters are moving in space and time most of the time; sometimes they may be at rest, sewing at home, sitting in a park, having visions. Their minds are never at rest. Nevertheless, beside this continuous flow of impressions, there are fixed landmarks in the novel, in space (London, the pillar box); in time (Big Ben striking), but these landmarks rather help to show how the human mind constantly strays from fixity, how it is elusive, how life itself is elusive.

The characters wander both in space and in time. Their movement accompanies their thoughts; life is a passage, with streets to be crossed, parks in which to dream, memories surreptitiously invading the mind. Although the plot is contained in one day, from morning to evening, the wandering mind transcends clock time, objective time, and embraces huge periods, – years, and even centuries, if we consider the literary references (Dante, Shakespeare, the Greek world of myth and tragedy). The subjective intuition, in its infinite flow, triumphs over monumental time (the expression was coined by Paul Ricœur in his study of time in *Mrs. Dalloway*; the philosopher adapted Nietzsche's phrase, "monumental history", associated with epic grandeur[24]). It also prevails upon the duty imposed by authority: life cannot be "dealt with, she felt positive, by Acts of Parliament for that very reason: they love life".[25] In the first version of what was to become *Mrs. Dalloway*, Virginia Woolf more explicitly referred to Proust: "A leaf of mint brings it back: or a cup with a blue ring." This is a direct reference to the process of reminiscence described in *In Search of Lost Time*.

If subjective intuition shall be given precedence over objective chronology, Virginia Woolf cannot pretend to impart the reader with any objective viewpoint. She would not capture reality in this way. There is not one single piece of truth but a myriad of subjective viewpoints. We shift from one to the other: Clarissa's, that of people in the street, Septimus', his wife Rezia's, Clarissa's former lover Peter Walsh's, her husband Richard Dalloway's, Miss Kilman's, and Clarissa's daughter Elizabeth's. It is to be noticed that we do not penetrate the minds of those definitely on the side of authority and monumental time: William Bradshaw's, or Hugh Whitbread's.

---

[24] Paul Ricœur, "Entre le temps mortel et le temps monumental: *Mrs. Dalloway*", in *Temps et récit : 2. La configuration dans le récit de fiction*, 192-212.
[25] Woolf, *Mrs. Dalloway*, 4.

Sometimes, it is not clear whose viewpoint is considered. When the characters talk to each other, the outlook quickly shifts; the reflections sometimes mingle and communication is elusive. Words can be unreliable. Too many words and people are quarrelling (this is the case of Peter and Clarissa). Solitude is the keyword to the human plight and people should not jeopardize the dignity of such separation. As Lucretius says, between the atoms there is a void. Symbols can be used, "objective correlatives" (Eliot's term), instead of words (for instance: Clarissa, Richard and the bunch of roses). The hat plays the same role between Rezia and Septimus in their final scene.

And language is as elusive since a character's words only provide us with his view of the situation. The reader of this novel has to put the fragments together in order to reach an understanding of such many-sided truth. The narrative itself is highly elusive. We find no transitions from one viewpoint to the other. For example, at the beginning, we shift from Clarissa's standpoint to Scrope Purvis' without notice. The latter will not re-appear in the novel. She provides us here with an outside view of the main protagonist, whom she likens to a "jay".[26] Birds have a significant presence in the novel. Septimus is compared to a crow, or a hawk.[27] What mostly recalls Katherine Mansfield is his remark on Rezia: "... he could feel her mind, like a bird, falling from branch to branch, and always alighting, quite rightly."[28] We think, in "The Garden-Party", of the guests who "like bright birds that had alighted in the Sheridans' garden for this one afternoon, on their way to – where?".[29] In *Mrs. Dalloway*, the characters generally first appear as simple names. The reader is not given any extent physical description but only sketches. The protagonists can also appear as "They", an unidentified third person, as is the case with the Morrises.[30] Not introduced, these individuals are atoms in the flow of time, offered to immediate perception and assuring the perceiver of the reality of life.

The syntax can also be elusive. When Clarissa comes home for instance: "'What are they looking at?' said Clarissa Dalloway to the

---

[26] *Ibid.*, 3.
[27] *Ibid.*, 126.
[28] *Ibid.*, 124.
[29] Mansfield, *The Edinburgh Edition of the Collected Works of Katherine Mansfield*, II, 410; *The Collected Stories*, 256-57.
[30] Woolf, *Mrs. Dalloway*, 135.

maid who opened the door."[31] "They" is surprising since the reference is not direct. We must ponder a while to connect the elements and understand that Clarissa means the people in the street. At the end of the next paragraph, the sentence, referring to Clarissa's inner thoughts, is interrupted:

> ... while Lucy stood by her, trying to explain how
> 'Mr. Dalloway, ma'am – '

In the moments of vision, the syntax is particularly fluid and cumulative.[32] The rhythm of prose conveys the flow of visual perception based upon a deeper structure of analogies in time and space. This is how the work of the mind is revealed.

The stream of consciousness as captured by Virginia Woolf (mostly through indirect speech) consists of two movements, one of dissolution, the other of piecing together. The first enhances erasing, disappearing: after Big Ben has struck, the "leaden circles dissolve in the air". The symbolism of water, the waves, streams and floating pervades the novel. The sea is also a decisive presence in Katherine Mansfield's work. It means desire, and the appeal of the infinite. In *Mrs. Dalloway*, it is linked with another element, the air, which is invisible, as Clarissa's body is.[33] So are the logical links in the novel, invisible. Bradshaw's sense of proportion, a notion redolent of Stoic philosophy, and conversion[34] is dissolved for the sake of freedom, freedom of being at different levels. Subjectivity with its lightness opposes the leaden objectivity of power. Virginia Woolf wrote, in her *Journal* in June 1923:

> ... its only the old argument that character is dissipated into shreds now: the old post-Dostoievsky argument. I dare say its true, however, that I haven't that 'reality' gift. I insubstantise, wilfully to some extent, distrusting reality – its cheapness.[35]

And Septimus' tragedy, imposed upon him by the advocates of duty and authority – the real world –, is at the core of the novel: "I'll give it

---

[31] *Ibid.*, 25.

[32] *Ibid.*, 49 and 19.

[33] *Ibid.*, 9.

[34] *Ibid.*, 84-85.

[35] Quoted in Woolf, *The Mrs. Dalloway Reader*, 94.

you!"[36] he says when jumping out of the window. But Rezia has preserved his subjective world, as contained in his drawings and writings.

The meanings of the book are conveyed to the reader through the analogies suggested between the scenes. We can find a parallelism between Peter's "final scene" with Clarissa and Clarissa's talk with Richard, at three, years after. Some types of objects also recur, as objective correlatives, the "white apron", the "flag", the "curtain", all flapping in the air or blowing out. The double movement of falling and rising is constant. The body may fall unless it is invisible but the mind is a bird, perfectly at ease in the air as is Rezia's.[37]

Therefore, if the whole novel is elusive as reality is, some clues can be grasped through assembling the scattered elements. These analogies are landmarks that help us build the meaning, or rather the meanings. From this we may gather that the general outlook is existential and apart from the contrast between monumental time and authority on the one hand (the passage staging William Bradshaw is much less elusive than the rest of the novel: the author clearly wants to deliver a message here), individual duration and the subjective love for life on the other hand, a significant subject in this novel is age. Putting together some similar scenes, we find a representation of the ages of life: three women, Elizabeth, Clarissa, the old lady; three men, Septimus, Peter Walsh, the old man. These figures of youth, middle and old age emerge from the elusive movement of transience, from this myriad of elusive characters which Clarissa calls "life": if the reader manages to piece the atoms together, her parties and Virginia Woolf's novel are an "offering".

To a certain extent, the reader is the screen on which Septimus sees the visions.[38] This screen recalls Katherine Mansfield's animated curtains whether it be leopards marching or birds singing. However she only gives life to what she can see while Septimus is the victim of his own hallucinations. As for the party, it provides a unity of time. It is a contraction in time, comparable to the contraction in Clarissa's face when she looks at herself in the mirror, drawing "the parts together" and composing "one centre".[39] We find two movements in

---

[36] Woolf, *Mrs. Dalloway*, 127.
[37] *Ibid.*, 124.
[38] *Ibid.*, 123.
[39] *Ibid.*, 32.

the novel: the centrifugal dispersion of units of being, individuals, moments, visions, all elusive, and the inward movement of the mind which gathers the fragments through rhythm, analogy, composition, the elusiveness being mirrored in one centre, from which it may then radiate. The process is dialectical and also involves the two different notions of space and time.

Space and time

The sense of continuity is the mark of the individual who has chosen himself, and therefore life, which means his, and the others', personal history. In "The Wind Blows" Katherine Mansfield opposes the break in space (leaving the "little island"[40]) to the continuity in time:

> There's the esplanade where we walked that windy day. Do you remember? I cried at my music lesson that day – how many years ago! Goodbye, little island, good-bye ....

Through imagination and memory, the mind transcends the break in space; communication and continuity in time are one and the same process ("Do *you* remember?"). The process is dialectic since the reflexive consciousness separates before it is able to unite again. We have noticed that, in "The Wind Blows", the process of estrangement from the origins through the wind and time starts when the main character looks at herself in the mirror:

> Hooking the collar she looks at herself in the glass. Her face is white, they have the same exciting eyes and hot lips. Ah, they know those two in the glass. Good-bye, dears; we shall be back soon.[41]

The separation from oneself is made up for by the brother and sister relationship:

> 'Hook on,' says Bogey.
> They cannot walk fast enough. Their heads bent, their legs just touching, they stride like one eager person through the town, down the asphalt zigzag where the fennel grows wild and on to the esplanade.[42]

---

[40] Mansfield, *The Edinburgh Edition of the Collected Works of Katherine Mansfield*, II, 229; *The Collected Stories*, 110.
[41] *Ibid.*, 228; 109.
[42] *Ibid.*, 228-29; 109.

In Virginia Woolf's novel, there is no such close relationship. Peter and Clarissa have broken off; Richard cannot tell Clarissa he loves her. He needs an "objective correlative"; he needs the flowers. But, remember, Katherine Mansfield said: "The words are like flowers."[43] Yet Clarissa's mind can overcome such powerlessness, and helplessness and loneliness, through bringing them all together at the party. Peter and Clarissa broke off at three o'clock in the past; Richard visits her at three with his bunch of roses; she sees the old lady for the second time at three in the morning during her party. She had seen her for the first time after Elisabeth had gone with Miss Kilman:

> Big Ben struck the half-hour.
> How extraordinary it was, strange, yes, touching to see the old lady (they had been neighbours ever so many years) move away from the window, as if she were attached to that sound, that string.[44]

Even then she has a sense of someone familiar to her. The second time the old lady appears when the clock strikes three:

> It was fascinating to watch her, moving about, that old lady, crossing the room, coming to the window. Could she see her? It was fascinating, with people still laughing and shouting in the drawing-room, to watch that old woman, quite quietly, going to bed alone. She pulled the blind now. The clock began striking. The young man had killed himself; but she did not pity him; with the clock striking the hour, one, two, three, she did not pity him, with all this going on.[45]

Septimus sees an old man at the very moment when he jumps out of the window:

> He did not want to die. Life was good. The sun hot. Only human beings? Coming down the staircase opposite an old man stopped and stared at him.[46]

The relationship is reversed since Clarissa sees the old lady and then watches her while Septimus is being stared at by the old man. Clarissa

---

[43] *The Katherine Mansfield Notebooks*, II, 33.
[44] Woolf, *Mrs. Dalloway*, 108.
[45] *Ibid.*, 158.
[46] *Ibid.*, 127.

is subject; Septimus, object. Moreover what follows immediately is: "Holmes was at the door."

Septimus' suicide is a debased version of the Greek tragedy. Among his drawings are these: "Diagrams, designs, little men and women brandishing sticks for arms, with wings – were they? – on their backs."[47] We may think of demons and harpies. Moreover, among his writings are Evans' "messages from the dead". Although Rezia is metamorphosed into "a flowering tree" sheltered in a "sanctuary where she feared no one"[48] – and this recalls Katherine Mansfield's trees of life –, Septimus has to face the "judges", Holmes and Bradshaw, which transform Rezia's new Paradise into Hell. The crow, a prophetic bird, is also a guide of the souls to the Underworld: "She sat down beside him and called him by the name of that hawk or crow which, being malicious and a great destroyer of crops, was precisely like him." The impending threat, expressed by the repetition of "would" ("Holmes would burst open the door. Holmes would say, 'In a funk, eh?' Holmes would get him."), hurries the tragic end: "It was their idea of tragedy, not his or Rezia's (for she was with him)." Yet it is a modern tragedy; he "flung himself vigorously, violently down on to Mrs. Filmer's area railings".[49] And Rezia must be preserved: "It seemed to her as she drank the sweet stuff that she was opening long windows, stepping out into some garden. But where?" We think of Clarissa at the beginning of the novel:

> What a lark: What a plunge! For so it had always seemed to her when, with a little squeak of the hinges, which she could hear now, she had burst open the French windows and plunged at Bourton into the open air.[50]

The scene of Septimus' suicide is connected with the "final scene, the terrible scene" between Peter and Clarissa, "at three o' clock". Virginia Woolf conveys the same suggestion of Paradise (the garden at Bourton) transformed into Hell:

> The fountain was in the middle of a little shrubbery, far from the house, with shrubs and trees all around it. There she came, even

---

[47] *Ibid.*, 125.
[48] *Ibid.*, 126.
[49] *Ibid.*, 127.
[50] *Ibid.*, 3.

before the time, and they stood with the fountain between them, the spout (it was broken) dribbling waters incessantly. How sights fix themselves on the mind! For example, the vivid green moss.[51]

Peter was the prey to "revelations", an important notion for Katherine Mansfield (see Chapter 3), the sense of an impending threat being expressed with "would": "This one – that she would marry Dalloway – was blinding – overwhelming at the moment."[52] The reference to Hell is explicit: "Never, never had he suffered so infernally! …. He almost cried out that he couldn't attend because he was in Hell!"[53]

Septimus' suicide occurs just before six o'clock but Virginia Woolf insists on the first three strokes:

> The clock was striking – one, two, three: how sensible the sound was; compared with all this thumping and whispering; like Septimus himself. She was falling asleep. But the clock went on striking, four, five, six, and Mrs. Filmer waving her apron (they wouldn't bring the body in there, would they?) seemed part of that garden; or a flag.[54]

The garden is a decisive place in Katherine's Mansfield's work; the pastoral world provides continuity while sacrifice means an unbridgeable break in time:

> 'There's miles of it,' quavered old Woodifield, 'and it's all as neat as a garden. Flowers on all the graves. Nice broad paths.' It was plain from his voice how much he liked a nice broad path.[55]

As his name shows, Woodifield belongs to the world of pastoral poetry, transcending death through the continuity of speech and nature. The tree of life is blossoming. The boss belongs to the tragic world and imposes upon the fly a desperate struggle against fate, which he embodies: "But just then the boss had an idea." The fly becomes the victim of a mind so disengaged from any form of

---

[51] *Ibid.*, 54.
[52] *Ibid.*, 52.
[53] *Ibid.*, 53.
[54] *Ibid.*, 127.
[55] Mansfield, "The Fly", in *The Edinburgh Edition of the Collected Works of Katherine Mansfield*, II, 477; *The Collected Stories*, 414.

empathy through its capacity for abstraction that the mechanics of necessity works unhampered by feeling:

> And while the old dog padded away he fell to wondering what it was he had been thinking about before. What was it? It was … He took out his handkerchief and passed it inside his collar. For the life of him he could not remember.[56]

The suspension points recall those used before:

> He's a pluck little devil, thought the boss, and he felt a real admiration for the fly's courage. That was the way to tackle things; that was the right spirit. Never say die; it was only a question of …[57]

The effect is cathartic as is Septimus' suicide for Clarissa: "… but she did not pity him."[58] And then: "She felt somehow very like him – the young man who had killed himself. She felt glad that he had done it; thrown it away while they went on living." As W.B. Yeats affirmed in his Preface to the *Oxford Book of Modern Verse* in 1936: "In all great tragedies, tragedy is a joy to the man who dies."[59] Clarissa is cured of her feelings of pity and fear: "Fear no more the heat of the sun." The quote from Cymbeline (IV, 2, 259-60)[60] is a leitmotiv through the book. The boss' son's death had stopped the flow of time:

> And he had left his office a broken man, with his life in ruins.
>   Six years ago, six years …. How quickly time passed! It might have happened yesterday.

What remains is the insuperable separation in the outer fixity of space:

> He decided to get up and have a look at the boy's photograph. But it wasn't a favourite photograph of his; the expression was unnatural. It was cold, even stern-looking. The boy had never looked like that.[61]

---

[56] *Ibid.*, 480; 418.

[57] *Ibid.*, 479; 417.

[58] Woolf, *Mrs. Dalloway*, 158.

[59] W.B. Yeats, *The Oxford Book of Modern Verse* (1936), xxxiv-xxxv, quoted by Jon Silkin, *Out of Battle* (1972), 2nd edn, London: Macmillan, 1998, 177.

[60] Shakespeare, *Cymbeline*, 208.

[61] Mansfield, "The Fly", in *The Edinburgh Edition of the Collected Works of Katherine Mansfield*, II, 479; *The Collected Stories*, 416.

Nothing can ever change. But as Blake said in *Milton*: "Time is the mercy of Eternity; without Time's swiftness, / Which is the swiftest of all things, all were eternal torment."[62]

In the same way, Clarissa and Septimus have no other connection apart from a fortuitous coincidence in space. The choice of death is eccentric: the centre is elusive; the centre is empty. Catharsis, the purgation of the feelings of pity and fear, implies separation in space while empathy means a strong sense of continuity in time. Giving a "sweet" drink to Rezia, Holmes protects her from feeling. His aim is cathartic.

Katherine Mansfield's wish to renew the lives of her ancestors discloses her choice of life, in spite of all. She chooses continuity while Virginia Woolf, or so it seems in *Mrs. Dalloway*, and we think of the various traumas in her childhood, had to wrestle to achieve her own tree of life.

Cenotaphs and trees of life

The "empty tomb"[63] on Whitehall, as well as the war monuments, which were built from 1920 on in the countries involved in World War One[64] exteriorize and reify memory to the point of annihilating it in the collective mind. "The monument makes up for amnesia; the means deprives the end of all worth",[65] wrote Abraham Heschel in *Les Bâtisseurs du temps* (*The Builders of Time*). We may even say that the monuments, as they glorify what is called the soldiers "sacrifice", legitimize war, and mass-murder. Since 1920 they have become part of our mental landscape but they say nothing on the soldiers' suffering, which only some of the poems and narratives of the period make real to us. There is no memory in space, no continuity in fixed images.

"Boys in uniform, carrying guns, marched with their eyes ahead of them, marched, their arms stiff, and on their faces an expression like the letters of a legend written round the base of a statue praising duty, gratitude, fidelity, love of England":[66] such legend calls for oblivion

---

[62] William Blake, *Milton*, in *Complete Writings*, 510.
[63] Woolf, *Mrs. Dalloway*, 43.
[64] On this question, see George L. Mosse, *Fallen Soldiers: Reshaping the Memory of World Wars*, Oxford: Oxford University Press, 1990.
[65] "Le monument supplée à l'amnésie; le moyen fait perdre toute valeur à la fin" (Abraham Heschel, *Les Bâtisseurs du temps*, Paris: Minuit, 1957, 100).
[66] Woolf, *Mrs. Dalloway*, 43.

of individual pain. Catharsis, a means of "escape from emotion",[67] is such oblivion, as Jon Silkin points out in his anthology of First World War Poetry (1979):

> There is in this poetry [the war poets'] something so profoundly *real* that I find myself questioning the idea of catharsis. And this is because I think, as the war poets did, that we must not dispel others' suffering, but, on the contrary, absorb it.[68]

The war poets all expressed how difficult it was to make themselves understood by the civilians, whose pity was often obliterated by the heroic legend in the making, and Virginia Woolf herself, for instance, failed to understand and sympathize with Robert Graves' attitude when he came to visit her in 1925 as the Hogarth Press had published some of his books and was just about to publish a new one:[69]

> ... cant travel on a train without being sick; is rather proud of his sensibility. No I don't think he'll write great poetry: but what will you? The sensitive are needed too; the halfbaked, stammering stuttering, who perhaps improve their own quarter of Oxfordshire.[70]

We may connect this very severe irony with a feature of Clarissa's character as emphasized by Peter Walsh: "That was the devilish part of her – this coldness, this woodenness, something very profound in her, which he had felt again this morning talking to her; an impenetrability."[71] Impenetrability, or the absence of empathy, is Hell. And fear is the cause for such withdrawal as the Shakespearean leitmotiv suggests:

---

[67] T.S. Eliot, "Tradition and the Individual Talent" (1979), in *Selected Prose*, 43.
[68] *The Penguin Book of First World War Poetry*, ed. Jon Silkin, London: Penguin, 1979, 46.
[69] Three collections of Graves' poems were published by the Hogarth Press: *The Feather Bed*, 1923; *Mock Beggar Hall*, 1924; *The Marmosite's Miscellany*, 1925. The Hogarth Press also published three of his books on poetry: *Contemporary Techniques of Poetry: A Political Analogy*, 1925; *Another Future of Poetry*, 1926; *Impenetrability; or, The Proper Habit of English*, 1926.
[70] Monday, 27 April 1925, in *The Diary of Virginia Woolf*, Vol. III, 1925-30, ed. Anne Olivier Bell, Harmondsworth: Penguin, 1987, 14.
[71] Woolf, *Mrs. Dalloway*, 51-52.

> But with Peter everything had to be shared; everything gone into. And it was intolerable, and when it came to that scene in the little garden by the fountain, she had to break with him or they would have been destroyed, both of them ruined, she was convinced; though she had borne about for years like an arrow sticking in her heart the grief, the anguish …. Cold, heartless, a prude, he called her. Never could she understand how he cared.[72]

Yet such remark about her feeling when facing Peter after the "revelation" provided by Sally Seton's kiss contradicts her refusal to share, unless what is denied is empathy, that is sharing the other's feelings: "It was like running one's face against a granite wall in the darkness! It was shocking; it was horrible!"[73] As far as Sally Seton is concerned, the quality of her voice is stressed, which recalls D.H. Lawrence in "The Blind Man" and Maurice's "velvety" voice: "... the sound of his voice seemed to touch her."[74] And then the kiss is like the gift of a flower:

> Sally stopped; picked a flower; kissed her on the lips. The whole world might have turned upside down! The others disappeared; there she was alone with Sally. And she felt that she had been given a present, wrapped up, and told just to keep it, not to look at it – a diamond, something infinitely precious, wrapped up, which, as they walked (up and down, up and down), she uncovered, or the radiance burnt through, the revelation, the religious feeling![75]

This sudden revelation is that of her power to assemble ("one centre, one diamond, one woman", see above on page 144); such centre is no longer empty but radiant.[76] The scene with Sally recalls the two significant scenes of communion and revelation of the radiant power of life in Katherine Mansfield's "Bliss" and "Prelude", the visions of the pear-tree and the aloe. Through the character of Rezia, Virginia Woolf emphasizes the engendering character of the "human voice":

---

[72] *Ibid.*, 7.
[73] *Ibid.*, 30.
[74] Lawrence, "The Blind Man", in *England, My England*, 62.
[75] Woolf, *Mrs. Dalloway*, 30.
[76] *Ibid.*, 32.

> 'K ... R ...' said the nursemaid, and Septimus heard her say 'Kay Arr' close to his ear, deeply, softly, like a mellow organ, but with a roughness in her voice like a grasshopper's, which rasped his spine deliciously and sent running up into his brains waves of sound, which, concussing, broke. A marvellous discovery indeed – that the human voice in certain atmospheric conditions (for one must be scientific, above all scientific) can quicken trees into life![77]

A close link is set between the microcosm (Septimus' spine and brain) and the macrocosm (the trees). In the scene with Sally Seton, such connection extends to the stars, with Peter's casual remark: "'Star-gazing?' said Peter."[78] Both the aloe and the pear-tree seem to reach the full moon. If "words are like flowers" (see above on page 146) as Katherine Mansfield said, the human voice is a blossoming tree of life. The following passage is connected to the previous one through the enumeration of the letters drawn by the smoke, "like something mounting in ecstasy, in pure delight":[79]

> She heard the click of the typewriter. It was her life, and, bending her head over the hall table, she bowed beneath the influence, felt blessed and purified, saying to herself, as she took the pad with the telephone message on it, how moments like this are buds on the tree of life, flowers of darkness they are, she thought (as if some lovely rose had blossomed for her eyes only).[80]

The "religious feeling"[81] she expresses in the Sally Seton moment of revelation has nothing to do with a belief in God, which she makes clear after describing the hesitations of the "seedy-looking nondescript man"[82] outside St Paul's Cathedral: "not for a moment did she believe in God."[83] She would not rely on predetermined images and monuments, petrified symbols "of something which had soared beyond seeking and questing and knocking of words together and has become all spirit, disembodied, ghostly",[84] a feeling shared by D.H.

---

[77] *Ibid.*, 19.
[78] *Ibid.*, 30.
[79] *Ibid.*, 24.
[80] *Ibid.*, 25.
[81] *Ibid.*, 30.
[82] *Ibid.*, 24.
[83] *Ibid.*, 25.
[84] *Ibid.*, 24.

Lawrence who remarked, in *The Rainbow* (see Chapter 7): "God burned no more in that bush. It was dead matter lying there."[85] The radiancy lies in the quest, in the renewal of life through words.

What would remain scattered and meaningless in the immediacy of the present moment of living, in the immediacy of space, can only be assembled through the radiant power of the mind – which T.S. Eliot found quite hard to do in *The Waste Land*. The idea of modernity as a break from the traditional way of living, speaking and thinking, induces a feeling of disconnection from the origins, and debasement as far as the glorious past is concerned. Once the sense of continuity is snapped, the past is reified within "the ideal order" of "existing monuments"[86] and any sort of renewal is highly thwarted: "From the point of view of immediacy, everything is lost." The radiance, as Kierkegaard says, may take the form of a "thunderstorm" – a sudden revelation – a leap into the future:

> When everything has stalled, when thought is immobilized, when language is silent, when explanation returns home in despair – then there has to be a thunderstorm. Who can understand this? And yet who can conceive of anything else?

The radiant quest, induced by the inner power of transcending the inert immediacy of space and responding to the present moment's power of revelation, reconciles past and future within the instant of reflexive consciousness, of a return on oneself in the infinite, what Rudolf Kassner, the dedicatee of Rilke's Eighth Duino Elegy, called *Umkehr*: "Job is blessed and has received everything *double*."[87] Katherine Mansfield ends both "Prelude" and "Feuille d'Album" with a suggestion of such restored integrity. Virginia Woolf ends *Mrs. Dalloway* with these words, through Peter Walsh's viewpoint:

> It is Clarissa, he said.
> For there she was.[88]

---

[85] Lawrence, *The Rainbow*, 203. See Chapter 7.
[86] Eliot, "Tradition and the Individual Talent", in *Selected Prose*, 38.
[87] Søren Kierkegaard, *Repetition* (1843), in *Fear and Trembling, Repetition*, 212 (Kierkegaard's emphasis).
[88] Woolf, *Mrs. Dalloway*, 165.

Her integrity is the party's gathering; Virginia Woolf's is the novel: "She heard the click of the typewriter."[89] The revelation comes from the individual, transcending both the lack of communication and the limits of immediate communication: "And it was an offering; to combine, to create; but to whom?"[90] It means being "in an active state of grace".[91] Katherine Mansfield's sense of continuity was certainly enhanced by exile (although leaving New Zealand to sail to London was voluntary on her part); it even seemed to have been renewed by her brother's death although she had already sketched *Maata* in 1913, in which we find some of her later motifs:

> Chapter IV. The arrival of the piano. The room transformed. The blue bed cover stitched with gold towers & minarets & borders of leopards. Chrysanthemums. A tiny fire. Maata in a grey and pink gown, in <u>curious</u> mood. She had spent yesterday shopping. She felt like she used to when she was a little girl & spoke her name & address outside the sweet shop. She pokes up the fire and sits down at the piano. 'Mon cœur s'ouvre à ta voix."[92]

"My heart opens to your voice." She too stresses the significance of the voice as a means to rouse empathy. She very soon felt detached from the immediate life[93] although she is able to wonder without restraint:

> You cannot think what pleasure my invisible, imaginary companion gave me. If he had been alive it would never have possibly occurred, but – its a game I like t play – to walk & and talk with the dead who smile and are silent – and <u>free</u> quite finally free.[94]

When her brother died, she reacted with empathy, like "old Woodifield" in "The Fly". The first pear tree she wrote about was the pear tree at the back of the garden in their childhood, a memory revived in Acacia Road during her brother's visit there:

---

[89] *Ibid.*, 25. See above on page 155.
[90] *Ibid.*, 103.
[91] *The Katherine Mansfield Notebooks*, II, 58.
[92] *Ibid.*, I, 248-49.
[93] See also Chapter 1.
[94] *The Katherine Mansfield Notebooks*, II, 13.

> He puts his arm round her. They pace up and down. A thin round moon shines over the pear tree & the ivy walls of the garden glitter like metal.[95]

From the immediate impression to its transformation within memory, there is no break: everything is transfigured at once. Contemplating the possibility of returning, she uses the same syntax as Kezia about her grandmother's death ("You couldn't not be there"[96]), which would be "awful": "I couldn't not come back, you know that feeling. Its awfully mysterious."[97] The double negative is not a simple assertion; it asserts "everything *double*".[98] Septimus Warren Smith sees the "old man"[99] staring at him once, and dies. Clarissa Dalloway sees the "old lady"[100] twice, and lives, renewed. Moreover, the first time she sees her, her figure is doubly connected with time, since she appears when "Big Ben struck the half hour" and the past is linked to the present: "... they had been neighbours ever so many years." Her appearance is familiar; the definite article is used, "the old lady" while Septimus' "old man" is only "an old man".[101]

The second time, the old lady becomes a figure of wonder since she "stared straight at her"[102] and she feels connected to the place where she lives: "It held, foolish as the idea was, something of her own in it, this country sky, this sky over Westminster." In Katherine Mansfield's "Feuille d'Album", romance starts when Ian French the painter looks out of the window and sees "a strangely thin girl in a dark pinafore",[103] who "simply did not see the house opposite". The cathartic element to be found in *Mrs. Dalloway* with Septimus' sacrifice is absolutely unknown to Katherine Mansfield, who

---

[95] *Ibid.*, 15.

[96] Mansfield, *The Edinburgh Edition of the Collected Works of Katherine Mansfield*, II, 358; *The Collected Stories*, 227.

[97] *The Katherine Mansfield Notebooks*, II, 15.

[98] Søren Kierkegaard, *Repetition* (1843), in *Fear and Trembling, Repetition*, 212 (Kierkegaard's emphasis). See above on page 156.

[99] Woolf, *Mrs. Dalloway*, 127.

[100] *Ibid.*, 108 and 158.

[101] *Ibid.*, 127.

[102] *Ibid.*, 157.

[103] Mansfield, *The Edinburgh Edition of the Collected Works of Katherine Mansfield*, II, 95; *The Collected Stories*, 164.

pondered over it in "The Fly", a story which she *"hated* writing",[104] she wrote in June 1922. Her subject is the individual and life while Virginia Woolf's is the individual and society. If the latter may long for the Open, she finds difficult to reach it while Katherine Mansfield has the natural gift of it.

---

[104] To William Gerhardi, 14 June 1922, in *The Collected Letters of Katherine Mansfield*, V, 206 (Mansfield's emphasis).

CHAPTER 9

MARVELLOUS GARDENS: KATHERINE MANSFIELD, COLETTE, CATHERINE POZZI, DOROTHY RICHARDSON

> J'ai craché du sang, mais si peu qu'à peu je croirais, comme l'autre jour, que j'ai une dent qui saigne .... Et c'est parce que l'on "m'a fait parler" hier. Et c'est en me levant, au réveil, à chaque fois, *just like Katherine Mansfield* : tout y est, jusqu'à la douleur de la jambe. Le soir, je lis les lettres de cette fille qui ont – ironie ! – un succès de librairie ....[1]

In November 1914, Katherine Mansfield wrote in her Notebook:

> I feel very happy and free. Colette Willy is in my thoughts tonight. I feel my own self awake and stretching – stretching so that Im on tiptoe; full of happy joy. Can it be true that one <u>can</u> renew oneself.[2]

A few days later: "I don't care a fig at present for anyone I know except her." She was reading *L'entrave*, a novel Colette (1873-1954) published in 1913, the year when she gave birth to her daughter, Colette de Jouvenel, called Bel-Gazou. The first-person narrator, Renée Néré, has a love affair with a man called Jean and tells how what was only sensual delight at the beginning is transformed into love. Then there is "no remedy to his mystery". Colette gives such definition of love: "Love is that painful, ever-repeated bump against a

---

[1] "I've spat up blood, but so little that I would almost think, as the other day, that I have a tooth which is bleeding .... And this is because I 'was made to talk' yesterday. And it happens when I wake up and stand up, each time, *just like Katherine Mansfield*: the whole thing, the pain in my leg. At night, I read that girl's letters, which – ironically – sell well ..." (Catherine Pozzi, *Journal 1913-1934*, eds Lawrence Joseph and Claire Paulhan, Paris: Ramsay, 1987, 589-90).
[2] *The Katherine Mansfield Notebooks*, I, 284 (Mansfield's emphasis).

wall which cannot be burst."[3] Some sort of wrestling replaces the first
embrace until a new feeling of confidence follows words of reproach.
The narrator briefly remembers her childhood, saying that from that
period she has kept the gift of emotion.[4]

For the brief comparative study I wish to carry out in this chapter I
have chosen a novel she published earlier, in 1907, under the name of
Colette Willy, at the time when she was playing pantomime at the
Moulin-Rouge. In *La retraite sentimentale* (*A Sentimental Retreat*),
the main character, Claudine, lives apart from her husband who is ill
and has to stay in a sanatorium until he comes back and dies. Her
garden and the animals which live in it enable her to transcend that
tragic break in her life.

The marvellous gardens described in this chapter are all linked
with the wonders and joys of childhood: "Can it be true that one can
renew oneself?" That sensitiveness to the outer world of trees, flowers
and animals as revelations of being is a common feature to the four
women's voices I wish to gather in this chapter. In the excerpt quoted
in the epigraph, Catherine Pozzi (1882-1934) wrote she felt "just like
Katherine Mansfield". She too was ill and died of tuberculosis.
Dorothy Richardson (1873-1957), one of the Modernists, even if she
may be less famous than Katherine Mansfield or Virginia Woolf,
recorded with great sensitiveness the marvellous details of the past.
Pointed Roof (1915), the first novel in the long series, *Pilgrimage*, she
dedicated her energy from 1912 to her death, in 1957, is the first
example of the use of the stream of consciousness technique in
English. She preferred the term "interior monologue" however. I am
going to consider a short story she published in August 1924, called
"The Garden".

"Refleurir":[5] Colette's garden of plenitude

After her husband's death, Claudine wishes to renew herself, to forget
the pain and remember the happy moments of her past life. Her
garden, the animals in it, the blossoming flowers keep a promise of

---

[3] Colette, *L'Entrave* (1913), Paris: Librio, 2013, 113: "Il n'y a pas de remède à son
mystère" and "L'amour, c'est ce choc douloureux et toujours recommencé, contre une
paroi qu'on ne peut pas rompre".
[4] *Ibid.*, 66.
[5] "Blossoming again", in Colette, *La retraite sentimentale* (1907), Paris: Gallimard
Folio, 1977, 228.

plenitude: "Je me penche, je ramasse les roses éparses et j'en *comble* les mains de mon amie."[6] At the beginning of the novel, Claudine, whose relationship with her husband is only epistolary, feels lonely in his absence. Her husband's style in his letters is Colette's: the words used to describe his illness "bound against the smooth walls of my bedroom like beautiful lepidopterous insects".[7] Katherine Mansfield displays the same gift of animating things in "Prelude", in "Feuille d'Album", or in her poem "Florian nachdenklich". However, she expresses sensuality and desire differently. She is much more allusive than Colette who writes quite directly about sexual pleasure – "I suppose Colette is the only woman in France who does just this":[8]

> Moi, je ne cherche pas la volupté, c'est elle qui me cherche, me trouve, m'assaille et me terrasse d'une main, d'une bouche si rudes que j'en tremble après .... Ou bien elle rôde lentement autour de moi, me fatigue d'une approche invisible, contre laquelle lutte en moi un sourd orgueil ....[9]

Her description of the cat Péronnelle on heat dancing like a maenad partakes of this readiness not to conceal such reality of the flesh.

Another difference lies in the fact that Katherine Mansfield chooses third persons in her stories while Colette creates a first-person narrator, partly herself, partly a persona, which is a centre of consciousness. This makes Katherine Mansfield's work dramatic (and we think of Shakespeare, particularly in *A Midsummer Night's Dream*, *As You Like It* and *The Winter's Tale*) while Colette remains more private and lyrical. The "I" in *La retraite sentimentale* is quite assertive, almost sovereign with the other characters – her husband's son and her friend Annie. Apart from Marthe, Annie's sister-in-law,

---

[6] "I bend down, gather the scattered roses and *fill* my friend's hands with them" (*ibid.*, 228; my emphasis).

[7] *Ibid.*, 14: "... rebondissent contre les parois de ma chambre comme de beaux lépidoptères."

[8] *The Katherine Mansfield Notebooks*, I, 284. Colette was not the only writer to claim freedom of speech and behaviour in France at that time. We may also mention Renée Vivien (1877-1909) and Lucie Delarue-Mardrus (1874-1945), the former was a friend of Colette's and the latter is named in *La retraite sentimentale*, 152.

[9] "I do not seek for voluptuous pleasure; it seeks me, finds me, assails me and triumphs over me with such rough hand and mouth that I shiver afterwards .... Or it slowly prowls about me and its coming closer unseen exhausts me while my muted pride wrestles against it" (Colette, *La retraite sentimentale*, 135-36).

there are three important female figures in the novel, Claudine, who passionately loves her husband but does not resent his cheating on her since she thinks he should remain free; Annie who got a divorce and became quite promiscuous; and Willette Collie "who played the Faun"[10] appears in Annie's narrative of her playing pantomime. Colette Willie draws from her own experience. In that part of the novel there is a suggestion of lesbian love.

A literary character is real in a special way. It transcends the immediate reality. Her relations with her friends, and even with her husband when he comes back from the sanatorium, an old man, do not fulfill Claudine's wishes. People talk too much. Society is a very narrow world, a closed world. In the silent company of flowers, trees and animals, Claudine finds the infinity which is the condition for her personal renewal. This is a trait Virginia Woolf must have felt when a sentence in the first version of *Mrs. Dalloway's Party*, the short story she sketched in 1922, "Mrs. Dalloway said she would buy the gloves herself"[11] was changed into "Mrs. Dalloway said she would buy the flowers herself".[12]

The garden is the place of renewal since it is the place of the origins. It is significant that Claudine should remember the garden of her childhood in a dream in which it is summer while she recognizes outside "the silky murmur of snow".[13] The garden of childhood is an enchanted place; it is linked with the pleasure of the "goûter" at four in the afternoon (the afternoon snack), "le pain de quatre heures"[14] ("the four o'clock bread"). When Katherine Mansfield remembers her childhood garden in her Notebook in 1915, she also refers to the sense of taste, so important to a poet like Keats. Her description is very precise:

> First you pulled out the little stem & sucked it. It was faintly sour & then you ate them always from the top – core & all.
> The pips were delicious.
> Do you remember sitting on the pink garden seat.
> I shall never forget that pink garden seat. It is the only garden seat for me.

---

[10] *Ibid.*, 128.
[11] Virginia Woolf, "Mrs. Dalloway in Bond Street", in *The Mrs. Dalloway Reader*, 15.
[12] Woolf, *Mrs. Dalloway*, 3.
[13] Colette, *La retraite sentimentale*, 161: "... le murmure soyeux de la neige."
[14] *Ibid.*, 162.

> Where is it now. Do you think we shall be allowed to sit in it in Heaven.[15]

The moment, unique and so recreated in memory, looks like paradise regained. "Assise au seuil du jardin, je goûte à longs soupirs ma solitude, comme si je m'étais sentie en danger de la perdre ...."[16] Such comparisons as "Like two little stray cats they followed the courtyard to where the doll's house stood"[17] recall Colette's way of mixing animal figures and human life: "Il lui jette un regard de crabe fâché."[18] The description of the sheep at the beginning of "At the Bay" recalls Colette's empathetic way of describing animals.

The garden is the place of personal renewal. The future gives the past a new shape. Memory and imagination make life real.

Catherine Pozzi: the "summit of time"[19]

Catherine Pozzi was a great reader and she loved English literature. John Middleton Murry was a friend of Paul Valéry's and Katherine Mansfield mentions the French poet in a letter to her husband on 20 April 1920,[20] but it is not likely that she met Catherine Pozzi, who was Valéry's mistress from 1920 to 1928. Catherine Pozzi felt close to Katherine Mansfield. They had both started writing a Journal as young children and went on doing so when grown-ups. They both felt lonely. Catherine Pozzi's marriage was a failure. Both idealized love but met with disappointment.

Throughout her life, Catherine Pozzi worked on a book which she at first called the *De Libertate*. Then it became *Le Corps de l'Ame* and finally *Peau d'Ame* (*Soul-Skin*), a pun on the title of Charles Perrault's tale in verse, *Peau d'âne* (*Donkey-Skin*). She was very interested in

---

[15] *The Katherine Mansfield Notebooks*, II, 14.

[16] Colette, *La retraite sentimentale*, 235-36: "I was sitting at the entrance of the garden, relishing my solitude with long sighs as though I had felt in danger of losing it."

[17] Mansfield, *The Edinburgh Edition of the Collected Works of Katherine Mansfield*, II, 419; *The Collected Stories*, 390.

[18] Colette, *La retraite sentimentale*, 232: "He casts an upset crab's look at her."

[19] Catherine Pozzi, *Peau d'Ame*, ed. Lawrence Joseph, Paris: La Différence, 1990, 109: "... le sommet du temps." For more details on the comparison between Katherine Mansfield and Catherine Pozzi, see Anne Mounic, "Du jardin de juillet aux fruits d'automne: de Katherine Mansfield à Catherine Pozzi. Pourquoi écrire ?", in *Psyché et le secret de Perséphone*, 103-33.

[20] *Letters between Katherine Mansfield and John Middleton Murry*, 303.

science and had read about the principle of entropy, discovered by Sadi Carnot (1796-1832) and Clausius (1822-1888). Her research was concerned with the origin of our sensations. She affirmed that one could feel because one had already felt. The connection with the universe was established in time. "Je sens ce que j'ai déjà senti":[21] she deduces this assertion from Weber's law [Weber (1795-1878), a German physiologist] which says that an impression is more intense if it has been preceded by similar impressions. Between the subject who perceives and the object which is perceived time intervenes: "Il n'y a pas de perception où il n'y a pas de masse résonante, et la masse est du temps."[22] The soul is the surface which transforms the immediate sensation into the magic of perception: "magie (ré bémol, rose, salé)."[23] The human mind is connected with the universe through time and "the ENCHANTED SUM ... has the value of Paradise lost".[24] Memory and perception renew the universe within their subjective synthesis of time. The garden is the place for such metamorphosis. The description is given in the second person. Throughout the book, Catherine Pozzi talks to her reader. Such epiphanies as occur in Katherine Mansfield's stories, or even in her Notebook, are also presented by Pozzi as intersubjective achievements:

> Le jardin de Juillet s'étendait sans limites, car les paysans de ce pays n'élèvent pas de murs entre leurs vignes, seulement des haies qui sont aux pampres confondues.
> Un espace de fleurs divisé par quatre allées droites, de quoi marcher cent pas, laissait marcher la fantaisie sur cent hectares, des ceps au ciel .... Vous étiez assis sur un banc.
> C'était les dahlias que vous regardiez, ils jouaient déjà dans l'automne, ils étaient déjà, ce matin, dans le faste soir; ils accompagnaient déjà de cris épanouis les raisins qui n'étaient pas mûrs, comme au chant des vendanges passées.
> Soudain vous entendîtes les jours passés.[25]

---

[21] Pozzi, *Peau d'Ame*, 42: "I can feel what I have already felt."

[22] *Ibid.*, 120: "There is no perception where there is no resonant mass, and that mass is time."

[23] *Ibid.*, 115: "magic (D flat, pink, salted)."

[24] *Ibid.*, 110: "la SOMME ENCHANTEE ... a précisément la valeur du paradis perdu."

[25] *Ibid.*, 41-42: "The garden in July lay boundless, since the peasants in this country do not build walls between the vineyards, only hedges undistinguished from the vine branches. / A flower bed divided by four straight paths, you could walk a while, let fantasy go for a hundred hectares, from the branches to the sky .... You were sitting on

The garden is boundless and even reaches the sky. The fullness of time brings plenitude in space. Immediate life is transcended through the subjective mind whose sphere is time. We may speak of an epic conversion as we did when commenting upon the vision of the aloe in "Prelude".

"It was safe here with the flowers":[26] Dorothy Richardson

Dorothy Richardson's story starts with: "There was no one there."[27] And this solitude is bliss because it gives the possibility of getting the revelation provided by the flowers. The main character is a third person – "She". Then she is called Nelly and we understand that she identifies with the beautiful flowers: "Wherever she looked she could see this one different flower, growing taller. It was Nelly on a stalk."[28] The garden is really the world of the origins since the little girl grows aware of her presence in the world although neither the flowers nor the bees seem to notice. Yet they reveal their presence to her only: "*They* had never seen them like this, standing quiet all together in this little piece."[29]

Such revelation is linked to perception: "She could see the different smells going up into the sunshine. The sunshine smelt of the flowers." The flowers are protective: "They all put their arms round her without touching her." In this part of the garden, nothing "could come":[30] "It could not get there. The flowers kept it away." "It" remains vague, not defined. We imagine some threat, some presence the girl would deem unpleasant: "Outside the garden it was dark and cold." She runs and falls:

> Bang. The hard gravel holding a pain against her nose. Someone calling. She lay still hoping her nose would be bleeding to make them sorry.

---

a bench. / You were looking at the dahlias, already playing in autumn, already this morning in the prosperous evening, already accompanying of their radiant cries the grapes not yet ripe, as with the song of past harvests. / Suddenly you could hear the days past."
[26] Dorothy Richardson, "The Flowers" (1924), in *Journey to Paradise*, London: Virago Press, 1989, 23.
[27] *Ibid.*, 21.
[28] *Ibid.*, 22.
[29] *Ibid.*, 21 (Richardson's emphasis).
[30] *Ibid.*, 23.

But solitude seems to mean plenitude in spite of all: "Someone would come, not knowing about the flowers; the pretty, pretty flowers. The flowers were unkind, staying too far off to tell them how happy and good she was."[31] She shares a special knowledge with the flowers although they could not follow her while she was running.

"Dear little flower."[32] The new intimacy with this particular part of the garden makes her aware of herself, of her subjective integrity. This means communion with the world and a sense of blissful separateness, of freedom:

> It had a deep smell. She touched it with her nose to smell more. It kissed her gently, looking small.

Such an affectionate link with the world gives evidence of the individual's presence. The present moment of the vision, or the dream, gathers all times as if the girl were in paradise:

> The smell of the dark pointed trees in the shrubbery. Raindrops outside the window falling down in front of the dark pointed trees. The snowman alone on the lawn, after tea, with a slanted face.
> Shiny apples on the trees on Sunday with pink on one side.
> The slippery swing seat, scrubby ropes, tight. Tummy falling out, coming back again high in the air ....
> The apples were near this part. In the sun. Where the cowslip balls hung in a row on the string.

Such a garden is a metaphor of the spirit of the narrative as it assembles several impressions, different seasons, the continuity of being and its distinct moments. As Catherine Pozzi so acutely understood, the world achieves its marvellous presence within the subjective mind as it opens, "transparent"[33] to itself, to its wonder, which is also the wonder of life as it takes shape in each individual:

> Then something immense came into view; an enormous shock-haired giant with his arms stretched out. It was the big gum-tree outside Mrs Stubb's shop, and as they passed by there was a strong whiff of eucalyptus. And now big spots of light gleamed in the mist. The

---

[31] *Ibid.*, 24.

[32] *Ibid.*, 22.

[33] Kierkegaard, *Either ... or ...*, 549.

shepherd stopped whistling; he rubbed his red nose and wet beard on his wet sleeve and, screwing up his eyes, glanced in the direction of the sea. The sun was rising.[34]

The trees and plants acquire a dramatic stance of their own. As in Hopkins' poems, each creature is singular within the drama of Creation: "And, for all this, nature is never spent."[35] The subjective mind can induce new beginnings, and "freedom is compatible with necessity".[36]

[34] Mansfield, *The Edinburgh Edition of the Collected Works of Katherine Mansfield*, II, 343; *The Collected Stories*, 206.
[35] Gerard Manley Hopkins, "God's Grandeur" (1877), in *The Major Works*, 128.
[36] Gerard Manley Hopkins, Letter to Robert Bridges, 4 January 1883, in *ibid.*, 258.

CHAPTER 10

A FLAVOUR OF PARIS
IN KATHERINE MANSFIELD'S STORIES

I now wish to study the "spirit of place" (Lawrence's phrase in his *Studies in Classic American Literature*[1]) in Katherine Mansfield's stories, either located or written in Paris ("Feuille d'Album", "Je Ne Parle Pas Français", the beginning of "An Indiscreet Journey", or "The Fly", among others[2]), through enumerating and analysing the typical details she emphasizes. For instance, in "An Indiscreet Journey", the famous Paris concierge is compared to St Anne. This is striking at the very beginning of the story, but not gratuitous, as I have already suggested and will consider in detail in this chapter. As the "spirit of place" is also conveyed by literary reminiscences, I also wish to study Katherine Mansfield's connection with Baudelaire, often considered as the first Modernist poet in France, through another of her stories, "The Doll's House", which she mentions in November 1921 in a letter written in Switzerland. We shall connect this affinity with the "cry" in her letter to her husband in December 1922: "*I want to be REAL.*"[3] This will help us to get a better understanding of her Modernism.

The spirit of place
In the first chapter of his *Studies in Classic American Literature*, Lawrence connects two notions, what he calls the "spirit of place" and genuine freedom: "Men are free when they are in a living homeland, not when they are straying and breaking away."[4] Breaking away means breaking away from oneself, not from the conscious self but

---

[1] Lawrence, "The Spirit of Place", in *Studies in Classic American Literature*, 7-14.
[2] For the list of stories written in Paris, or dealing with France, see Kimber, *Katherine Mansfield: The View from France*, 235-36.
[3] To J.M. Murry, [26 December 1922], in *The Collected Letters of Katherine Mansfield*, V, 341 (Mansfield's emphasis). See Chapters 1 and 8.
[4] Lawrence, "The Spirit of Place", 12.

from the deep source of "practical truth".[5] Lawrence then evinces a second paradox:

> Men are not free when they are doing just what they like. The moment you can do what you like, there is nothing you care about doing. Men are only free when they are doing what the deepest self likes.

And he adds: "We are free only so long as we obey." Calling the subjective inner being "IT",[6] he gives it an impersonal, objective character, which is, I think, highly objectionable.[7] I prefer to speak of what Robert Graves called anyone's "genius"[8] as a supra-personal entity – the utmost individual linked with the others in time. However, the link Lawrence sets between these three notions – place, freedom, the inner self – is certainly at the root of an artist's sense of reality, as opposed to abstract idealism and the rule of the dissociated intellect:

> The world doesn't fear a new idea. It can pigeon-hole any idea. But it can't pigeon-hole a real new experience. It can only dodge.[9]

It is likely to be easier for an exile to capture the "spirit of place" than for someone who has never moved and has only known his native place, since the acquaintance with the "deeper self" is originally an experience of otherness. The contrast involves a comparative viewpoint. This reality comes across in Katherine Mansfield's stories. In "Feuille d'Album", the main character, an artist called Ian French, is first viewed through the others' eyes as a very strange fellow: "It can't all be as innocent as it looks! Why come to Paris if you want to be a daisy in the field?"[10] To that we may retort that it is appropriate to "come to Paris" when your name is "French". The painter is a figure of the "deeper self" and otherness: "How surprised those tender women would have been if they had managed to force the door."[11] His studio is as neat as a pin" but the exotic element – "An Indian curtain

---

[5] *Ibid.*, 8.
[6] *Ibid.*, 13.
[7] See Mounic, *Monde terrible où naître*, 426-33.
[8] Robert Graves, "Genius" (1969), in *Some Speculations on Literature, History and Religion*, Manchester: Carcanet, 2000, 268-79.
[9] Lawrence, "The Spirit of Place", 7.
[10] Mansfield, *The Collected Stories*, 162.
[11] *Ibid.*, 163.

that had a fringe of red leopards marching round it" – gives the idea of a wild living energy.

Paris is the place where John Middleton Murry, who had come to attend Bergson's lectures in the Collège de France, and J.D. Fergusson, who found the city was "a place of freedom", met in 1910, and founded the magazine *Rhythm*. The rhythm they thought of was the rhythm of the deeper life. One of the contributors, Frederick Goodyear, spoke of "neo-barbarians", or people who intended to "familiarize us with our outcast selves"[12] (see Chapters 1 and 6). Katherine Mansfield was one of those "neo-barbarians" contributing to the short-lived magazine created by her husband. We have already mentioned how aware she was of the variety of cultural values. "Feuille d'Album" (written in London in September 1917 but set in Paris) wittily tells of the inevitability of desire in the present moment, and its redeeming quality. And it is the role of some chosen objects (the Indian curtain) or plants to disclose such intensity: "His heart fell out of the side window of his studio, and down to the balcony of the house opposite – buried itself in the pot of daffodils under the half-opened buds and spears of green ...."[13] The metonymy (the heart for the feelings) is given a dynamic impulse. Thinking of Hopkins, we could call it "sprung" metonymy. We find the same energy in things – the energy to move and not to break – at the end of "Prelude", so often referred to in this book and originally written in May 1915 in Paris as "The Aloe": "And the top of the cream jar flew through the air and rolled like a penny in a round on the linoleum – and did not break."[14]

In the stories written in Paris from December 1913 ("Something Childish But Very Natural") to May 1915 ("The Little Governess", "An Indiscreet Journey", "Spring Pictures"), we may find some elements in common – the existential rhythm of the train (see also Chapter 6), the protective character of the *concierge*, the energy of some particular elements. In "Something Childish But Very Natural", the girl Henry falls in love with in the train has "marigold-coloured hair"[15] like "The Little Governess" and with the same fascinating attraction:

---

[12] Smith, "Paris Is Simply a Place of Freedom", *Temporel* n° 7, May 2009: http://temporel.fr/Rhythm-par-Angela-Smith.

[13] Mansfield, *The Collected Stories*, 164.

[14] *Ibid.*, 60.

[15] *Ibid.*, 598.

> Alas! how tragic for a little governess to possess hair that made one
> think of tangerines and marigolds, of apricots and tortoiseshell cats
> and champagne! Perhaps that was what the old man was thinking as
> he gazed and gazed, and that not even the dark ugly clothes could
> disguise her soft beauty.[16]

The story may look like a variation, with only one old man, on the
Biblical episode of Susan and the elders, a Greek addition to the Book
of Daniel (13) so often represented by painters:

> It was a dream! It wasn't true! It wasn't the same old man at all. Ah,
> how horrible! the little governess stared at him in terror.[17]

Susan is accused of adultery; the young flying governess is derided by
old fat women on the bus.

In "Something Childish But Very Natural" as in other stories
mentioned in Chapter 6, the rhythm of the train gives the emotional
impulse to the tale:

> The train had flung behind the roofs and chimneys. They were
> swinging into the country, past little black woods and fading fields
> and pools of water shining under an apricot sky. Henry's heart began
> to thump and beat to the beat of the train.[18]

It sets the world in motion, changing it into a fairy world of dream and
faith. The rhythm opens the field of possibility and freedom against
fatalism ("But then I've been a fatalist for a long time now",[19] says the
young girl on the train). And this is linked with spring, with
primroses, jonquils, roses and violets as well as butterflies. Those
teenagers hate life as it is; the girl's Hungarian mother is the strange
element of otherness in the tale, suggesting the possibility of another
life: "She hates our life just as much as I do",[20] says the girl. They
wish to live the simple, natural life but their prelapsarian happiness
nevertheless comes to an end. The story is a variation on *Paradise
Lost* (see also Chapter 3). In Chapter 1, we saw how Katherine

---

[16] *Ibid.*, 180.
[17] *Ibid.*, 188.
[18] *Ibid.*, 599.
[19] *Ibid.*, 600.
[20] *Ibid.*, 603.

Mansfield loved Paris and as she was very young the idea she had of its Bohemia. It was freedom for her. The girl's name is Edna: "'Are all those trees down there – apple?' she asked in a shaky voice."[21] The little girl in the pinafore brings Henry a telegram: "Perhaps it's only a make-believe one, and it's got one of those snakes inside it that fly at you."[22] The final "web of darkness" that spreads over the garden restores the fatalist outlook and puts an end to their dream of timelessness:

> "We oughtn't to wait for things. What's age? You're as old as you'll ever be and so am I. You know," he said, "I have a feeling often and often that it's dangerous to wait for things – that if you wait for things they only go further and further away."[23]

We may wonder whether the final break of their happiness came from the fact that Henry was waiting for her return or that he had kissed her under the apple trees, saying they were "full of angels".[24]

This sense of doom – of a disquieting reality beneath the simple everyday texture of life, later expressed at the end of "The Canary" – is more obviously conveyed in "Spring Pictures". The title is deceptive since the lilies, roses, and violets the "old hag" wishes to sell will not sell, and are decaying instead: "But the lilies, bunched together in a frill of green, look more like cauliflowers."[25] Beauty is defaced for lack of "Hope!":

> "You misery – you sentimental, faded female! Break your last string and have done with it. I shall go mad with your endless thrumming; my heart throbs to it and every little pulse beats in time. It is morning. I lie in the empty bed – the huge bed big as a field and as cold and unsheltered."[26]

---

[21] *Ibid.*, 614.
[22] *Ibid.*, 616.
[23] *Ibid.*, 610.
[24] *Ibid.*, 614.
[25] *Ibid.*, 633.
[26] *Ibid.*, 635.

In "Something Childish But Very Natural", written in December 1913, Henry says: "We ought to be building nests instead of houses, I always think."[27] Lack of hope comes from lack of love:

> Is this my room? Are those my clothes folded over an arm-chair? Under the pillow, sign and symbol of a lonely woman, ticks my watch. The bell jangles. Ah! At last! I leap out of bed and run to the door. Play faster – faster – Hope!
> "Your milk, Mademoiselle," says the concierge, gazing at me severely.
> "Ah, thank you," I cry, gaily swinging the milk bottle. "No letters for me?"[28]

Waiting for things simply means they go further away from you, Henry suggests. There is a reminiscence of Ophelia in the description of the woman coming "down the steps from the Quay, walking slowly, one hand on her lip. It is a beautiful evening; the sky is the colour of lilac and the river of violet leaves."[29] The violets are for faithfulness. "I would give you some violets" says Ophelia in *Hamlet*, "but they withered when my father died".[30]

In December 1913, Katherine Mansfield had stayed in Paris with her husband, who hoped he would be able to make a living in France, which proved a deceptive idea: "But, Henry, money! You see we haven't any money." And Henry answered: "Don't you feel that money is more or less accidental – that if one really wants things it's either there or it doesn't matter?"[31] In "Je Ne Parle Pas Français", the narrator Raoul Duquette, modelled on Francis Carco, says: "... and Paris behind us nothing but a great trap we had set to catch these sleepy innocents."[32]

In May 1915, she was alone in Paris, in Francis Carco's flat on the Ile de la Cité after difficult moments with her husband. Their estrangement was exacerbated by the fact that she thought she was in love with Carco. She had already come to Paris in February and March 1915, when she went to see the French writer and poet in the

---

[27] Mansfield, "Something Childish But Very Natural", in *ibid.*, 603.
[28] Katherine Mansfield, "Spring Pictures", in *ibid.*, 635-36.
[29] *Ibid.*, 636.
[30] Shakespeare, *Hamlet*, IV, v, 184-85, 308.
[31] Mansfield, "Something Childish But Very Natural", in *The Collected Stories*, 610.
[32] Mansfield, "Je Ne Parle Pas Français", in *ibid.*, 77.

"Zone des Armées" in Gray. Thus she wrote "An Indiscreet Journey".[33] She refers to her visit in her Notebook. On the 20 February, she writes: "I don't really love him now I know him, but he is so rich and so careless – that I love."[34] And then:

> It was like an elopement .... Laughing and trembling we pressed against each other a long long kiss – interrupted by a clock on the wall striking five. He lit the fire. We sighed together a little, but always laughing. The whole affair seemed somehow so ridiculous and at the same time so utterly natural. There was nothing to do but laugh.

The word "journey" in the title gives the "elopement" an epic tint. The adjective "indiscreet" is interesting since it may have several meanings: "Imprudent in speech or action; inconsiderate; unadvised", derived from the Latin *indiscretus* – "which cannot be distinguished, similar, indiscreet". A sense of adventure comes out of the title. The tale is divided into three sections: first of all, the waking up and hurrying to the station for a trip to nowhere, or at least into the unknown; then the account of an evening at the café, followed by a talk with some soldiers. This is Katherine Mansfield's way of catching the reality of war but the tale is also a parody of initiation.

"An Indiscreet Journey"

At the beginning of the story, we meet a *concierge* again. She is waking the narrator up and bringing a cup of milk like the concierge in "Spring Pictures". Yet, the essential difference is that she is not called "the concierge" at once but first submitted to comparison: "She is like St. Anne." The pronoun, "She", through being indefinite, opens a field of possibilities, starts the story *in medias res*, and gives more importance to St Anne (the symbolical figure) than to the real character. Throughout the story, the real world is being contrasted with the world of the mind, which secures the continuity of time in spite of the disruptive quality of the war. We may say that Katherine Mansfield uses a comparative technique for the genuine quality of the event – its deeper meaning – to emerge. She immediately affirms the accuracy of the simile: "Yes, the concierge is the image of St. Anne,

---

[33] For a full analysis of the story, see Anne Mounic, "'An Indiscreet Journey': Katherine Mansfield et la Grande Guerre", in *Monde terrible où naître*, 193-210.
[34] *The Katherine Mansfield Notebooks*, II, 9.

with that black cloth over her head, the wisps of hair hanging, and the tiny smoking lamp in her hand." We may say that the comparison is based on visual evidence, in the same way as our knowledge of the story of Susan and the elders mostly comes from the numerous paintings of the subject we may have seen.

There is a painting in the Louvre in which Rembrandt represents Saint Anne with a "black cloth over her head" leaning over Jesus on Mary's lap. The character of Mary's mother was given its particular significance by Jacques de Voragine in his *Légende dorée*. The comparative quality of the story is obvious throughout: "I jumped out of my pyjamas and into the basin of cold water like any English lady in any French novel." The narrator herself is not totally herself but shares in an archetypal identity, which is literary. Therefore, religious history is associated with literature, as part and parcel of an archetypal narrative likely to come across through everyday life. The Burberry she puts on also belongs to several worlds: "It did not belong to me. I had borrowed it from a friend." It is "significant" because it is the "perfect and adequate disguise". It was what the soldiers wore in the trenches, which she does not mention, but says: "Lions have been faced in a Burberry." The figure of Blandine and the lions comes to mind. Moreover she felt that she had to wear the "perfect and adequate disguise". And a Burberry is "the token of the undisputed venerable traveller". Her position is heroic; she is going to get involved in an epic adventure and she should pluck up courage. She invokes a lot of mythic models and figures; her Burberry is "age-old". She is deviating from the usual path of everyday routine. The concierge does not think much of her chance of getting there. Her fears are ominous.[35]

The comparative element recurs: "... the tall black trees on the far side, grouped together like negroes conversing"; and "I ran down the echoing stairs – strange they sounded, like a piano flicked by a sleepy housemaid – and on to the Quay".[36] The world into which she is hurled is an echoing world. Should we think of Blake's "The Ecchoing Green", which echoes the mirth of little ones from one generation to the other? It gives us further evidence of Katherine Mansfield's sense of continuity (see Chapter 1).

Once she arrives at "the big station", the reality of the war takes an allegorical aspect. What may be recognized and named in the civilian

---

[35] Mansfield, "An Indiscreet Journey", in *The Collected Stories*, 618.
[36] *Ibid.*, 617.

world ("The Commissaire of Police") takes a strange appearance in the world of war: "a Nameless Official." The place names lose any kind of geographical substance, becoming geometrical landmarks: "X.Y.Z." And the narrator has no watch. As a perfect initiate, she reaches a domain which lies out of space and time but is subjected to a particular rhythm, that of the train, a recurrent element in the stories of that time: "Ah! the train had begun to move. The train was on my side."[37] Such rhythm, as we noticed in Chapter 6, is endowed with the same subjective quality in "The Little Governess": "The train seemed glad to have left the station."[38] Movement is welcome; movement brings revelation: "It swung out of the station, and soon we were passing the vegetable gardens, passing the tall, blind houses to let, passing the servants beating carpets."[39] Everyday life is thus revealed from this comparative viewpoint: when the soldiers appear and the scene becomes a scene of war, its reality is being questioned: "Is there really such a thing as war? Are all these laughing voices really going to the war?"

Appearance clashes with reality:

> What beautiful cemeteries we are passing! They flash gay in the sun. They seem to be full of cornflowers and poppies and daisies. How can there be so many flowers at this time of the year? But they are not flowers at all. They are bunches of ribbons tied on to the soldiers' graves.[40]

We remember that in "The Fly", her story written in Paris in February 1922, Katherine Mansfield connected the pastoral reminiscence with the memory of the Great War. Woodifield, the boss's friend, who pipes like the pastoral figure his name suggests, says about the war cemeteries:

> "There's miles of it," quavered old Woodifield, "and it's all as neat as a garden. Flowers growing on all the graves. Nice broad paths." It was plain from his voice how much he liked a nice broad path.[41]

---

[37] *Ibid.*, 618.
[38] Mansfield, "The Little Governess", in *ibid.*, 179.
[39] Mansfield, "An Indiscreet Journey", in *ibid.*, 618.
[40] *Ibid.*, 619.
[41] Mansfield, "The Fly", in *ibid.*, 414.

The comparative technique stresses the ridiculous quality of the drama: "But really, *ma France adorée*, this uniform is ridiculous. Your soldiers are stamped upon your bosom like bright irreverent transfers."[42] The comparison suggests childishness ("transfers" being like toys for children) and childlike figures ("stamped upon your bosom") seeking their mother's protection. We have an overall impression of chaos. Things seem to be out of place, and the time "out of joint", as Hamlet said.

The comparative feature is never dropped: "He looked as though he had escaped from some holy picture, and was entreating the soldiers' pardon for being there at all ...."[43] And the narrator's "unfamiliar letter in the familiar handwriting" contrasts with the old woman's letter: "Slowly, slowly she sipped a sentence, and then looked up and out of the window, her lips trembling a little, and then another sentence, and again the old face turned to the light, tasting it ...."[44] The fake character of her own letter, although "Aunt Julie" had added "in a corner of the empty back page: '*Venez vite, vite*' Strange impulsive woman!",[45] contrasts with the genuine quality of the old mother's attention. Therefore it is as if the sea-gull on the second woman's "black velvet toque" were disclosing the deception: "I was terrified."[46] The initiation takes a more decisive turn then when the station with a "fatal name", not disclosed, is reached. The two colonels, looking "omnipotent", one of them smoking "what ladies love to call a heavy Egyptian cigarette" are named "God I" and "God II".[47] This chaos is absolutely ambivalent. The man with the fish "looked as though he had escaped from some holy picture" but, at the same time, the narrator is sensitive to what is comic in her own predicament. There is also pretence on her part, and therefore a paradox – with the necessary "suspension of disbelief" required by fiction: "suddenly they were there with me, more real, more solid than any relations I had ever known."[48] The narrator gives the impression of being in a world of make-believe, a stage on which human passions are being dramatized.

---

[42] Mansfield, "An Indiscreet Journey", in *ibid.*, 620.
[43] *Ibid.*, 621.
[44] *Ibid.*, 618-19.
[45] *Ibid.*, 621-22.
[46] *Ibid.*, 623.
[47] *Ibid.*, 623-24.
[48] *Ibid.*, 621.

In such a situation, in the "Zone des Armées", the two images on the wall of the café look out of place, "Premier Rencontre" and "Triomphe d'Amour", and evince the parodying quality of the narrator's love date. The dissociated feature of the present moment induces a further dissociation, brought about by rhythm: "I heard the ghostly clatter of the dishes." We may think again of Blake's "The Ecchoing Green" but the echo discloses the apocalyptic feature of the moment:

> And years passed. Perhaps the war is long since over – there is no village outside at all – the streets are quiet under the grass. I have an idea this is the sort of thing one will do on the very last day of all – sit in an empty café and listen to a clock ticking until –[49]

The narrator sets one last comparison:

> The faces lifted, listening. "How beautiful they are!" I thought. "They are like a family party having supper in the New Testament ..." The steps died away.[50]

The explicit reference to the New Testament leads us to think back of the symbolical pattern woven through the tale. The figure of St. Anne at the beginning, the narrator's haste to fly away, the two figures of God omnipotent, one of them smoking an Egyptian cigarette, the holy picture of the old man with a pail of fish, recall the Flight into Egypt, linking therefore the Nativity to the end of times (the Apocalypse) in a continuous archetypal narrative, transcending the tragic disruption of the war. Katherine Mansfield does not pass direct judgement on the event, only questioning its reality and showing its ridiculous feature. Yet, if we follow the underlying narrative – the New Testament reminiscence – we understand that the war is a Massacre of the Innocents, as it was what the Holy Family fled from into Egypt. The soldiers are not only described as children when their ludicrous uniform is derided but the description of the crying soldier with sore eyes is really pathetic. He is as deprived in his suffering as a child would be. The comparative technique enables the real quality of the event to emerge.

---

[49] *Ibid.*, 627.
[50] *Ibid.*, 632.

The individual's helplessness is emphasized:

> In and out of them walked the Red Cross men; the wounded sat
> against the walls sunning themselves. At all the bridges, the crossings,
> the stations, a *petit soldat*, all boots and bayonet. Forlorn and desolate
> he looked, like a little comic picture waiting for the joke to be written
> underneath.[51]

Among the guests at the café, in the Zone des Armées, she described
the crying soldier with the eyes "pink as a rabbit's":

> His comrades watched him a bit, watched his eyes fill again, again
> brim over. The water ran down his face, off his chin on to the table.
> He rubbed the place with his coat-sleeve, and then, as though
> forgetful, went on rubbing, rubbing with his hand across the table,
> staring in front of him. Ant then he started shaking his head to the
> movement of his hand. He gave a loud strange groan and dragged out
> the cloth again.[52]

The soldier rubs his eyes with his sleeve like a child, groaning like a
child, and certainly as innocent as a child. Through the very discreet
allusion to the massacre of the innocents,[53] Katherine Mansfield
conveys her impression of the war and her empathy as regards the
others' suffering.

As regards initiation, the place in which she is staying with the
"little corporal" looks like a labyrinth: "What an extraordinary thing.
We had been there to lunch and to dinner each day; but now in the
dusk and alone I could not find it."[54] Reality seems to be dissociated
once again: "And then quite suddenly the waiting-boy came out of just
such place."[55] Inside we find a parody of civilian life: "And he
followed me up the café to our special table, right at the far end of the
window, and marked by a bunch of violets that I had left in a glass
there yesterday."[56] Flowers are signs of life. Just before, she had

---

[51] *Ibid.*, 619.
[52] *Ibid.*, 628-29.
[53] Henry James also makes such allusive use of the 28th December in *The Turn of the Screw*, since the story is told "on night the fourth" after Christmas Eve (Henry James, *The Turn of the Screw* [1898], London: Everyman's Library, 1975, 8).
[54] Mansfield, "An Indiscreet Journey", in *ibid.*, 625.
[55] *Ibid.*, 629.
[56] *Ibid.*, 626.

noticed: "Policemen are as thick as violets everywhere."[57] In *Hamlet* (IV, 5, 184-85), the violets symbolize faithfulness; in *The Winter's Tale* (IV, 4, 120), the renewal of the world in spring. In "Psychology", they associate presence and memory. Here they express the fact that the familiar place has been found again with its "warm light".[58]

The narrator is an observer in this place. First of all she insists on the character of parody of her own "indiscreet journey", with the two pictures hanging on either side of the clock (see above). Then, she is included in the conversation, which in the last part runs around eau-de-vie. It is significant that the last word of the story should be "whisky" since originally it means "eau-de-vie":

> "What do you think? Isn't it just as I said? Hasn't it got a taste of excellent – *ex-cellent* whisky?"[59]

Woodifield also drinks whisky in "The Fly".

Reality takes an even darker appearance in the two stories Katherine Mansfield wrote in Paris in February 1922, "The Fly"[60] and "Honeymoon", followed by "The Canary", which she wrote in Switzerland in July. In "The Fly", the part of God omnipotent is played by "the boss", who compensates for his grief over his son's death in action through the deliberate sacrifice he inflicts on the insect, wrestling in vain. In "Honeymoon", the beginning confronts the end through the young couple coming to the Mediterranean for their honeymoon and listening to this "thin, faint voice, the memory of a voice singing something in Spanish". Their end is contained within their beginning since the common experience gives evidence of their perfect misunderstanding: "But George had been feeling differently from Fanny."[61] The three stories are haunted by the same question: "And while the old dog padded away he fell to wondering what it was he had been thinking about before. What was it? It was ...."[62] But the answer has been cancelled through the fly's sacrifice, providing an accurate example of what catharsis means. In contrast, in

---

[57] *Ibid.*, 624.
[58] *Ibid.*, 626.
[59] *Ibid.*, 633.
[60] For a full analysis of "The Fly", see Mounic, *Monde terrible où naître*, 211-24.
[61] Mansfield, "Honeymoon", in *The Collected Stories*, 397.
[62] Mansfield, "The Fly", in *ibid.*, 418.

"Honeymoon" and "The Canary", it remains, unanswered, as some sort of gaping abyss underlying the reality of life:

> Had she and George the right to be so happy? Wasn't it cruel? There must be something else in life which made all these things possible. What was it?[63]

The end of Katherine Mansfield's last story, often quoted in this book, and part of its title, echoes that question:

> I must confess that there does seem to me something sad in life. It is hard to say what it is …. I often wonder if everybody feels the same. One can never know. But isn't it extraordinary that under his sweet, joyful little singing it was just this – sadness? – Ah, what is it, – that I heard?[64]

The reality of life comes across as something deeply ambivalent, the joyful song of the bird ringing against the dark abyss – this strong contrast being the deeper essence of life, its genuine quality.

Being true to life, being real
We know that in one of her last letters to her husband, in December 1922, she wrote: "You see Bogey if I were allowed one single cry to God that cry would be *I want to be REAL*."[65] What she describes then is some sort of Job-like condition:

> But this place has taught me so far how unreal I am. It has taken from me one thing after another (the things never were mine) until at this present moment all I know really really is that I am not annihilated and that I hope – more than hope – believe.

We remember what Henry said of faith in the story of December 1913 and how the persona in "Spring Pictures" longed for hope. Here faith and hope seem to emerge on the face of the abyss – of slow deprivation and the existential endeavour to transcend the sense of

---

[63] Mansfield, "Honeymoon", in *ibid.*, 397.
[64] Mansfield, "The Canary", in *ibid.*, 422.
[65] To J.M. Murry, [26 December 1922], in *The Collected Letters of Katherine Mansfield*, V, 341 (Mansfield's emphasis). See above on page 171, as well as Chapters 1 and 8.

loss – or, could we say paraphrasing Benjamin Fondane on Baudelaire,[66] out of the experience of the abyss ("l'expérience du gouffre"). Indeed it is striking that for Baudelaire, the work of art true to life ("l'œuvre vivante"), confronts the artistic enchantment and the terror of the abyss. This is clear in a prose poem included in *Le Spleen de Paris* (1863), "Une mort héroïque" ("A Hero's Death"):

> Fancioulle me prouvait, d'une manière péremptoire irréfutable, que l'ivresse de l'Art est plus apte que toute autre à voiler les terreurs du gouffre ; que le génie peut jouer la comédie au bord de la tombe avec une joie qui l'empêche de voir la tombe, perdu, comme il est, dans un paradis excluant toute idée de tombe et de destruction.[67]

The repetition of the word "tombe" ("grave"), three times, seems to ward off the idea of death but does not ignore it; it is part of the rhythm of life, wrestling with the negative, which produces a genuine work of art: "Personne ne rêva plus de mort, de deuil, ni de supplices. Chacun s'abandonna, sans inquiétude, aux voluptés multipliées que donne la vue d'un chef-d'œuvre d'art vivant."[68] The artistic rapture of the work of art which is true to life veils the terrors of the abyss as the sense of wonder prevails.

The word "vivant" ("living, true to life, alive") is significantly used by Baudelaire in his sonnet "Correspondances",[69] in which he speaks of the "vivants piliers" ("living pillars") of Nature, compared to a temple, and in another prose poem called "Le Joujou du pauvre" ("The Poor Child's Toy"), in which the poor child's toy, drawn from life itself, is a living rat. It is contrasted with the wealthy child's beautiful toy. Yet the latter, instead of playing with his "splendid toy",

---

[66] Benjamin Fondane, *Baudelaire et l'expérience du gouffre* (1942), Brussels: Complexe, 1994. On the comparison between Baudelaire and Katherine Mansfield, see Anne Mounic, "Joujou du pauvre et Maison de poupée : de Baudelaire à Katherine Mansfield", Chapter 23, in *L'Esprit du récit ou La chair du devenir*, 416-28.

[67] Baudelaire, *Le Spleen de Paris*, 83: "Fancioulle was peremptorily and irrefutably proving to me that the rapture of Art is abler than any other to veil the terrors of the abyss; that genius may act on the brink of death with a joy which prevents it from seeing the tomb, lost as he is in a paradise which rules out any idea of a tomb or ruin."

[68] *Ibid.*: "No one any longer dreamt of death, bereavement and torture. Each of them, unworried, indulged in the multiplied voluptuous delights which seeing a work of art true to life gives."

[69] Baudelaire, *Les Fleurs du Mal*, 21.

is fascinated by the poor child's, and the wonder at the "living rat", shared by both children, makes them equal:

> Or, ce joujou, que le petit souillon agaçait, agitait et secouait dans une boîte grillée, c'était un rat vivant ! Les parents, par économie sans doute, avait tiré le joujou de la vie elle-même.
>   Et les deux enfants se riaient l'un à l'autre fraternellement, avec des dents d'un *égale* blancheur.[70]

In "The Doll's House", Katherine Mansfield, who mentioned Baudelaire in a story published in 1907, "In a Café",[71] and who remarks that "one can't see Beaudelaire" [*sic*] in Swinburne's "Ave Atque Vale"[72], stages the same type of shared fascination for a real presence, that of the lamp, in "The Doll's House", a story written in October 1921[73] in Switzerland.[74] We have often referred to this passage in the present book. The object opens suddenly like an instant revelation: "Perhaps it is the way God opens houses at the dead of the night when He is taking a quiet turn with an angel ...." And the perfect resemblance of a lamp stands out against God's night searching for genuine souls opening to him like the doll's house.

> But the lamp was perfect. It seemed to smile at Kezia, to say, "I live here." The lamp was real.[75]

And as far as Kezia is concerned, that sense of a real presence has to be shared with the Kelveys, those poor children who should not be spoken to, Lil and "our Else".[76] When, disobeying the order, the little girl asks the Kelveys to come and see the house, the enchantment is confirmed by Else's understanding. When Isabel is talking about the house with the Kelveys overhearing her, Kezia's insistence has not

---

[70] Baudelaire, *Le Spleen de Paris*, 57: "Now, that toy which the little slut teased, moved, and shook in a barred box, was a living rat! The boy's parents, to save money undoubtedly, had drawn the toy of life itself. / And both children smiling welcomed each other like brothers, with teeth of an *equal* whiteness."
[71] *The Katherine Mansfield Notebooks*, I, 172.
[72] *The Collected Letters of Katherine Mansfield*, IV, 300.
[73] *The Katherine Mansfield Notebooks*, II, 290.
[74] *The Collected Letters of Katherine Mansfield*, IV, 310.
[75] Mansfield, "The Doll's House", in *The Collected Stories*, 384.
[76] *Ibid.*, 386.

been paid attention to.[77] When Kezia opens the house to them, she is interrupted by Beryl's voice and the word "lamp" remains unsaid: "There's the drawing-room and the dining-room, and that's the – ."[78] Yet the wonder has been mutual: "She put out a finger and stroked her sister's quill; she smiled her rare smile. 'I seen the little lamp,' she said softly."[79]

Such wonder transcends social barriers; it may be shared although the poor children were shooed out of the garden "as if they were chickens". Just before they had been compared to "two little stray cats". Then seen through Beryl's mind, they become "those little rats of Kelveys". Katherine Mansfield's doll's house is not the poor child's toy, the "living rat", but its real presence must be confirmed through being shared: "Et les deux enfants se riaient l'un à l'autre fraternellement, avec des dents d'un *égale* blancheur" ("And both children smiling welcomed each other like brothers, with teeth of an *equal* whiteness"). Else's "I seen the little lamp" is such acceptance of sisterhood: "... she smiled a rare smile." "Se rire à quelqu'un" means welcoming someone and suggests a smile. Chasing them out of the garden, Beryl plays the part of the archangel forbidding entrance to the Garden of Eden: "Burning with shame, shrinking together, Lil huddling along like her mother, our Else dazed, somehow they crossed the big courtyard and squeezed through the white gate."[80]

If we compare the end of Baudelaire's "Joujou du pauvre" with another of his prose poems, "Le Gâteau" ("The Cake"), in which two poor children struggling for a piece of bread put an end, through envy, to an Eden-like enchantment, we may say that the two boys' mutual fascination for the living rat is Paradise regained, and can be compared to the spell the jester's art, so true to life, casts upon the fascinated audience. Baudelaire thus captures the paradox of plenitude – the epic conversion of the tragic abyss. Such conversion is conspicuous in "La vie antérieure" ("Life Before") in which the land of the origins is some sort of Eden-like place by the sea, a paradise of echoes and resonant correspondences. From the Greek root of the word "gouffre" ("abyss") is also derived the word "golfe" ("gulf"). The first meaning of the Greek *kolpos* is the mother's breast.

---

[77] *Ibid.*, 387.
[78] *Ibid.*, 390.
[79] *Ibid.*, 391.
[80] *Ibid.*, 390.

Thinking of other possible analogies between Baudelaire to Katherine Mansfield, we may also refer to "La chevelure" ("The Hair"),[81] poem 23 in *Les Fleurs du Mal*. The woman's hair opens on the infinite and, like the sea, is an invitation to travel away. Katherine Mansfield insists on the attractive character of the little governess's hair. Henry is fascinated by Edna's hair. "He could not keep his eyes off that beautiful waving hair." The word "waving" refers to the first description of "a long wave of marigold-coloured hair".[82] In "Honeymoon", George and Fanny do not consider the sea in the same way: "George, too, gazed at the bright, breathing water, and his lips opened as if he could drink it. How fine it was!"[83] The reader grasps how the two of them fail to understand each other since he remembers these lines:

> Fanny's heart sank. She had heard for years of the frightful dangers of the Mediterranean. It was an absolute death-trap. Beautiful, treacherous Mediterranean. There it lay curled before them, its white, silky paws touching the stones and gone again.[84]

The sea, although white, seems to be one of those red leopards on the Indian curtain. Fanny sees the abyss in it, like Baudelaire: "Homme libre, toujours tu chériras la mer ! / ... Et ton esprit n'est pas un gouffre moins amer."[85]

Yet the perception of the ambivalence of the abyss, which is also the infinite of the deeper self, provides the right ground for a work of art true to life, "une œuvre vivante": "It is there, deep down, deep down, part of one, like one's breathing."[86] Such tragic sadness lies in the deeper self, in which are also rooted Katherine Mansfield's figures of wonder such as the pear tree in "Bliss", the aloe in "Prelude", or any plant ready to attract what I called a "sprung" metonymy, denoting the terrible effort to remain alive – the fly's wrestling against the "dark drop",[87] a miniature epiphany of the abyss: "Pascal avait son

[81] Baudelaire, *Les Fleurs du Mal*, 37.
[82] Mansfield, "Something Childish But Very Natural", in *The Collected Stories*, 598.
[83] Mansfield, "Honeymoon", in *ibid.*, 397.
[84] *Ibid.*, 393.
[85] Baudelaire, *Les Fleurs du Mal*, 29: "Free man, you will always cherish the sea! / ... And your mind is as bitter an abyss."
[86] Mansfield, "The Fly", in *The Collected Stories*, 422.
[87] *Ibid.*, 417.

gouffre, avec lui se mouvant" ("Pascal had his abyss, moving with himself").[88] In this poem, "Le gouffre", Baudelaire wishes for a finite world of circumscribed knowledge (as defined in Aristotle's *Metaphysics*, Θ 6) since the infinite (the *apeiron* as the origin of the world for Anaximander) looks so dreadful to him. Yet in other poems he can bridge the abyss and convert it into possibility when sharing with the beloved his "Invitation au voyage".[89]

Katherine Mansfield cherishes the same type of hope. On Sunday, 30 August 1914, she wrote: "Ah, I wish I had a lover to nurse me – love me – hold me – comfort me – to stop me thinking."[90] Being "REAL" means being able to convert the ambivalence of joy and fear into a work of art through what Kierkegaard, thinking of Job, called "repetition" – a renewal of life in art. In 1921, she wrote:

> You see – to me – life and work are two things indivisible. It's only by being true to life that I can be true to art. And to be true to life is to be *good, sincere, simple, honest.*[91]

Kezia, the name chosen by Katherine Mansfield to refer to herself, is really the right name to achieve his purpose since, as we have seen, it is the name of Job's second daughter when he gets "twice as much as he had before" (Job, 42, 10).

The sense of freedom that, according to D.H. Lawrence, one can feel when obeying one's deeper self certainly derives from the feeling that one has fully identified with life in its awful, dreadful, horrible (adjectives so often used by Katherine Mansfield) yet wonderful ambivalence. The spirit of place then is the spirit of life; to be real is to be free, within the "sprung", reflexive spirit of the tale.

---

[88] Charles Baudelaire, "Le gouffre", in *Les Fleurs du Mal*, 204.
[89] Baudelaire, *Les Fleurs du Mal*, 66, and *Le Spleen de Paris*, 53-55.
[90] *The Katherine Mansfield Notebooks*, I, 284.
[91] *The Collected Letters of Katherine Mansfield*, IV, 170 (Mansfield's emphases).

CHAPTER 11

KATHERINE MANSFIELD
AND THE SPIRIT OF THE NARRATIVE

The notion which I defined in my Introduction, the "spirit of the narrative", involves an existential approach to the tale, a subjective viewpoint, and therefore what we could call, after Kierkegaard, an ethical choice. It also implies a definite conception of time and of the links between the immediate, contingency, and the work of art. The epic outlook, with its sense of a soul-making continuity, transcends the tragic. It should be associated with Katherine Mansfield's taste for the pastoral mode – "Et in Arcadia ego",[1] as she wrote in her Notebooks at the time of her brother's death.

The subjective viewpoint in Katherine Mansfield's stories and poems
In her first collection of stories as in her poems, Katherine Mansfield uses the first person. In *In a German Pension* (1911), the "I" is not very different from herself staying in Pension Müller in Bad Wörishofen near Munich while she was pregnant, in 1909. She finally experienced a miscarriage. The thirteen stories the book contains are much concerned with physical life, food or birth. The first person's outlook is mainly ironical, and even satirical, as regards the members of the German middle class she describes in the small pension in which she is accommodated. We could speak of a comedy of manners with the attacks on middle-class family life, and even of a comedy of morals, with the deriding, for instance, of "Ridiculous dignity".[2] The pension provides the scene for the drama. We may also think of the prologue to the *Canterbury Tales*, not only because of the setting, but also because some characters are named only through their social

---

[1] *The Katherine Mansfield Notebooks*, II, 17.
[2] Katherine Mansfield, "The Luftbad", in *The Edinburgh Collection of the Collected Works of Katherine Mansfield*, I, 175; in *The Collected Stories*, 729.

roles, such as the "Widow" or the "Traveller" in "Germans at Meat".[3] Those names may also be given in German, such as "Oberlehrer" or "Oberregierungsrat" in "The Baron" – "ober" (expressing high status or power) hinting at those people's conceit. Some family names may reveal an ironical intention, such as "Frau Stiegelauer" and "Herr Rat" in "Germans at Meat" – "Stiege" means "narrow stairs" in German, and "Lauer" is used in phrases meaning "to be on the lookout"; "Rat" means "council" but the homonymy with the English "rat" may have a comic effect, all the more because the character is depicted as rather grotesque: "Prompted by the thought, he wiped his neck and face with his dinner napkin and carefully cleaned his ears."[4] The remark, similar to a stage direction, has been prepared by others, revealing a gradation, from "He tucked his napkin into his collar and blew upon his soup as he spoke"[5] to "He turned up his eyes and his moustache, wiping the soup drippings from his coat and waistcoat".

The Widow also has very delicate ways of behaving, "picking her teeth with a hairpin as she spoke"[6] and then speaking "contemptuously, replacing the hairpin in the knob which was balanced on the top of her head". What is striking is that the caricature is not static; it may develop throughout the tale. Movement is one of the main qualities of Katherine Mansfield's art. Another funny name is Brechenmacher, in "Frau Brechenmacher Attends a Wedding", since "machen" means "to make" while "brechen" means "to break". In "Frau Fischer", the eponymous character as well as the Catholic church are being derided:

> I was reading the 'Miracles of Lourdes', which a Catholic priest – fixing a gloomy eye on my soul – had begged me to digest; but its wonders were completely routed by Frau Fischer's arrival. Not even the white roses upon the feet of the Virgin could flourish in that atmosphere.
> '... It was a simple shepherd-child who pastured her flocks upon the barren fields...'
> Voices from the room above: 'The washstand has, of course, been scrubbed over with soda.'

---

[3] Katherine Mansfield, "Germans at Meat", in *ibid.*, 165-166; 684-85.
[4] *Ibid.*, 166; 686.
[5] *Ibid.*, 165; 683.
[6] *Ibid.*, 166; 684.

'... Poverty-stricken, her limbs with tattered rags half covered ....'[7]

This exchange of words and their responses recalls the Catholic mass, the author resorting to situation comedy.

Some stories in *In a German Pension* are told in the third person, such as "At 'Lehmann's'", whose main character, Sabina, is a young maid; "Frau Brechenmacher's Attends a Wedding", "A Birthday", whose main character is Andreas Binzer, worried about his wife's suffering as she is giving birth to a son, and "The Swing of the Pendulum", whose main character has a Shakespearian name, Viola (*Twelfth Night*). Yet since the first person is used in some of the tales gathered in this collection marked by its unity of place (even the Chekhovian "The-Child-Who-Was-Tired" is transferred to Germany), the first-person viewpoint gives a subjective unity to the whole.

What are the characteristics of this subject? Katherine Mansfield's irony relies on the fact that she is a foreigner and feels so. In "Germans at Meat", she remarks: "I wanted to say that was only the preliminary canter, but could not translate it, and so was silent."[8] In "The Sister of the Baroness", she complains: "I felt a little crushed. Not at the prospect of losing that vision of diamonds and blue velvet bust, but at the tone – placing me outside the pale – branding me as a foreigner."[9] Moreover her situation is odd, being alone in a foreign country, and she has to account for it:

> 'Then, dear child, where is your husband?'
> I said he was a sea-captain on a long and perilous voyage.
> 'What a position to leave you in – so young and so unprotected.'
> She sat down on the sofa and shook her finger at me playfully.
> 'Admit, now, that you keep your journeys secret from him. For what man would think of allowing a woman with such wealth of hair to go wandering in foreign countries?'[10]

Katherine Mansfield's imagination resorts to the books she has read and the "sea-captain" invented in "Frau Fischer" recalls Stevenson, mentioned in the tales of the "Thoughtful Child" (see Chapter 1). The outlook is epic. Frau Fischer's remark about her hair heralds other

---

[7] Katherine Mansfield, "Frau Fischer", in *ibid.*, 194; 698.
[8] Mansfield, "Germans at Meat", in *ibid.*, 165; 684.
[9] Mansfield, "The Sister of the Baroness", in *ibid.*, 190; 692.
[10] Mansfield, "Frau Fischer", in *ibid.*, 197; 702.

stories by Katherine Mansfield, such as "The Little Governess", written in Paris in May 1915 (see Chapter 6), or "Something Childish But Very Natural", also written in Paris, in December 1913 (also see Chapter 6).

One feature of this narrator and these characters is their vulnerable innocence. Sabina is one of them:

> They stood opposite to each other, hands still clinging. And again that strange tremor thrilled Sabina.
>
> 'Look here,' he said roughly, 'are you a child, or are you playing at being one?'
>
> 'I – I''
>
> Laughter ceased. She looked up at him once, then down at the floor, and began breathing like a frightened animal.[11]

Katherine Mansfield's young girls are sometimes compared to kittens or owls and are afraid of bigger animals, rushing animals (see Chapters 3 and 5). Sabina's identity is roughly questioned by the lascivious "Young Man", and the "I", as she stammers, is split, with the same dash as reveals life's essential sadness in "The Canary", or the boss's oblivion in "The Fly". Each time some kind of rushing violence is involved; it is fairly obvious with the fly's sacrifice; in "The Canary", the violence of death and mourning is coupled with the young men's cruel indifference. The break in the subject ("I – I") is the result of such rushing violence, which brings about the signs of a nascent reflexive consciousness, accompanied with anguish.

Another rushing element in Katherine Mansfield's life is her illness. The verb "breathing" is significant here – even though she knew she was ill only in December 1917 – since it heralds how she will symbolically handle her suffering later, with William's "gnawing" pain, for instance, in "Marriage à la Mode" (1921),[12] or in a poem like "The Wounded Bird", in which we find the dashes again:

> Oh, waters – do not cover me!
> I would look long and long at those beautiful stars!
> O my wings – lift me – lift me![13]

---

[11] Katherine Mansfield, "At Lehmann's", in *ibid.*, 183; 728.
[12] Mansfield, "Marriage à la Mode", in *ibid.*, II, 331; 310.
[13] Mansfield, *Poems*, 82.

The movement is reverberated through the epizeuxis (immediate repetition), which is given some sort of visually transcribed rhythm with the dashes. In her effort to overcome her weakness, she arranges her words two by two: "long and long", and there are other examples in the same poem: "the leaves and flowers", "Timidly, timidly", "two stars", and "I am not dreadfully hurt" in Stanza 2 becomes "I am not so dreadfully hurt" in the last line. We find the same kind of reflexive pattern in "Out in the Garden", a poem written in 1917. The rhythmical echoes are combined with a healing movement: "Someone is secretly putting in order." [14]

The dashes reveal the tragic, the unspeakable void, as Virginia Woolf would have it (see Chapter 8; Chekhov also displays a very powerful sense of the tragic in his tales, and irony as regards the human, and social, response to it), but the break prompted by the rushing energy of the mind which then sees the abyss ("I – I"; "Oh, waters – do not cover me!") is overcome by the synthesis provided by the capacity of uniting life and the mind in writing:

> And the top of the cream-jar flew through the air and rolled like a penny in a round in the linoleum – and did not break.
> But for Kezia it had broken the moment it flew through the air, and she picked it up, hot all over, and put it back on the dressing table. Then she tiptoed, far too quickly and airily ....[15]

It is clear from the end of "Prelude" that there are two levels of consciousness – the immediate, contingency (Kezia thinking the jar had broken, "I – I", the abyss, the "waters") and the creative instant, which is reflexive, and synthetic: "and did not break", hence the effects of repetition and the echoing rhythm. And the reflexive endeavour finally opens onto the infinite. Virginia Woolf makes the same distinction in *Mrs. Dalloway* between Septimus, who stammers, cannot communicate ("'I – I —' he stammered. ... 'I – I —' Septimus stammered."[16]) and therefore feels "the impossibility of reaching the centre which, mystically, evaded"[17] him, and Clarissa, who is

---

[14] *Ibid.*, 64.
[15] Mansfield, "Prelude", in *The Edinburgh Collection of the Collected Works of Katherine Mansfield*, II, 92; *The Collected Stories*, 60.
[16] Woolf, *Mrs. Dalloway*, 83.
[17] *Ibid.*, 156.

"pointed"[18] and able to bring people together, "to combine, to create"[19].

The narrator's young age is stressed in "The Luftbad":

> From the pine forest streamed a wild perfume, the branches swayed together, rhythmically, sonorously. I felt so light and free and happy – so childish! I wanted to poke my tongue out at the circle on the grass, who, drawing close together, were whispering meaningly.[20]

As is usual in Mansfield's work, happiness is connected with nature and its perception, with rhythm and sound, with a sense of lightness and freedom. In the stories collected in *In a German Pension*, the narrator is set apart from the others. She is isolated; she is different. And it is not only because she is a foreigner; her youth and her critical stand in respect to social conformity also account for her awkward position.

She shares some distinctive traits with the character of Jane Eyre at the beginning of Charlotte Brontë's novel – her remaining apart from the family in Gateshead and, as a sign of her growing older and more independent, her irony as regards Brocklehurst in Gateshead and then in Lowood. The latter is first introduced as "a black pillar!".[21] The phrase ironically answers the question: "a man or a woman?". Later, in Lowood, he is said to be "the same black column"[22] and "this piece of architecture". The metaphor reifies and caricatures the dreadful character and denies his authority. The young girl does not acknowledge Brocklehurst's claim for power over her. In "The Luftbad", the narrator calls one of the women "the Coral Necklace"[23] and another "the Vegetable Lady" because she had declared she lived "entirely on raw vegetables and nuts".[24] In each case, the metonymy both reifies and caricatures women with whom the narrator feels no affinities. Such story-writing partakes of the *Bildungsroman*: writing deals with learning about life, which cannot be dissociated from

---

[18] *Ibid.*, 32.
[19] *Ibid.*, 103.
[20] Mansfield, "The Luftbad", in *ibid.*, I, 177; 732.
[21] Charlotte Brontë, *Jane Eyre* (1847), London: Penguin, 1985, 63.
[22] *Ibid.*, 94.
[23] Mansfield, "The Luftbad", in *The Edinburgh Collection of the Collected Works of Katherine Mansfield*, I, 177; *The Collected Stories*, 732.
[24] *Ibid.*, 176; 731.

learning how to write. The double move towards subjective independence is fairly obvious in *Jane Eyre*, and also characterizes *In a German Pension*.

One of the stories, "The Child-Who-Was-Tired", borrows from a Chekhov story (as already mentioned). In "The Sister of the Baroness", Katherine Mansfield refers to Mörike (1804-1875) who, among his poems, wrote idylls in the manner of Theocritus. The pastoral mode is decisive in the stories of her maturity as a writer. The fact that she mentions Ibsen, the author of *Hedda Gabler* (1890) and *A Doll's House* (1879), is also significant. Impressed by Kierkegaard's philosophy, the Norwegian playwright created strong individual female characters in both plays, and Katherine Mansfield called one of her stories "The Doll's House" (1921). Therefore writing and reading belong to a writer's education to life; they are part of the epic quest. Writing means embracing the existential reality of life and transforming the contingent quality of the immediate into a memorable moment, an enchanted instant. The resort to the pastoral element as a means of redemption – since, in spite of everything, it secures the ever renewed possibility of blossoming – is her distinctive trait. *In a German Pension* may be indebted to Chekhov to a certain extent but in the following tales she found her own particular voice. However, reading Chekhov's "After the Theatre" (1892), where the young protagonist, Nadia Zelenine, dreaming of love after seeing *Eugene Onegin*, thinks that, if she did not fear upsetting her mother and her brother, she would take the veil, one thinks of Mansfield's "Taking the Veil" (1922) – but the association may be sheer coincidence and chance.

Pastoral empathy and the epic embrace of reality

In most of the stories collected in *Bliss* (1920), *The Garden-Party* (1922), and in the posthumous collections (except, for instance, for "A Journey to Bruges" and "An Indiscreet Journey"), Katherine Mansfield sheds the first-person narrator and speaks in the third person. The choice of Kezia as the name of her childhood *alter ego* encapsulates her effort to recreate what has been lost (see Chapter 3) and to give a new life to the dead. Her narrative voice, more humorous than ironical, gives its unity to quite different stories. In some of them she identifies with the main character (William in "Marriage à la Mode"; the female character in "Psychology"); in others, she mocks the protagonist (Raoul Duquette in "Je Ne Parle Pas Français"; Reginald Peacock in "Mr. Reginald Peacock's Day"). We could say that in those stories she had grown out of her self-centred viewpoint and developed the qualities already disclosed in the first collection, or a capacity to give a true-to-life rendering of the existential drama. The epic outlook magnifies the moments of being and the pastoral mode secures the continuity of time and the tender relationship between people.

Katherine Mansfield borrows the motif of the sea voyage from the ancient epic but her view of life as a journey belongs to the Christian tradition. The influence of Bunyan's *Pilgrim's Progress* (1678) pervades English literature. Yet she renews all those motifs so as to render her own view of life. The irony and the distance to be found in *In a German Pension* helped her to find her own voice and, from that moment on, her viewpoint was widened with new confidence. The aloe transformed into an ancient vessel gives shape to the movement of the mind transcending time. Thus this epic view of life is comparable to the outlook which is sketched in "The Wind Blows". In "The Voyage", the Picton boat carries young Fenella to her new life after her mother's death, as if, sailing across waters, she were leaving Hades and coming back from the dead. The true-to-life feature of Katherine Mansfield's stories is secured by the fact that mythic reminiscences rest on personal experience. The Picton boat (see Chapter 6) is decisive in her tales and in her childhood, and is described as a bright appeal to the unknown and its promises, over the seas.

The author's childhood in New Zealand is significant not only because she chose to revive it in her tales but also since she very soon experienced the questioning of otherness (see Chapter 6), which provides tender comfort in "How Pearl Button Was Kidnapped" but instils a notion of wildness and barbarity (the idea developed in the magazine *Rhythm*) in "The Woman at the Store" (1912), a story written in the first person but in which the "I" does not seem to be the author:

> "There is no twilight to our New Zealand days, but a curious half-hour when everything appears grotesque – it frightens – as though the

savage spirit of the country walked abroad and sneered at what it saw. Sitting alone in the hideous room I grew afraid."[25]

This is the first story Katherine Mansfield had written for *Rhythm*,[26] where it was published in spring 1912. The story is cruel and suggests there is no age of innocence:

> The kid tore out a page and flung it at me.
> 'There you are,' she said. 'Now I done it ter spite Mumma for shutting me up 'ere with you two. I done the one she told me I never ought to. I done the one she told me she'd shoot me if I did. Don't care! Don't care!'
> The kid had drawn the picture of a woman shooting at a man with a rook rifle and then digging a hole to bury him in.[27]

Katherine Mansfield drew from her "memories of a camping trip through the central North Island in December 1907".[28]

"Ole Underwood" (1913) is also a cruel story although Katherine Mansfield seems to show some compassion for the old man rejected by everybody because he killed his wife and served a prison sentence for the murder. She reveals the extreme ambivalence of life's impulse, "the old, old lust"[29] as she calls it, which has its peculiar rhythm:

> Something inside Ole Underwood's breast beat like a hammer. One two – one two – never stopping, never changing. He couldn't do anything. It wasn't loud. No, it didn't make a noise – only a thud. One, two – one, two – like someone beating on an iron in a prison, – someone in a secret place – bang – bang – trying to get free.[30]

In *Bliss* (1920), her third-person main characters are varied: Kezia and Linda in "Prelude"; Raoul Duquette in "Je ne Parle Pas Français"; Bertha Young in "Bliss"; "she" in "Psychology"; Miss Ada Moss in "Pictures"; Robert in "The Man Without a Temperament"; the artist in

---

[25] Katherine Mansfield, "The Woman at the Store", in *ibid.*, 271; 554.
[26] *The Edinburgh Collection of the Collected Works of Katherine Mansfield*, I, 276, n.
[27] Mansfield, "The Woman at the Store", in *The Edinburgh Collection of the Collected Works of Katherine Mansfield*, I, 276; *The Collected Stories*, 561.
[28] *The Edinburgh Collection of the Collected Works of Katherine Mansfield*, I, 276, n.
[29] Mansfield, "Ole Underwood", in *The Edinburgh Collection of the Collected Works of Katherine Mansfield*, I, 321; *The Collected Stories*, 565.
[30] *Ibid.*, 319; 562-63.

"Mr. Reginald Peacock's Day"; two children, brother and sister, in "Sun and Moon"; Ian French in "Feuille d'Album"; "she" in "A Dill Pickle"; "she" in "The Little Governess"; Monica Tyrell in "Revelations"; "he" in "The Escape". And we find the same variety of characters and situations in *The Garden-Party* (1922) and the other stories. The self acquires its full integrity through adopting a great variety of standpoints and voices, each of them corresponding to the moment of writing the tale whether it is based on memories or current experience.

The continuity of time is thus secured in two ways – through remembering and recreating the figures of the past and the present, and through complying with the flow of becoming and adapting to each individual moment. Then the dash splitting the I ("I – I") with the rushing, bewildering energy of life and desire is no longer a void, an abyss (Baudelaire) but the inter-subjective space in which empathy can develop. However life remains ambivalent. Ole Underwood's lust, beating inside himself, is a thirst to harm and kill:

> "I will! I will! I will!" he muttered. He tore the little cat out of his coat and swung it by its tail and flung it out to the sewer opening. The hammer beat loud and strong.[31]

The same destructive impulse is described by the "Married Man": "– for there is – I swear there is – in the very best of us – something that leaps and cries 'A-ahh!' for joy at the thought of destroying."[32] He also perceives a deeper self beyond the conscious will:

> It is the owner, the second self inhabiting them, who makes the choice for his own particular purposes, and – this may sound absurdly far-fetched – it's the second self in the other which responds.[33]

This viewpoint is not very different from D.H. Lawrence's in *Women in Love*.

The feeling of life deep inside may be a feeling of pain, a terrible sadness, as the narrator of "The Canary" describes it at the end of the tale or a feeling of contented desire, as in "A Dill Pickle": "As he

---

[31] *Ibid.*, 321; 565-66.
[32] Mansfield, "A Married Man's Story", in *ibid.*, II, 382; 426.
[33] *Ibid.*, 383; 427.

spoke she lifted her head as though she drank something; the strange beast in her bosom began to purr ....".[34] Katherine Mansfield quite often says life is awful – in "Revelations", for instance:

> Oh, how terrifying life was, thought Monica. How dreadful. It is the loneliness which is so appalling. We whirl along like leaves, and nobody knows – nobody cares where we fall, in what black river we float away.[35]

We may find here an echo of Gloucester's famous speech in *King Lear* ("As flies to wanton boys, are we to th' Gods; / They kill us for their sport"),[36] which also comes to mind while reading "The Fly". However, in "The Wind Blows", while the young girl is in Mr Bullen's sitting-room playing the piano, Katherine Mansfield writes: "'Life is so dreadful,' she murmurs, but she does not feel it's dreadful at all."[37]

The pastoral world provides figures of renewal and fruitfulness which make up for the inner experience of the abyss (Sun's experience at the end of "Sun and Moon", Miss Brill's sadness, or Leila's revelation of the cruelty of time, among other examples). The pear tree in "Bliss" is blossoming in the full moon's light; the violets restore some kind of hope in "Psychology" and in "An Indiscreet Journey". There are numerous instances of Katherine Mansfield's sensitive response to plants, trees, and flowers in her *Notebooks* and letters. In "The Fly", the pastoral world, to which old Woodifield belongs, transcends tragedy's dead end: "All the same, we cling to our last pleasures as the tree clings to his last leaves."[38] The old man "pipes" like a shepherd in Arcadia and the renewal of nature in the broad alley of the cemetery which looks like a well-tended garden secures the continuity of time in spite of his son's death. Two worlds are opposed, that of sacrifice and tragedy, embodied by the boss and his "idea",[39] that of nature and renewal, embodied by Woodifield.

---

[34] Mansfield, "A Dill Pickle", in *ibid.*, 102; 173.

[35] Mansfield, "Revelations", in *ibid.*, 217; 195.

[36] William Shakespeare, *King Lear*, IV, i, 36-37, ed. Kenneth Muir, London: Methuen, 1982, 140.

[37] Mansfield, "The Wind Blows", in *The Edinburgh Collection of the Collected Works of Katherine Mansfield*, II, 228; *The Collected Stories*, 109.

[38] Mansfield, "The Fly", in *ibid.*, 476; 412.

[39] *Ibid.*, 479; 417.

"Et in Arcadia ego": those words may be found in a painting by Guercino, *The Shepherds of Arcadia* (1620) and two paintings with the same title by Nicolas Poussin, one of which, painted in 1638, is in the Louvre. Walter Pater places the words "Et in Arcadia ego fui"[40] as an epigraph for his essay on Wincklemann in *The Renaissance* (1873): "I have also been in Arcadia." Katherine Mansfield's subjective voice ("ego") is pastoral, which means that her poetic aim is the recreation of life and its continuity in spite of death. The poem, or the tale, should transcend tragedy and the dead end of sacrifice. "Can art represent men and women in these bewildering toils so as to give the spirit at least an equivalent for the sense of freedom?"[41] Walter Pater wonders in his essay on Winckelmann. In his conclusion, he writes:

> To such a tremendous wisp constantly re-forming itself on the stream, to a single sharp impression, with a sense in it, a relic more or less fleeting, of such moments gone by, what is real in our life fines itself down. It is with this movement, with the passage and dissolution of impressions, images, sensations, that analysis leaves off – that continual vanishing away, that strange perpetual, weaving and unweaving of ourselves.[42]

These lines proleptically provide a good account of Katherine Mansfield's voice and way of writing. We know that she was a reader of Walter Pater. From the opposite point of view, looking ahead, I find a comparable sensitive account of life in Carson McCullers' *The Ballad of the Sad Café* (1951), for instance:

> But the hearts of small children are delicate organs. A cruel beginning in this world can twist them into curious shapes. The heart of a hurt child can shrink so that afterward it is hard and pitted as the seed of a peach.[43]

Carson McCullers' style is not impressionistic; the tale develops in a more linear way, and is generally longer, but the attention to people, the empathy, is the same.

---

[40] Pater, *The Renaissance*, 114.
[41] *Ibid.*, 148-49.
[42] *Ibid.*, 151-52.
[43] Carson McCullers, *The Ballad of the Sad Café* (1951), London: Penguin, 1963, 36.

Katherine Mansfield's last story, "The Canary", is written in the first person, clearly not the author but a simple sensitive woman who found a companion in her canary. The persona helps the author to dramatize a personal feeling without risking the solipsistic danger of confession. The existential meaning is dramatized, not the immediate anecdote. This very simple story acquires an epic significance. We move from "I – I" to:

> On can never know. But isn't it extraordinary that under his sweet, joyful little singing it was just this – sadness? – Ah, what is it? – that I heard.[44]

The dashes reveal the abyss and the song as if they were inseparable. The subject ("I") is connected to those depths through her capacity to probe reality and to listen to the song – the pastoral song of life and death. Her empathy goes deeper than the simple compassion for pain; she sympathizes with the core of life, what we cannot depart from unless we cease to exist.

At the beginning of *The Sickness Unto death* (1849), Kierkegaard described "the state of the self when despair is completely eradicated"[45] as the result of a reflexive process opening onto the infinite: "the self is grounded transparently in the power that established it" (see Chapter 2). What we cannot control, the flow of becoming, otherness, the origin of life, gives its strength to the artist. The abyss is being converted into the powerful ability to breathe and to be free. In *The White Goddess* (1948), Robert Graves said that the poet's mind transcended time and could have the intuition of the past and the memory of the future:

> But an interesting feature of prolepsis and analepsis is that the coincidence of the concept and the reality is never quite exact: Gamma coincides with Zeta, but not so closely that either loses its identity.[46]

Time means an everlasting absence of coincidence: "The wind – the wind",[47] Katherine Mansfield wrote in "The Wind Blows" as a

---

[44] Mansfield, "The Canary", in *The Edinburgh Collection of the Collected Works of Katherine Mansfield*, II, 514; *The Collected Stories*, 422.
[45] Kierkegaard, *The Sickness Unto death*, 44.
[46] Graves, *The White Goddess*, 344.

leitmotiv. In "Revelations", the wind is more threatening. Yet, the artistic rapture of the work of art (Baudelaire) transcends the abyss but does not deny it in an ideal world in which reality would lose its identity, and life would cease to be. The abundance of dashes in Katherine Mansfield's work could be interpreted as a sign of such accepted absence of coincidence. And she moves from absence of coincidence within the personal subject ("I – I") to its existential manifestation ("The wind – the wind") through a process of revelation which is part and parcel of the spirit of the narrative.

The narrative self is manifold, "chameleon"[48] as Keats said in one of his letters. The spirit of the narrative transcends personal experience to dramatize it and give it its full existential significance. We leave the sphere of the immediate, and Schopenhauer's everlasting present floating like a rainbow over the abyss,[49] for a world in which the individual magnifies the instant of living through inserting it in the flow of becoming, in the existential history of individuals. "Therefore it needs courage to choose oneself", Kierkegaard wrote in *Either... or...,* "for just when he seems to be becoming more isolated, he is entering more deeply than ever into the roots through which he is linked with the whole".[50] In "The Wind Blows", the "ribbons" to be found at the beginning ("Now my best little Teneriffe-work teacloth is simply in ribbons"[51]), which are the result of the wind's tearing violence, are metamorphosed into language at the end of the story: "The wind carries their voices – away fly the sentences like little narrow ribbons."[52] Thus the destructive fugacity of immediate life is converted into the subjective reality of spoken words rhythmically arranged into written sentences. Do they not look like "narrow ribbons" on paper? Those words connect the individuals together both in space and time. The fact that Katherine Mansfield should have chosen the same word, "ribbons", to refer to immediate destruction and to the subjective conversion of time into a radiating instant

---

[47] Mansfield, "The Wind Blows", in *The Edinburgh Collection of the Collected Works of Katherine Mansfield,* II, 229; *The Collected Stories,* 110.
[48] John Keats, *Selected Letters,* ed. George Gittings, rev. with an Introduction and Notes by John Mee, Oxford: Oxford World's Classics, 2002, 232.
[49] Arthur Schopenhauer, *The World as Will and Representation,* 54, 356.
[50] Kierkegaard, *Either... or...,* 518. See Chapter 1.
[51] Mansfield, "The Wind Blows", in *The Edinburgh Collection of the Collected Works of Katherine Mansfield,* II, 226; *The Collected Stories,* 106.
[52] *Ibid.,* 229; 110.

through the power of the voice, is a sure sign of what she meant her poetic task to be. In the tale, life reaches its splendour while immediate life is not denied but subjectively acknowledged, which means plenitude of being. Being real may therefore mean to identify with life in its metamorphic identity, its individual history, and its fluid ambivalent depth, its rhythm at the heart. And the mind coincides with it in its fruitful, luminous, generous epiphanies. A tale, a poem, are such epiphanies.

CHAPTER 12

THE SEQUENCE OF SENSES AND THE UNITY OF BEING:
KATHERINE MANSFIELD AND FRENCH LITERATURE

For Baudelaire, the "rapture of art"[1] may at some favourable moments overcome, yet not cancel, the terrors of the abyss. In *Time Regained*, Marcel Proust explains how he decided to undertake the nightly task of responding to the "feeling of vertigo"[2] he felt in himself when considering the work of time on the faces of his acquaintances. The process of reminiscence is based upon the involuntary memory the senses may induce as the famous passage on the *madeleine* in the first volume of *In Search of Lost Time* suggests. He speaks of "This notion of Time embodied"[3] in *Time Regained*. For Baudelaire, the correspondences within Nature are accompanied with correspondences between the senses. In each case, the sequence of senses is also a sequence of times, from immediate perception to the descent into the self induced by involuntary memory, as far as Proust is concerned; from the "terrors of the abyss" in one of Baudelaire's prose poems, "Une mort héroïque" ("A Hero's Death"), to the delights of "La vie antérieure" ("Life Before"), the abyss becoming a bay as the etymology of the French "gouffre" may induce, the first meaning of the Greek *kolpos* being the motherly breast, then a gulf or a bay and the pit. I would like to show how relevant for the analysis of Katherine Mansfield's work those notions are. The sea is an inspiring poetic element for her, which also tells her of the infinite. The sequence of senses and times generates a genuine unity of being in spite of the "sadness" in life. This is also perceptible in Colette's work, with her

---

This chapter is based on a paper written for the Paris Katherine Mansfield Conference held in June 2014 at Paris 3 Sorbonne nouvelle.

[1] Baudelaire, "Une mort héroïque", in *Le Spleen de Paris*, 83. See also Chapter 10 in this volume.

[2] Proust, *Time Regained*, 531.

[3] *Ibid.*, 529.

taste for gardens and the world of her childhood.[4] The Englishness of Katherine Mansfield's pastoral outlook (she was a great reader of Shakespeare and the Romantics) is heightened through her awareness of French modernity. Thinking of Baudelaire, should Katherine Mansfield's short stories not be read with his prose poems in mind, which would provide a new view of the unity of her work? In this chapter I intend to develop what I only briefly sketched in Chapter 10.

Sequence of senses, sequence of tenses

Let me start from this almost complete homophony of words, senses and tenses, to show how the poetic restoration of things past as embodied in the instant of reminiscence relies on the truth of sensitive perception. The subjective viewpoint, incarnate in the work of art, should resist the temptation of abstraction from the immediate which the use of language induces. And, simultaneously, a work of art which would not convert immediate existence into figures of wonder would not give the intimate feeling of life's splendour. The link with immediate life needs to be ascertained for the subjective freedom of metamorphic perception to be fully achieved. Language should not be emancipated from the senses. Lost time should be remembered with the full power of creation and plenitude to be found in the present moment and the tenses be related to the senses. The medieval order of the five senses, from the most intimate to the most distant, namely touch, taste, smell, hearing, and eyesight, is idealistic and favours distance and abstraction. The poets, like Baudelaire, Keats, or Rilke, who rely on the subjective correspondences between Man and the world as well as between the senses, favour the close unity of synaesthesia.

In *Sodome et Gomorrhe* (*Sodom and Gomorrah*, 1922), Marcel Proust tackles the issue of the translations into French of the *Arabian Nights*, a work which is decisive as far as his own work, *In Search of Lost Time*, is concerned. He does not deal with the problem in the abstract but relates it to a significant character in the novel, the narrator's grandmother, and her relationship with her daughter, his mother. The *Arabian Nights* is linked with memories of Combray and its "pretty painted plates";[5] the debate concerning which translation should be preferred, Galland's or Mardrus', is related to the

---

[4] See Chapter 9.
[5] Proust, *Sodome et Gommorhe*, 268: "jolies assiettes peintes."

personality of his grandmother and her relationship with her daughter and grandson. It is viewed in connection with the passing of time and the generations. Literature is appropriated and made as familiar as the usual objects of everyday life. Language, the choice of words and the transcriptions of proper names cannot be dissociated from the feelings and the voices of distinct individuals. Therefore, language, as well as Time, is "embodied";[6] the tenses and the senses may achieve a unity which also reveals strong correspondences between individuals.

Katherine Mansfield stages the relations between generations. The correspondence of senses, tenses, and generations is clear in the famous passage of the aloe in "Prelude". The character of Linda's mother, Kezia's grandmother, is linked with the sense of hearing: "but her mother's voice answered from the veranda."[7] Their intercourse involves a special voice: "and she spoke to her mother with the special voice that women use at night to each other as though they spoke in their sleep or from some hollow cave."[8] The eyesight is connected with vision in the moonlight at night. The immediate impressions are metamorphosed into figures of the present moment as restored through memory. Proust speaks of "a quite different sort of three-dimensional psychology",[9] which includes some sort of gravitation of individuals, like heavenly bodies, in space and time. Chronological time is cancelled through memory and is replaced by interrelated time and the "awareness" of "different planes". The past is recounted in the preterite, with a recollection of the beginning of the story in the pluperfect: "The moon that Lottie and Kezia had seen from the store-man's wagon was full, and the house, the garden, the old woman and Linda – all were bathed in dazzling light." [10] Three generations are gathered in the previous sentence. The impression of plenitude does not come from the full moon only but also from the sequence of tenses and senses. The youngest generation, Lottie and Kezia, are referred to in the pluperfect, linked with the beginning of the story. All the characters are set in space. We move from the children to the "old woman" and then to the intermediate generation, embodied by Linda. Visual perception ("had seen") becomes vision: "all were bathed in

---

[6] Proust, *Time Regained*, 529.
[7] Mansfield, "Prelude" (1915), in *The Collected Stories*, 52.
[8] *Ibid.*, 53.
[9] Proust, *Time Regained*, 505.
[10] Mansfield, "Prelude" (1915), in *The Collected Stories*, 52.

dazzling light." Seeing the full moon, the characters remain distant from this image of plenitude; when they participate in sublunary vision, they are gathered and wrapped in its fullness.

In the centre of the circles of time stands the grandmother; the two girls gravitate around her, and Linda shares the vision she induces: "'I have been looking at the aloe', said Mrs. Fairfield." The "old woman" also refers to a moment before, closely connected to the present moment through the present-perfect progressive, and Linda describes the epic vessel in the present, in her "special voice", until the moment when she achieves a synthesis of times and tenses: "I like that aloe. I like it more than anything here. And I am sure I shall remember it long after I've forgotten other things." And immediately after: "She put her hand on her mother's arm and they walked down." The sense of touch is involved at the moment when time is endowed with the power of vision. In the same way as space is transfigured by the power of the mind at night ("How much more real this dream was than that they should go back to the house where the sleeping children lay and where Stanley and Beryl played cribbage."), time revolves around the present moment of subjective awareness. Linda projects herself into the future which she predicts and she returns midway to the present moment with the present-perfect. In this future of promise, the aloe stands alone in her mind as it did in the vision, "coming towards" them, and catching her "out of the cold water into the ship" with an oblique reference to the sense of touch. It is a protective image of plenitude: "Nobody would dare to come near the ship or to follow after."[11] Her integrity of being is secured in this subjective centre moving in time and space.

In "The Wind Blows", the same inter-subjective synthesis of space and time is achieved. The close relationship between brother and sister, "arm in arm",[12] makes up for the new distance in space and time, conveyed through the shift from the I and You dialogue to the use of the third person of absence: "... Who are they?" The present moment becomes past: "I cried at my music lesson that day – how many years ago!" Visual perception becomes vision because of the dark: "It's the light that makes her look so beautiful and mysterious ...." The moment which is referred to as "Now" is as uncertain as it should be, considering such adverbs only take their

[11] *Ibid.*, 53.
[12] Mansfield, "The Wind Blows", in *ibid.*, 110.

substance in speech. "Now" refers to the present moment of speech. The story is told in the present tense, linked with an emphasis on the sense of touch: "Mr. Bullen takes her hand."[13] Or later: "Their heads bent, their legs just touching, they stride like one eager person through the town."[14] Although the wind tears things, diction, and the moment, "The wind – the wind",[15] the tale ensures closeness within the realm of embodied memory, even if such achievement is highly paradoxical:

> Now the dark stretches a wing over the tumbling water. They can't see those two any more. Good-bye, good-bye. Don't forget ... But the ship is gone, now.

Through the epanalepsis (the repetition of the first word of the paragraph "Now" at the end), the dissolution of vision into the chaos of the origins is enclosed within the present moment of the tale. Only speech remains as in the instant which preceded creation, and vision: "Let there be light" (Genesis 1, 3). And what remains at the very end is the principle of movement, split as it is in the process of telling and becoming: "The wind – the wind."

In "Psychology", the Book of Genesis is explicitly mentioned; it is connected with the sense idealism places at the basest rank after touch, taste: "Let there be cake. And there was cake. And God saw that it was good."[16] Katherine Mansfield suggests that there can be vision in taste also: "Eat it imaginatively. Roll your eyes if you can and taste it on the breath." The perception should be literally inspired and experienced in the centre of being with a feeling of plenitude, which implies sharing: "It's a queer thing but I always do notice what I eat here and never anywhere else." Yet such plenitude is incessantly threatened by an abyss of darkness ready to open. The lovers are connected to it through the sense of hearing:

> Again they were conscious of the boundless, questioning dark. Again, they were – two hunters, bending over the fire, but hearing suddenly from the jungle beyond a shake of wind and a loud, questioning cry...[17]

---

[13] *Ibid.*, 108.
[14] *Ibid.*, 109.
[15] *Ibid.*, 110.
[16] Mansfield, "Psychology", in *ibid.*, 113.
[17] *Ibid.*, 115.

And they fail to find the accurate language which would give shape to such impalpable mystery, impossible to approach through the "'spiritual' vision",[18] or the idealistic viewpoint split from the invisible core of life and the individual. If it is not rightly apprehended, such mysterious darkness becomes "nothingness" and life, a mechanical void: "They saw themselves as two little grinning puppets jigging away in nothingness."[19] Nothingness and life's mechanical void of meaning result from the subjective voice's failure.

The narrative should ensure such continuity from darkness to vision in spite of possible "maddening chatter". In "Bliss", personal integrity is secured through sensitive perception and vision. The sense of taste sets a correspondence with the world: "you are overcome, suddenly, by a feeling of bliss – absolute bliss! – as if you'd suddenly swallowed a bright piece of that late afternoon sun and it burned in your bosom, sending out a little shower of sparks into every particle, into every finger and toe ...."[20] Such participation in the outer creation makes of the self a radiating centre of fullness. As compared to this inner feeling, the mirror is "cold".[21] Katherine Mansfield associates the body and her character's baby through the repetition of similar words: "Why be given a body if you have to keep it shut up in a case like a rare, rare fiddle?" And then, later: "Why have a baby if it has to be kept – not in a case like a rare, rare fiddle – but in another woman's arm?"[22] The baby is eating; it is also connected to the sense of touch through the anecdote of the dog whose ear she clutched. The feeling of bliss comes from close contact to bodily impressions, such as kissing the baby, or smelling the jonquils: "How strong the jonquils smelled in the warm room."[23] Vision is achieved through the combination of eyesight and memory: "At the far end, against the wall, there was a tall, slender pear tree in fullest, richest bloom." It becomes: "And she seemed to see on her eyelids the lively pear tree with its wide open blossom as a symbol of her own life." She absorbs the pear tree in her memory as she had pretended to devour the sun. In spite of the guests' superficial talk, the vision reaches plenitude when

---

[18] *Ibid.*, 117.
[19] *Ibid.*, 116.
[20] Mansfield, "Bliss", in *ibid.*, 91-92.
[21] *Ibid.*, 92.
[22] *Ibid.*, 94.
[23] *Ibid.*, 96.

shared and crowned with the full moon. The sense of hearing is appealed to through such contrasted sounds as Miss Fulton's "murmur"[24] and the light being "snapped on", as a return to uninspiring reality.

Telling a story means to move upon the face of the abyss, which vision opens and renders fruitful through language and figures, or symbols, of life. Night is the privileged time for such mixture of continuity and conversion, for such plenitude of light and darkness, mystery and speech. In "Une mort héroïque" ("A Hero's Death"), Baudelaire stages a fool, named Fancioulle, from the Italian *fanciullo*, meaning "child", who dances over the abyss. Before considering the decisive poetic significance of night and darkness, I would like to compare Katherine Mansfield's tales to Baudelaire's prose poems as regards both poets' ethical standpoint.

From Baudelaire to Katherine Mansfield: a shared ethics
Whether it be in "Le Joujou du pauvre" ("The Poor Child's Toy") or "Le Gâteau" ("The Cake"), Baudelaire ironically stages poor children with a mixture of irony and compassion. The "poor child's toy" is a rat, which recalls Beryl's calling the Kelveys "little rats".[25] The rat is life as it truly is, neither good or bad, simply alive. Baudelaire rejects the rich child's sophisticated toy as artificial. The two children's mutual admiration for the rat unites them. Baudelaire provides an ironical comment on life and the work of art. Yet in the first paragraph of his prose poem, he describes the wonder of poor children when given small inexpensive toys. He compares them to cats running away from their benefactor because they do not trust man. Katherine Mansfield writes: "Like two little stray cats they followed across the courtyard to where the doll's house stood." She describes with accuracy the interaction between the rich and the poor girls: "The children stood together under the pine trees, and suddenly, as they looked at the Kelveys eating out of their paper, always by themselves, always listening, they wanted to be horrid to them."[26] The reference to the sense of hearing suggests animal fear from danger. As the poor girls are weak, they are also the potential victims of the others' sarcasm. The future therefore is ominous, and disturbs the pleasure of

---

[24] *Ibid.*, 102.
[25] Mansfield, "The Doll's House", in *ibid.*, 390.
[26] *Ibid.*, 388.

taste: "Lil looked up from her dinner. She wrapped the rest quickly away. Our Else stopped chewing. What was coming now?"

The pleasure of seeing the doll's house is also forbidden to them. In Baudelaire's prose poem and in Katherine Mansfield's story, the children, rich and poor, are separated by a fence and a gate, and they look at each other:

> The Kelveys came nearer, and beside them walked their shadows, very long, stretching right across the road with their heads in the buttercups. Kezia clambered back on the gate; she had made up her mind; she swung out.[27]

With this beautiful image of their shadows so long that their heads reach the buttercups, Katherine Mansfield suggests that they are connected to that mysterious, uncertain world she explores in her stories, and which traces back to the very essence of language: let there be light out of utmost darkness. The rich girls' dancing, giggling, and being horrid to the poor Kelveys betrays their fear of the unknown, while Kezia wants to bridge the social gap and, as the author's *alter ego*, face the unknown. The rich children's garden could be compared to Paradise if it could be opened to all: "'I'll open it for you,' said Kezia kindly. She undid the hook and they looked inside."[28]

The doll's house becomes a symbol of such a theme: Paradise is lost for them all if they acquiesce to such estrangement. The garden becomes a prison, whose limits Kezia trespasses. The fullness of personal relationship is suggested by the constant use of "our", implying common responsibility, with the name of Else. The incomplete present-perfect in the end: "I seen the little lamp", accompanied with the girl's smile means Paradise regained for a short while, or the present moment's brief ecstasy. The Kelveys are chased out of the garden by angry and frustrated Beryl:

> They did not need telling twice. Burning with shame, shrinking together, Lil huddling along like her mother, our Else dazed, somehow they crossed the big courtyard and squeezed through the white gate.

---

[27] *Ibid.*, 389.
[28] *Ibid.*, 390.

Yet such discord means Paradise lost for everyone: what remains is a brief moment of plenitude, Paradise on earth caught through transient but intense glimpses of wonder, still radiating in the whole being since seeing has become vision through keen desire and reminiscence. In "Le Gâteau" ("The Cake"), the marvel of the piece of bread so eagerly coveted that it is called "cake" crumbles away in "the hideous struggle",[29] the "utterly fratricidal war" between the two poor children. Both pleasure and vision are lost. One of Katherine Mansfield's stories is called "His Sister's Keeper".[30]

The Kelveys, when chased, are compared to "chickens".[31] The poultry means vulnerability. Katherine Mansfield's use of animals – cats, rats, birds – may recall the ancient, and then medieval, tradition of bestiaries, as well as her use of flowers and plants recalls the pattern of the millefleurs, as in the tapestry of the *Lady with the Unicorn* (Musée de Cluny, Paris), which stages the five senses. In both cases, such constant correspondences to the living world of creation implies a feeling of participation in the movement of life. In "Prelude", the beheaded duck prompts Kezia's awareness of and revolt against death. Virginia Woolf may have remembered Katherine Mansfield when she compared Rezia to "a little hen"[32] as she endeavours to prevent Holmes, a figure of irrevocable power, from entering their Paradise newly regained. In "Les Yeux des pauvres" ("Poor People's Eyes"), Baudelaire describes his own compassion for three poor persons, a father and his two boys, looking with admiring eyes to the café in which he is sitting with his beloved: "The little boy's eyes: 'How beautiful it is! so beautiful! but this is a house to which only those who are not like us can get access.'"[33] Yet the poet fails to find the same compassion in the eyes of his beloved, who wishes "those people",[34] whom she "cannot bear with their eyes opened like porte-cochères", were chased away.

---

[29] Charles Baudelaire, "Le Gâteau", in *Le Spleen de Paris*, 48.

[30] See Chapter 3, on p. 42.

[31] Mansfield, "The Doll's House", in *The Collected Stories*, 390.

[32] Woolf, *Mrs Dalloway*, 126.

[33] Charles Baudelaire, "Les Yeux des pauvres", in *Le Spleen de Paris*, 78: "Les yeux du petit garçon: 'Que c'est beau! que c'est beau! mais c'est une maison où peuvent seuls entrer les gens qui ne sont pas comme nous.'"

[34] *Ibid.*, 79.

Such lack of generosity, such "impermeability"[35] of feelings breaks the harmony of love, brings hatred, and therefore discord: "It is so hard to get on well, my dear angel, and thought is so impossible to communicate, even between people loving each other!"[36] In "The Garden-Party", Laura cannot bear the idea of having the party while a man was killed in an accident because she thinks it is "terribly heartless of us".[37] The world is divided into "we" and "they", into "poky little holes" surrounded with "garden patches"[38] in which "there were nothing but cabbage stalks, sick hens and tomato cans", and beautiful places full of marvellous flowers. Such happiness is connected with the sense of the open and the lightness of the air:

> The house was alive with soft, quick steps and running voices .... But the air! If you stop to notice, was the air always like this? Little faint winds were playing chase in at the tops of the windows, out at the doors.[39]

The description recalls a baroque painting. From this openness Laura derives a sense of personal unity and participation in the world outside: "She crouched down as if to warm herself at that blaze of lilies; she felt they were in her fingers, on her lips, growing in her breast." Katherine Mansfield suggests that social inequality is not only a material question of having or not, but a lack of fair balance in terms of access to existential plenitude, which is what Hopkins evinced in a letter to R.W. Dixon in 1881 when he spoke of "the misery of the poor in general, of the degradation even of our race, of the hollowness of this century's civilisation".[40]

Baudelaire insists on the contrast between poverty and wealth in his prose poem "Le vieux saltimbanque" ("The Old Performer"). He describes a holiday, a day in which workmen "forget everything, pain and work" and retrieve children's capacity to wonder:

---

[35] *Ibid.*, 77.
[36] *Ibid.*, 79: "Tant il est difficile de s'entendre, mon cher ange, et tant la pensée est incommunicable, même entre gens qui s'aiment!"
[37] Mansfield, "The Garden-Party", in *The Collected Stories*, 255.
[38] *Ibid.*, 254.
[39] *Ibid.*, 249.
[40] Hopkins, *The Major Works*, 252.

For the small ones it is a day of vacation, the horror of school postponed twenty-four hours later. For the grown-ups, it is armistice signed with the malevolent powers of life; it is a relief in the universal contention and wrestling.[41]

In the end, he sees in the old performer the character of "the old friendless poet, without a family, without children, degraded by his own misery and public ingratitude".[42]

Nevertheless Baudelaire is also aware of what demoniac perversion can mean. He tells about such experience in "Le mauvais vitrier" ("The Bad Glazier") and calls "high deed" ("action d'éclat"[43]) a nasty trick he plays on the poor glazier, breaking all "his poor wandering fortune"[44] out of sheer malice, in the same way as Katherine Mansfield ironically called Lena's teasing the Kelveys "a marvellous thing to have said".[45] Such "active Demon, or fighting Demon",[46] in "Assommons les pauvres!" ("Let Us Knock Out the Poor!"), incites the narrator to test his philosophical theories and punch a beggar in the face in order to "give him back his pride and his energy of life".[47] The tale derides all utopian theories of "public happiness";[48] the poet refuses to be taken in by an idealistic view of life. The grotesque image of the "living rat" is closer to the truth.

In "Ole Underwood" and "The Woman at the Store" Katherine Mansfield does not idealize people either but discloses "the savage spirit"[49] of the grotesque. She uses the same adjective, "hideous", as Baudelaire in "Le Gâteau": "Sitting alone in the hideous room I grew afraid." And perturbed innocence (the kid with the "diseased"[50] mind) finally reveals the horror of murder and its dissimulation. "Ole Underwood", the sick old man, like the Kelveys, is compared to a cat:

---

[41] Charles Baudelaire, "Le vieux saltimbanque", in *Le Spleen de Paris*, 43: "Pour les petits c'est un jour de congé, c'est l'horreur de l'école renvoyée à vingt-quatre heures. Pour les grands c'est un armistice conclu avec les puissances malfaisantes, un répit dans la contention et la lutte universelles."
[42] *Ibid.*, 45.
[43] Charles Baudelaire, "Le mauvais vitrier", in *Le Spleen de Paris*, 30.
[44] *Ibid.*, 31.
[45] Mansfield, "The Doll's House", in *The Collected Stories*, 388.
[46] Charles Baudelaire, "Assommons les pauvres!", in *Le Spleen de Paris*, 140.
[47] *Ibid.*, 141.
[48] *Ibid.*, 139.
[49] Mansfield, "The Woman at the Store", in *The Collected Stories*, 554.
[50] *Ibid.*, 559.

"Ole Underwood sneaked on one side, like a cat."[51] Then he is likened to a rat: "Somebody kicked him: he scuttled like a rat."[52] The temptation of violence, irresistible, "the old, old lust"[53], picks out a victim, a cat:

> Ole Underwood sat up and took the kitten in his arms and rocked to and fro, crushing it against his face. It was warm and soft, and it mewed faintly. He buried his eyes in its fur. My God! My Lord! He tucked the little cat in his coat and stole out of the woodyard and slouched down towards the wharves.

The fact of satisfying his "old lust" with an animal "in his *own* image" (Genesis 1, 27) cancels his own life's experience, renews him, and restores "his pride and his energy of life" as Baudelaire said of the attacked beggar:

> He tore the little cat out of his coat and swung it by its tail and flung it out to the sewer opening. The hammer beat loud and strong. He tossed his head, he was young again.[54]

Such behaviour partakes of the violence of sacrifice, and the delusive idea that it may overcome individual helplessness:

> Something inside Ole Underwood's breast beat like a hammer. One, two – one, two – never stopping, never changing. He couldn't do anything.[55]

The hens emphasize how personal lack of power means discord with the world:

> Under one veranda yellow hens huddled out of the wind. "Shoo!" shouted Ole Underwood, and laughed to see them fly, and laughed again at the woman who came to the door and shook a red, soapy fist at him.[56]

---

[51] Mansfield, "Ole Underwood", in *The Collected Stories*, 563.
[52] *Ibid.*, 564.
[53] *Ibid.*, 565.
[54] *Ibid.*, 566.
[55] *Ibid.*, 562.
[56] *Ibid.*, 563.

Being unable to find a centre in oneself and to make up for loss through finding one's personal rhythm, as Katherine Mansfield does in "The Wind Blows", means remaining an outcast: "and no sign of anybody – anybody at all."[57] She insists on the disquieting presence of the wind at the beginning of the story:

> The pine trees roared like waves in their topmost branches, their stems creaked like the timber of ships; in the windy air flew the white manuka flowers. "Ah-k!" shouted Ole Underwood, shaking his umbrella at the wind bearing down upon him, beating him, half strangling him with his black cape.[58]

The sea also looks insatiable: "The sea sucked against the wharf-poles as though it drank something from the land."[59] In such unhinged world, devoid of any subjective centre, the threat is everywhere: "Ole Underwood looked once back at the town, at the prison perched like a red bird, at the black webby clouds trailing." There is no escape. "Red – red – red – red! beat the hammer."[60] Sacrifice means failure of the inner voice to find light over the abyss.

Such a contrast of harmony and discord, as expressed by Shakespeare in *A Midsummer Night's Dream* (1595-96), in which Theseus wonders: "How shall we find the concord of this discord?",[61] is handled by both poets in the same way as the contrast between light and darkness. They both rule out the dualistic viewpoint and highlight the ambivalence feature of life. Night is the appropriate moment for such utopian achievement of life's fullness.

Night, openness, and freedom

> Oh night! oh refreshing darkness! for me you are the signal of an inner celebration, you are my release from anguish! In the loneliness of plains, in the stony mazes of a capital city, with the stars' twinkling and the burst of lanterns, you are the fireworks of the Goddess Liberty.

---

[57] *Ibid.*, 566.
[58] *Ibid.*, 562.
[59] *Ibid.*, 566.
[60] *Ibid.*, 564.
[61] Shakespeare, *A Midsummer Night's Dream* (V, 1, 60), 107.

Twilights, how soft and tender you are![62]

The last line of this excerpt of Baudelaire's "Crépuscule du soir" ("Evening Twilight") recalls Keats' "Ode to a Nightingale" (1819) : "tender is the night".[63] Such night is suffused with perfumes, soft sounds, and appeals to the sense of taste. Although the poet "cannot see", night "brings light"[64] into his mind and the twilight, connected to the sense of touch ("the heavy draperies an invisible hand draws from the depths of the Orient"[65]), dramatizes "all the complex feelings which wrestle in man's heart at the solemn hours of life". Considering Katherine Mansfield's nightly figures as the aloe, the pear-tree, or the Picton boat in this perspective, we reach a synthetic view of her endeavour to catch the ambivalent mystery of life. Such poetic language dances over the abyss with all the power of our wondering mind. The "rapture of art"[66] dominates the abyss. Baudelaire advises us to get drunk on "wine, poetry or virtue"[67] in "Enivrez-vous" ("Get Drunk"): "One should always be drunk." Such intoxication helps the soul to wrestle against the objective impermeability of clock time. When waking up from the reverie induced by rapture, we should ask "the wind, the wave, the star, the bird, the clock" what time it is and they will answer: "It is time to get drunk!"

Katherine Mansfield also wishes to keep constantly the inner magic of life that the nightly return to the dark self makes possible. In "A Dill Pickle", the female character leaves the place when her interlocutor starts speaking of a "Mind system"[68] which would make plain all the mystery of life. The author's mistrust of psychology is obvious in "Psychology": "What dreadfully dismal outlook",[69] the woman answers the man who speaks of "making an exhaustive study of" the symptoms and "trying to get at the root of the trouble". In "Her

---

[62] Charles Baudelaire, "Le Crépuscule du soir", in *Le Spleen de Paris*, 68: "O nuit! ô rafraîchssante ténèbres! vous êtes pour moi le signal d'une fête intérieure, vous êtes la délivrance d'une angoisse! Dans la solitude des plaines, dans les labyrnthes pierreux d'une capitale, scintillement des étoles, explosion des lanternes, vous êtes le feu d'artifice de la déesse Liberté .... Crépuscule, comme vous êtes doux et tendre!"

[63] Keats, *Poetical Works*, 208.

[64] Baudelaire, "Le Crépuscule du soir", in *Le Spleen de Paris*, 68.

[65] *Ibid.*, 69.

[66] Baudelaire, "Une mort héroïque", in *ibid.*, 83.

[67] Charles Baudelaire, "Enivrez-vous", in *ibid.*, 106.

[68] Mansfield, "A Dill Pickle", in *The Collected Stories*, 174.

[69] Mansfield, "Psychology", in *ibid.*, 115.

First Ball", the young girl withstands the fat man's attempt to spoil her happiness and gets intoxicated again on the music and the ravishing movement of dancing:

> But in one minute, in one turn, her feet glided, glided. The lights, the azaleas, the dresses, the pink faces, the velvet chairs, all became one beautiful flying wheel.[70]

The magic, often suggested through the repetition of word (an epizeuxis here), provides a sense of unity as if all life were suddenly gathered in one radiating centre of energy, the sun's power absorbed into the soul's darkness, a way to "flame into being",[71] as D.H. Lawrence called it in his poem "Wedlock", in *Look! We have come through!* (1917).

In "Sun and Moon", taste and touch are connected: "She always wanted to touch all the food."[72] Seeing becomes vision in the children's dream aroused by the sounds of the party. When the vision is destroyed, such disenchantment is horror, and loss of Paradise: "Off you go!"[73] The boy's pain recalls Fancioulle's fall in "Une mort héroïque" ("A Hero's Death"); both children are "awakened"[74] in their dreams and chased from Paradise, as symbolized by "a little house", as in "The Doll's House":

> Oh! Oh! Oh! It was a little house. It was a little pink house with white snow on the roof and green windows and a brown door and stuck in the door there was a nut for the handle.[75]

"Anywhere out of the world", exclaims Baudelaire in the poem of the same name. It is an invitation to travel far from the "hospital where each sick person is possessed by the desire to change beds"[76] to a place where "we could take long baths of darkness"[77] and see

---

[70] Mansfield, "Her First Ball", in *ibid.*, 343.

[71] Lawrence, *Complete Poems*, 245.

[72] Mansfield, "Sun and Moon", in *The Collected Stories*, 155.

[73] *Ibid.*, 160.

[74] Baudelaire, "Une mort héroïque", in *Le Spleen de Paris*, 84.

[75] Mansfield, "Sun and Moon", in *The Collected Stories*, 155.

[76] Charles Baudelaire, "Anywhere out of the world, N'importe où hors du monde", in *Le Spleen de Paris*, 137.

[77] *Ibid.*, 138.

"reflections of Hell's fireworks". The "Invitation to a Voyage", or the impulse to reach the unknown shores of inner plenitude, is shared by Katherine Mansfield as the end of "The Wind Blows", or "The Journey to Bruges", may suggest: "In the shortest sea voyage there is no sense of time."[78] The only thing left is the sense of rhythm, "the pendulum itself". Baudelaire was fascinated by the movement of ships, in which he perceived "the hypothesis of a vast, huge, complex but eurythmic being, of an animal full of genius, suffering and heaving all sighs and human ambitions".[79] The voyage's aim is the core of being, the centre of radiating energy in which the individual voice will find words to tell about the shared, complex, sensitive experience of life. The end of "A Married Man's Story" can be read as a successful access to this place which is to be found "Anywhere out of the world": "I had come into my world!"[80]

The return to the dark hidden self marks the end of the secluded self derided by the others: "But not as if she were angry, – as if she understood, and her smile somehow was like a rat – hateful!"[81] The process is the exact opposite of the fool's fall in "Une mort héroïque". It means Paradise regained through the power of the work of art, of the inner voice and speech: "I did not consciously turn away from the world of human beings; I had never known it; but I from that night did beyond words consciously turn towards my silent brothers ...."[82] It means a return to the origins, to a fruitful silence of harmony rather than discord. It sounds like a sudden revelation: "I saw it all, but not as I had seen before .... Everything lived, everything. But that was not all. I was equally alive ...." The feeling of plenitude is conveyed by the repetition of "everything" and the use of "all". Once this silent primeval world has been reached within the self, the mind can spread its wings and follow its original impulse to make darkness "palpable"[83] as D.H. Lawrence thought we should do, and "visible" as

---

[78] Mansfield, "A Journey to Bruges", in *The Collected Stories*, 528.
[79] Charles Baudelaire, *Fusées*, in *Œuvres complètes*, ed. Michel Jamet, Paris: Laffont, 1980, 398.
[80] Mansfield, "A Married Man's Story", in *The Collected Stories*, 437.
[81] *Ibid.*, 436.
[82] *Ibid.*, 437.
[83] Lawrence, *The Rainbow*, 230.

Milton described it in Paradise Lost: "yet from those flames / No light, but rather darkness visible."[84]

Such dark light is ambivalent as Baudelaire suggested in "Anywhere out of the world". It is radiating and engendered by the inner elusive night. Each flash of light is a new beginning, a return to oneself and an opening, an ecstasy of freedom, a miracle. It means yielding to the flow of life:

> ... yes, she had her moment! And it was not connected with anything she had thought or felt before, not even with those words the doctor had scarcely ceased speaking. It was single, glowing, perfect; it was like – a pearl, too flawless to match with another .... Could she describe what happened? Impossible. It was as though, even if she had not been conscious (and she certainly had not been conscious all the time) that she was fighting against the stream of life – the stream of life indeed! – she had suddenly ceased to struggle. Oh, more than that! She had yielded, yielded absolutely, down to every minutest pulse and nerve, and she had fallen into the bright bosom of the stream and it had borne her .... She was part of her room ....[85]

From the epigraph to this story, Shakespeare's quote, Hotspur's words in his soliloquy, also to be found on her grave in Avon (Seine-et-Marne, France), "But I tell you, my lord fool, out of this nettle, danger, we pluck this flower, safety",[86] we may infer how keenly and fully Katherine Mansfield felt the cruel ambivalence of life. But from that awareness she deduced her art of questioning such mystery without ever breaking the enchantment. The loss of Paradise means the loss of one's own domain of radiating energy. Being chased out of the original Eden means being chased from one's own power of being, choosing and creating, which is full freedom. Thus Katherine Mansfield returns, as Baudelaire, Keats, Hopkins, Proust, or Shakespeare, to the origins of language – this poignant contrast of light and dark following the alternate rhythm of night and day, of yielding to darkness and converting it into speech: "Let there be

---

[84] John Milton, *Paradise Lost*, Book I, 62-63, ed. Scott Elledge, New York, London: Norton, 1975, 8.
[85] Katherine Mansfield, "This Flower", in *The Collected Stories*, 660-61.
[86] William Shakespeare, *Henry IV*, Part I, II, 3, 8-9, ed. David Bevington, Oxford: Oxford University Press, 1998, 172.

light."[87] Poetic language is performative not only through calling things to the mind but also because it may generate fertile connections between people. Let there be what I wish to communicate and share; let there be a mutual fruitful concord within the depths of being, an openness to the manifold surges of the unknown. It means an everlasting questioning over the abyss: "Ah, what is it? – that I heard."[88]

---

[87] Henri Meschonnic argues that the syntax of the original Hebrew text implies that the first thing to be created was light, and not the sky and the earth. The performative feature of speech is thus still more emphasized (Henri Meschonnic, *Au Commencement*, A Translation of Genesis, Paris: Desclée de Brouwer, 2002, 243).
[88] Mansfield, "The Canary", in *The Collected Stories*, 422.

SO AS NOT TO CONCLUDE

KATHERINE MANSFIELD'S ART OF THE OPEN

> Mit allen Augen sieht die Kreatur
> das Offene. Nur unsre Augen sind
> wie umgekehrt und ganz um sie gestellt
> als Fallen, rings um ihren freien Ausgang. [1]

The end of this book is no conclusion; since it is presumptuous and not "REAL" to conclude. What I have developed is my reading of Katherine Mansfield's work until now. There have been, and shall be, other readings. And I may still improve mine. The sense of continuity should spare us the naivety of concluding. I only wish this book might help further readers in the generations to come. I would like to preserve a dynamic view of the individual and the work of art. In *Apocalypse*, D.H. Lawrence made this very accurate statement:

> Once a book is fathomed, once it is *known*, and its meaning is fixed and established, it is dead. A book only lives while it has power to move us, and move us *differently*; so long as we find it *different* every time we read it. [2]

This everlasting interaction between author and reader is part of the "spirit of the narrative"; it is the way a poet's work is renewed in each reader's soul, when his/her work opens new vistas. The process is not cathartic; the aim is not to get rid of the feelings of pity and fear but to penetrate with increased accuracy the existential depth of our lives. Through the reader's empathy, the poet's breathing becomes communicative.

---

[1] R.M. Rilke, "Die Achte Elegie" (1922), *Rudolf Kassner zugeeignet* (dedicated to Rudolf Kassner), *Les Elégies de Duino, Les Sonnets à Orphée*, 1974, 74: "With all eyes does the creature see / in the Open. Only our eyes, so to speak / turn the other way and set traps / around her, surrounding its free impulse."
[2] Lawrence, *Apocalypse*, 4 (Lawrence's emphases).

Unlike what Clarissa Dalloway thought in the last pages of Virginia Woolf's novel (see Chapters 2 and 8), there is no communication in death. Tragedy skirts the question of life, only intimidating us with a feeling of irrevocable helplessness, or irresponsible callousness. The result is an hedonistic praise of immediacy, the triumph of the aesthetic, eccentric character. Katherine Mansfield ironically attacked such would-be artists. The titles she imagines for their books indicates the existential void of such fall into the trivial: *False Coins*, *Wrong Doors*, *Left Umbrellas*[3] in "Je Ne Parle Pas Français", an implicit critical view of Carco's novels. I do not wish to insist on the choice of adjectives, "false" and "wrong". The former is used in *Love in False Teeth*,[4] a title given in "Bliss" while another is suggested: "Stomach Trouble", emphasizing the deceiving feature of trivia. In *Apocalypse*, D.H. Lawrence commented on that aspect of commercial literature:

> Owing to the flood of shallow books which really are exhausted in one reading, the modern mind tends to think every book is the same, finished in one ending. But it is not so .... It is, as usual, a question of values: we are so overwhelmed with *quantities* of books, that we hardly realize any more that a book can be valuable, valuable like a jewel, or a lovely picture, into which you can look deeper and deeper and get a more profound experience every time.[5]

The response is individual. Lawrence says that *War and Peace* little moved him when he read it once more. My own second reading of it a few months ago was a second revelation to me. The person who has chosen himself "does not try to erase the multiplicity or to disperse it":[6] "the thing is to see the task, to see that when someone tends to be distracted, that task is to summon up resistance, to keep hold of the infinite and not go on a wild goose chase."[7]

Through the character of Bertha in "Bliss" Katherine Mansfield manages to convert such trifling immediacy into resonant art:

---

[3] Mansfield, "Je Ne Parle Pas Français" (1918), in *The Edinburgh Edition of the Collected Works of Katherine Mansfield*, II, 119, 124; *The Collected Stories*, 71, 77.
[4] Mansfield, "Bliss", in *ibid.*, 148; 100.
[5] Lawrence, *Apocalypse*, 4-5 (Lawrence's emphasis).
[6] Kierkegaard, *Either ... or ...*, 549.
[7] *Ibid.*, 548.

No, they didn't share it. They were dears – dears – and she loved having them there, at her table, and giving them delicious food and wine. In fact, she longed to tell them how delightful they were, and what a decorative group they made, how they seemed to set one another off and how they reminded her of a play by Tchekof!⁸

Three years later, in "Marriage à la Mode" (1921), her outlook is much more painful. William is widely estranged from his wife, the "new Isabel".⁹ His loneliness weighs on him like fate. We remember that one of the characters is called Moira,¹⁰ after the name of the three Greek Fates (see Chapters 3 and 6), and she acts like fate on Isabel's mood, calling her "an exquisite little Titania",¹¹ thus even perverting Shakespeare's inspiring world. A title is derisively suggested for a painting: "'A Lady with a Box of Sardines,' said Dennis gravely."¹² A debased view of art is conveyed. The immediate has won over the "'inside' voice",¹³ which is able to convert shreds of material torn by the wind into ribbons (see Chapter 11):

> Bill and Dennis ate enormously. And Isabel filled glasses, and changed plates, and found matches, smiling blissfully. At one moment she said, 'I do wish, Bill, you'd paint it.'
> 'Paint what?' said Billy loudly, stuffing his mouth with bread.
> 'Us', said Isabel, 'round the table. It would be so fascinating in twenty years' time.'
> Bill screwed up his eyes and chewed. 'Light's wrong,' he said rudely, 'far too much yellow'; and went on eating. And that seemed to charm Isabel, too.
> But after supper they were all so tired they could do nothing but yawn until it was late enough to go to bed ....¹⁴

The attack is ironic but the spirit of the narrative ("'It would be so fascinating in twenty years' time'") even preserves author and reader

---

⁸ Mansfield, "Bliss" (1918), in *The Edinburgh Edition of the Collected Works of Katherine Mansfield*, II, 148; *The Collected Stories*, 100.
⁹ Mansfield, "Marriage à la Mode" (1921), in *ibid*., 330; 309.
¹⁰ *Ibid*., 332; 313.
¹¹ *Ibid*., 333; 313.
¹² *Ibid*., 335; 317.
¹³ Mansfield, "The Thoughtful Child", in *The Edinburgh Edition of the Collected Works of Katherine Mansfield*, I, 127.
¹⁴ Mansfield, "Marriage à la Mode", in *The Edinburgh Edition of the Collected Works of Katherine Mansfield*, II, 335-36; *The Collected Stories*, 317.

from any aesthetic complacency, so close it is to despair. Katherine Mansfield assembles as Clarissa Dalloway would say, but never judges, even when Isabel postpones her decision to write to her husband, whose letter to her has just been derided by the members of her little Bohemia:

> Oh, how could there be any question? Of course she would stay here and write.
> 'Titania!' piped Moira.
> 'Isabel?'
> No, it was too difficult. 'I'll – I'll go with them, and write to William later. Some other time. Later. Not now. But I shall *certainly* write,' thought Isabel hurriedly.
> And laughing in the new way, she ran down the stairs.[15]

In all those instances, we grasp that Katherine Mansfield thought that art should metamorphose the immediate life into the instant, taking its full shape in the movement of becoming. Her stories convey the impression of the extreme fluidity of time. What counts with her art is the movement, which preserves life in the infinite. From this viewpoint – the movement of life as captured through language – we cannot dissociate the stories and poems from the Letters and Notebooks, as the Italian writer, Cristina Campo (who, in an essay collected in *Sotto Falso Nome*, "La noce d'oro"[16] – "The Golden Nut" – recalled the doll's house in her own childhood) so aptly remarked in her Introduction to her translation of some of Katherine Mansfield's tales. She says that Katherine Mansfield's work is a creature gifted with blood, nerves, a heart, a brain, and a mind – a whole life.[17]

In Chapter 10, I have suggested some common points with Baudelaire's poems. The desire for the infinite, the *apeiron*, beyond the limits of logics and knowledge (see Aristotle, *Metaphysics*, Θ 6, which runs counter to Kassner's wish that the mind's movement should not contemplate an end[18]) is one of them: "Homme libre,

---

[15] *Ibid.*, 338; 320-321.
[16] Cristina Campo, "La Noce d'oro", in *Sotto Falso Nome* (1998), Milan: Adelphi Edizioni, 2010, 221.
[17] Cristina Campo, "Introduzione a Katherine Mansfield, 'Una Tazza di té e altri racconti'", in *ibid.*, 15.
[18] Kassner, *Evocations et paraboles*, 8.

toujours tu chériras la mer!"[19] When Baudelaire invites his beloved to
share a journey with him ("L'invitation au voyage"[20]), he seeks for the
infinite, and the infinite implies the I and You relationship and the
movement it triggers off – a return to oneself, as described by Rudolf
Kassner, while "I" radiates into "You": so it is at the end of
Baudelaire's prose poem, when the ships sailing the sea, or the
infinite, "sail back to their native harbour, those are still my enriched
thoughts which sail back from the Infinite towards you".[21] Katherine
Mansfield's "little island"[22] is not a closed world. Under the title "At
Sea", in her Notebook 1906, she wrote:

> Swiftly the Night came. Like a great white bird the ship sped onward
> – onward into the unknown. Through the darkness the stars shone, yet
> the sky was a garden of golden flowers, heavy with colour. I lay on
> the deck of the vessel, my hands clasped behind my head, and,
> watching them, I felt a complex curious emotion, a swift mysterious
> realisation that they were shining steadily & ever more powerfully
> into the very soul of my soul. I felt their still light permeating the very
> depths, and fear & ecstasy held me still, shuddering.
> There is some fearful magic in their shining, I thought.[23]

The stars' splendour seems to partially eclipse the "flame" of her
life and she faces the infinite in all its terror:

> ... and I thought before long it will go out and then. Even as I thought
> I saw there where it had shone – darkness remained.
> Then I was drifting, drifting – where – whence – whither. I was
> drifting in a great boundless purple sea. I was being tossed to and fro
> by the power of the waves, and the confused sound of many voices
> floated to me. A sense of unutterable loneliness pervaded my spirit. I
> knew the sea was eternal – I was eternal – this agony was eternal.

[19] Charles Baudelaire, "L'homme et la mer" ("Man and the Sea"), in *Les Fleurs du Mal*, 29: "Free man, you will always love the sea!"
[20] Charles Baudelaire, "L'invitation au voyage" ("The Invitation to a Journey"), in *ibid.*, 66 and *Le Spleen de Paris*, 53. Baudelaire wrote a poem in verse (in *Les Fleurs du Mal*) as well as a prose poem (in *Le Spleen de Paris*) with the same title.
[21] *Ibid.*, in *Le Spleen de* Paris, 55: "... quand ... ils rentrent au port natal, ce sont encore mes pensées enrichies qui reviennent de l'Infini vers toi."
[22] Mansfield, "The Wind Blows", in *The Edinburgh Edition of the Collected Works of Katherine Mansfield*, II, 229; *The Collected Stories*, 110.
[23] *The Katherine Mansfield Notebooks*, I, 78.

Then it seems that from the process of reflexive consciousness the notion of desire and fullness emerges:

> So, smiling at myself, I sit down to analyse this new influence, this complex emotion. I am never anywhere for long without a like experience. It is not one man or woman that a musician desires – it is the whole octave of the sex, & R. is my latest. The first time I saw him I was lying back in my chair & he walked past. I watched the complete rhythmic movement, the absolute self confidence, the beauty of his body, & that Quelque which is the everlasting & eternal in youth & creation stirred in me.[24]

I think we may find a reminiscence of those early thoughts in this often quoted passage of "Psychology" (1920):

> That silence could be contained in the circle of warm, delightful fire and lamplight. How many times hadn't they flung something into it just for the fun of watching the ripples break on, the easy shores. But into that familiar pool the head of the little boy sleeping his timeless sleep dropped – and the ripples flowed away, away – boundlessly far – into deep glittering darkness.[25]

The relationship involves three elements, "I", "You" and the "infinite", and the "I and You" relationship is also the inner relation of the "'inside' voice".[26] Kierkegaard made very subtle remarks on this issue:

> For if the individual man believes the universal man is situated outside him and will come to meet him from outside, then he is disoriented, he has an abstract conception, and his method will always be an abstract annihilation of the original self. Only from within himself can the individual obtain information about himself. Therefore the ethical life has this twofold nature, that the individual has himself outside himself within himself. However, the typical self is the imperfect self, for it is only a prophecy and therefore not the actual self.[27]

---

[24] *Ibid.*, 78-79.
[25] Mansfield, "Psychology", in *The Edinburgh Edition of the Collected Works of Katherine Mansfield*, II, 195; *The Collected Stories*, 114.
[26] Mansfield, "The Thoughtful Child", in *The Edinburgh Edition of the Collected Works of Katherine Mansfield*, I, 127.
[27] Kierkegaard, *Either ... or ...*, 550.

The infinite, or the possibility of the ideal embodied within the present moment without drying up its spring, keeps opening the soul to the marvellous and its ambivalence of a possible relationship ("the whole octave", see the quotation at the top of the previous page) or its failure. If it fails, the "deep glittering darkness" gapes like an abyss: "They faltered, wavered, broke down, were silent. Again they were conscious of the boundless, questioning dark."[28]

Writing implies such complex relationship with the world, the others and the second person, and with oneself. Katherine Mansfield's art of the open accounts for her trespassing the social barriers. We have noticed that in "The Doll's House", the lamp, that centre of belonging, is shared both by Kezia and "our Else": "'I seen the little lamp,' she said, softly."[29] Kezia refused to obey her mother's order not to invite the poor Kelvey girls to see the house. In "The Garden-Party" (1921), Laura also "seemed to be different from them all"[30] thinking that the party should be stopped because of the "man dead just outside the front gate".[31] Then what was horrible from the outside is converted into something else, something she did not expect, the peaceful view of a young man dreaming. Only a dash can express the complexity of the sensation:

> 'No,' sobbed Laura. 'It was simply marvellous. But, Laurie –' She stopped, she looked at her brother. 'Isn't life,' she stammered, 'isn't life –' But what life was she couldn't explain. No matter. He quite understood.
> *'Isn't* it, darling?' said Laurie.[32]

The similarity in the names, Laura and Laurie, suggests the same type of ternary relationship, her brother being an *alter ego* and both facing the ambivalence of the infinite – a promise of plenitude or an abyss. The dash makes the quivering suspension of the present moment in eternity visible. It remains open while tragedy is enclosed within the boundaries of necessity and fate. There is no relief but

---

[28] Mansfield, "Psychology", in *The Edinburgh Edition of the Collected Works of Katherine Mansfield*, II, 196; *The Collected Stories*, 115.
[29] Mansfield, "The Doll's House", in *ibid.*, 420; 391.
[30] Mansfield, "The Garden-Party", in *ibid.*, 411; 258.
[31] *Ibid.*, 407; 254.
[32] *Ibid.*, 413; 261 (Mansfield's emphasis).

escaping through "aesthetic detachment",[33] that is, catharsis. Empathy, which seeks for an "I and You" relationship within and without, arouses an epic conversion of the tragic. Ethics means resurrection: "It would be so fascinating in twenty years' time" (see above on p. 205). "The idea of resurrection stresses with emphasis the interest of temporality", Rachel Bespaloff writes. What is at stake is "the will to destroy death in time" as I have suggested in Chapter 4. The "ethical individual is transparent to himself"[34] and the world is transparent to him. The aesthetic view creates obstacles, impediments, and false excuses for not carrying out one's artistic task. The ethical choice means confidence in life and the "whole octave" of the "I and You" relationship.

The empty centre of tragedy is impenetrable but the radiating centre of the inner voice is transparent in its energy. In "Bénédiction" ("Blessing") Baudelaire called this inner spring of life "the holy source of primitive sunbeams" ("le foyer saint des rayons primitifs"[35]). The art of the open considers the beginning rather than the result instead of carrying on "an aesthetic flirtation with the result".[36] It means a new birth to oneself, among the others, within history, or the spirit of the narrative – a new awareness of oneself, a sense of belonging. The sense of continuity leads to the sense of belonging:

> I saw it all, but not as I had seen it before .... Everything lived, but everything. But that was not all. I was equally alive and – it's the only way I can express it – the barriers were down between us – I had come into my own world![37]

Katherine Mansfield ends this story with these words: "... but I from that night did beyond words consciously turn towards my silent brothers ...." The revelation of the complex individual's identity is expressed in opposition. The present moment of the new beginning stands in contrast: "But now." So does the "I", born to himself in the darkness of night. The nocturnal root of being calls for dawn, which is

---

[33] Rachel Bespaloff, *De l'Iliade* (1943), Paris: Allia, 2004, 77.
[34] Kierkegaard, *Either ... or ...*, 549.
[35] Charles Baudelaire, "Elévation" ("Elevation"), in *Les Fleurs du Mal*, 29.
[36] Kierkegaard, *Fear and Trembling* (1843), in *Fear and Trembling, Repetition*, 63.
[37] Mansfield, "A Married Man's Story" (1921), in *The Edinburgh Edition of the Collected Works of Katherine Mansfield*, II, 390; *The Collected Stories*, 437.

revelation – a gift from the infinite, within and without: "It looked as though the sea had beaten up softly in the darkness, as though one immense wave had come rippling, rippling – how far?"[38]

---

[38] Mansfield, "At the Bay", in *ibid.*, 342; 205.

BIBLIOGRAPHY

Works by Katherine Mansfield

The Collected Letters of Katherine Mansfield, eds Vincent O'Sullivan and Margaret Scott, 5 Volumes, Oxford: Clarendon Press, 1984-2008.

The Collected Stories, London: Penguin, 2001.

The Edinburgh Edition of the Collected Works of Katherine Mansfield, I, The Collected Fiction of Katherine Mansfield, 1898-1915; II, The Collected Fiction of Katherine Mansfield, 1916-1922, eds Gerri Kimber and Vincent O'Sullivan, Edinburgh: Edinburgh University Press, 2012.

The Katherine Mansfield Notebooks, ed. Margaret Scott, Minneapolis: University of Minnesota Press, 2002.

Letters between Katherine Mansfield and John Middleton Murry, ed. Cherry A. Hankin, New York: New Amsterdam Books, 1988.

Poems, ed. Vincent O'Sullivan, Oxford: Oxford University Press, 1988.

Works by other poets and philosophers

Agamben, Giorgio, *Le temps qui reste* (2000), Paris: Rivages Poche, 2004.

—, *Stanze* (1981), trans. Yves Hersant, Paris: Rivages, 1998.

Baudelaire, Charles, *Les Fleurs du* Mal (1857), Paris: Le Livre de Poche, 1967.

—, *Le Spleen de Paris* (1863), Paris : Le Livre de Poche, 1969.

—, *Œuvres complètes*, ed. Michel Jamet, Paris : Laffont, 1980.

Bergson, Henri, *Essai sur les données immédiates de la conscience* (1888), Paris : P.U.F., 2001.

—, *L'évolution créatrice* (1907), Paris: P.U.F. Quadrige, 1981.

—, *Matière et mémoire* (1896), Paris: P.U.F. Quadrige, 1982.

—, *Le rire* (1900), Paris: P.U.F. Quadrige, 1981.

Blake, William, *Complete Writings*, ed. Geoffrey Keynes, Oxford: Oxford University Press, 1989.

Brontë, Charlotte, *Jane Eyre* (1847), London: Penguin, 1985.

Campo, Cristina, *Sotto Falso Nome* (1998), Milan: Adelphi Edizioni, 2010.

Chekhov, Anton, *Le duel, Ma vie, Lueurs, Une banale histoire, La fiancée*, Paris: Le Livre de Poche, 1971.

—, *Œuvres*, I, II, and III, Paris: Gallimard Pléiade, 1970.

—, "Three Years", *The Literature Network*, http://www.online-literature.com/o_henry/1277/

Chestov, Léon, *Sur la balance de Job* (1929), Paris: Flammarion, 1971.

Coleridge, S.T., *Poems*, ed. John Beer, London: Everyman's Library, 1974.

Colette, *L'Entrave* (1913), Paris: Librio, 2013.

—, *La retraite sentimentale* (1907), Paris: Gallimard Folio, 1977.

Du Maurier, George, *Trilby* (1894), London: Everyman, 1992.

Eliot, T.S., *Collected Poems*, London: Faber, 1974.

—, *Selected Prose*, ed. Frank Kermode, London: Faber, 1984.

Flaubert, Gustave, *Trois contes* (1877), Paris: Garnier-Flammarion, 2001.

Fondane, Benjamin, *Baudelaire et l'expérience du gouffre* (1942), Brussels: Complexe, 1994.

Graves, Robert, *Poems and Satires 1951*, in *Collected Poems*, eds Beryl Graves and Dunstan Ward, Manchester: Carcanet, 1997.

—, *Some Speculations on Literature, History and Religion*, Manchester: Carcanet, 2000.

—, *The White Goddess* (1948), London: Faber, 1957.

Heschel, Abraham, *Les Bâtisseurs du temps*, Paris: Minuit, 1957.

Hölderlin, Friedrich, *Œuvre poétique complète*, trans. François Garrigue, A German/French edition, Paris: La Différence, 2005.

Hopkins, Gerard Manley, *The Major Works*, ed. Catherine Phillips, Oxford: Oxford University Press, 2002.

James, Henry, *Selected Tales*, eds Peter Messent and Tom Paulin, London: Everyman, 1982.

—, *The Turn of the Screw* (1898), London: Everyman's Library, 1975.

The Jewish Study Bible (1985), eds Adele Berlin and Marc Zvi Brettler, Oxford and New York: Oxford University Press, 1999.

Kassner, Rudolf, *Esquisse d'une physiognomonie universelle, Evocations et paraboles*, trans. Geneviève Bianquis, Paris: Plon, 1956.

Keats, John, *Poetical Works*, ed. H.W. Garrod, London, Oxford and New York: Oxford University Press, 1976.

—, *Selected Letters*, ed. George Gittings, rev. with an Introduction and Notes by John Mee, Oxford: Oxford World's Classics, 2002.

Kertész, Imre, *L'Holocauste comme culture*, Preface by Péter Nádas, trans. Natalia Zaremba-Huzsvai and Charles Zaremba, Arles: Actes Sud, 2009.

Kierkegaard, Søren, *Either... or...* (1843), trans. with an Introduction by Alastair Hannay, London: Penguin, 2004.

— , *Fear and Trembling* (1843), in *Fear and Trembling, Repetition*, ed. and trans. Howard V. Hong and Edna H. Hong, Princeton, NJ: Princeton University Press, 1983.

—, *Fear and Trembling*, eds C. Stephen Evans and Sylvia Walsh, Cambridge: Cambridge University Press, 2006.

—, *Post-scriptum aux Miettes philosophiques*, Paris: Gallimard Tel, 2001.

—, *The Sickness Unto Death* (1849), trans. and ed. Alastair Hannay, London: Penguin, 2004.

Lautréamont, Isidore Ducasse, Comte de, *Les Chants de Maldoror* (1869), Paris: Poésie Gallimard, 1988.

Lawrence, D.H., *Apocalypse* (1931), London: Penguin, 1981.

—, *Complete Poems*, eds Vivian de Sola Pinto and Warren Roberts, London: Penguin Books, 1993.

—, *England, My England* (1922), London: Penguin, 1960.

—, *Fantasia of the Unconscious* (1922), London: Penguin, 1986.

—, *The Man Who Died* (1929), in *Love Among the Haystacks* (1960), Harmondsworth: Penguin, 1986.

—, *The Prussian Officer and Other Stories* (1914), London: Panther Books, 1985.

—, *The Rainbow* (1915), London: Penguin, 1987.

—, *The Selected Letters of D.H. Lawrence*, ed. James T. Boulton, Cambridge: Cambridge University Press, 1997.

—, *Studies in Classic American Literature*, London: Penguin, 1977.

—, *Women in Love* (1920), London: Penguin, 1974.

McCullers, Carson, *The Ballad of the Sad Café* (1951), London: Penguin, 1963.

Maine de Biran, *Rapports du physique et du moral de l'homme*, Paris: Vrin, 1984.

Mallarmé, Stéphane, *Œuvres complètes*, I, ed. Bertrand Marchal, Paris: Gallimard Pléiade, 1998.

Mann, Thomas, *Joseph et ses frères: Les Histoires de Jacob* (1933), trans. L. Vic, Paris: Gallimard L'Imaginaire, 1985.

Meschonnic, Henri, *Au Commencement*, A translation of Genesis, Paris: Desclée de Brouwer, 2002.

Milton, John, *Paradise Lost*, ed. Scott Elledge, New York, London: Norton, 1975.

Misrahi, Robert, *Construction d'un château* (1981), Paris: Entrelacs, 2006.

The Norton Anthology of Poetry, Fourth Edition, New York and London: W.W. Norton, 1996.

O'Sullivan, Vincent, *Palms and Minarets*, Wellington: Victoria University Press, 1992.

——, *Cette voûte de si pur respire/That Vault of Such Pure Breath*, Poems, Bilingual edition, trans. Anne Mounic, Paris: Inventaire, 2006.

Pater, Walter, *The Renaissance: Studies in Art and Literature* (1868), Oxford: Oxford University Press, 1998.

Pozzi, Catherine, *Journal 1913-1934*, eds Lawrence Joseph and Claire Paulhan, Paris: Ramsay, 1987.

——, *Peau d'Ame*, ed. Lawrence Joseph, Paris: La Différence, 1990.

Proust, Marcel, *Contre Sainte-Beuve* (written in 1908, first published 1954), Paris: Folio Gallimard, 2004.

——, *In Search of Lost Time: I. Swann's Way* (1913), trans. C.K. Scott Moncrieff and Terence Kilmartin, rev. D.J. Enright, London: Chatto and Windus, 1992.

——, *In Search of Lost Time: VI. Time Regained* (1927), trans. Andreas Mayor and Terence Kilmartin, rev. D.J. Enright, London: Chatto and Windus, 1992.

——, *Sodome et Gomorrhe* (1921-1922), Paris: Gallimard Folio, 1972.

Richardson, Dorothy, *Interim* (1919), in *Pilgrimage 2*, London: Virago Press, 1992.

——, *Journey to Paradise*, London: Virago Press, 1989.

Ricœur, Paul, *Temps et récit: 2. La configuration dans le récit de fiction*, Paris: Seuil, 1984.

Rilke, Rainer Maria, *Les Elégies de Duino* (1912-1922), *Les Sonnets à Orphée* (1922), bilingual edition, Paris: Seuil Points, 1974.

Rossetti, Christina, *Selected Poems*, ed. C.H. Sisson, Manchester: Carcanet, 1984.

Schopenhauer, Arthur, *Le monde comme volonté et comme représentation* (1819-1851), Paris : P.U.F. Quadrige, 2004.

Shakespeare, William, *A Midsummer Night's Dream* (1595-1596), ed. Harold F. Brooks, London: Routledge, 1993.

—, *As You Like It* (1600), ed. Alan Brissenden, Oxford: Oxford University Press, 1993.

—, *Cymbeline* (1610), ed. Roger Warren, Oxford: Oxford University Press, 1998.

—, *Hamlet* (1600), ed. G.R. Hibbard, Oxford: Oxford University Press, 1998.

—, *Henry IV*, ed. David Bevington. Oxford: Oxford University Press, 1998.

—, *King Lear*, ed. Kenneth Muir, London: Methuen, 1982.

—, *The Winter's Tale* (1611), ed. Stephen Orgel, Oxford: Oxford University Press, 1998.

Silkin, Jon, ed., *The Penguin Book of First World War Poetry*, London: Penguin, 1979.

Stevenson, Robert Louis, *The Child's Garden of Verses* (1885), Ware: Wordsworth Edition, 1994.

Vigée, Claude, *L'art et le démonique*, Paris: Flammarion, 1978.

Wilde, Oscar, *The Picture of Dorian Gray* (1891), Harmondsworth: Penguin, 1986.

Winnicott, D.W., *Playing and Reality*, London: Tavistock, 1971.

Woolf, Virginia, *The Diary of Virginia Woolf*, Vol. III, 1925-30, ed. Anne Olivier Bell, Harmondsworth: Penguin, 1987.

—, *Mrs. Dalloway* (1925), London: Penguin, 1996.

—, *Mrs. Dalloway* (1925), Oxford: Oxford University Press, 2000.

—, *Mrs. Dalloway's Party*, in *The Mrs. Dalloway Reader*, ed. Francine Prose, New York: Harcourt, 2004.

Critical works

Armengaud, Françoise and Daniel Poirion, "Bestiaires", *Encyclopédie Universalis*, 2009.

Blanchot, Maurice, *Faux Pas* (1943), trans. Charlotte Mandell, Stanford: Stanford University Press, 2001.

Gusdorf, Georges, *Le savoir romantique de la nature*, Paris: Payot, 1985.

Henry, Anne, *La tentation de Marcel Proust*, Paris: P.U.F., 2000.

Katherine Mansfield Studies, *The Journal of the Katherine Mansfield Society*, I (2009), Edinburgh: Edinburgh University Press.

Kimber, Gerri, *Katherine Mansfield: The View from France*, Bern: Peter Lang, 2008.

—, and Janet Wilson, eds, *Celebrating Katherine Mansfield: A Centenary Volume of Essays*, Basingstoke: Palgrave Macmillan, 2011.

Mosse, George L., *Fallen Soldiers: Reshaping the Memory of World Wars*, Oxford: Oxford University Press, 1990.

Mounic, Anne, *Counting the Beats: Robert Graves' Poetry of Unrest*, Amsterdam: Rodopi, 2012.

—, *Jacob ou l'être du possible*, Paris: Caractères, 2009.

—, *L'Esprit du récit ou La chair du devenir: Ethique et création littéraire*, Paris: Champion, 2013.

—, *L'inerte ou l'exquis: Pensée poétique, pensée du singulier*, Paris: Champion, 2014.

—, *Monde terrible où naître: La voix singulière face à l'Histoire*, Paris: Honoré Champion, 2011.

—, *Psyché et le secret de Perséphone*, Paris: L'Harmattan, 2004.

—, "D.H. Lawrence: Darkness visible, ténèbres palpables, ou le puits de l'être. *Temporel*, n° 5, http://temporel.fr/D-H-Lawrence-Tenebres-palpables.

O'Sullivan, Vincent, "Katherine Mansfield's Canary, a 'wounded bird'", *Temporel* 2: http://temporel.fr

Pilditch, Jan, ed., *The Critical Response to Katherine Mansfield*, Westport, CT: Greenwood Press, 1996.

Sagar, Keith, *The Life of D.H. Lawrence*, London: Methuen, 1982.

Silkin, Jon, *Out of Battle* (1972), 2nd edn, London: Macmillan, 1998.

Smith, Angela, "Paris Is Simply a Place of Freedom", *Temporel* n° 7, May 2009, http://temporel.fr/Rhythm-par-Angela-Smith

Wright, T.R., *D.H. Lawrence and the Bible*, Cambridge: Cambridge University Press, 2000.

Yates, Frances, *The Art of Memory* (1966), London: Pimlico, 2000.

INDEX

Agamben, Giorgio, 24
Anaximander, 74n, 189
Aristotle, 189, 228
Armengaud, Françoise, 89n

Baisnée, Valérie, 5n
Barres, Georges, 15
Baudelaire, Charles, xi, 22, 78, 80, 102, 103n, 104, 112, 115, 184-89, 203, 207-23, 228, 229, 232
Beauchamp, Leslie Heron, 27
Becket, Samuel, xi
Beethoven, Ludwig van, 111
Bergson, Henri, xi, 31, 51, 53, 57, 58, 68, 84, 115, 142
Besnault-Levita, Anne, 5
Bespaloff, Rachel, 232
Blake, William, 105, 135, 139, 152, 178
Blanchot, Maurice, ix
Bowden, George, 7
Brett, Dorothy, 78
Brontë, Charlotte, 196
Bunyan, John, 198

Campo, Cristina, 228
Carco, Francis, 56, 106, 176, 226
Chekhov, Anton, 78-80, 193, 195, 197
Chestov, Léon, 74n

Clausius, Rudolf, 166
Coleridge, Samuel Taylor, 43, 62
Colette, xi, 5, 161-65, 207

D'Annunzio, Gabriele, 15
Dante, xi, 143
Degas, Edgar, 62
Delarue-Mardrus, Lucie, 163n
Dixon, R.W., 216
Du Maurier, George, 12

Eliot, T.S., 21, 23, 90, 144, 156

Fergusson, J.D., 13, 101, 173
Flaubert, Gustave, 90n
Fondane, Benjamin, 184
Forrest-Thomson, Veronica, 84
Freud, Sigmund, 120

Galvani, Luigi, 125
Goethe, Johann Wolfgang von, 22
Goodyear, Frederick, 13, 101
Graves, Robert von Ranke, 85, 97n, 153, 172, 203
Guercino, Giovanni Francesco Barbieri, 201
Gusdorf, Georges, 125n

Appeared earlier in the COSTERUS NS series

Irony and Idyll
Jane Austen's *Pride and Prejudice* and *Mansfield Park* on Screen
Volume 203 – *By Marie N. Sørbø*

Elizabeth Bowen and the Writing of Trauma: The Ethics of Survival
Volume 202 – *By Jessica Gildersleeve*

From Sight through to In-Sight
Time, Narrative and Subjectivity in Conrad and Ford
Volume 201 – *By Omar Sabbagh*

Wandering into *Brave New World*
Volume 200 – *By David Leon Higdon*

Dangerous Writing: The Autobiographies of Willa Muir,
Margaret Laurence and Janet Frame
Volume 199 – *By Carmen Luz Fuentes-Vásquez*

A Spectacular Failure: Robinson Crusoe I, II, III
Volume 198 – *By Virginia La Grand*

Opting Out: Deviance and Generational Identities in
American Post-War Cult Fiction
Volume 197 – *By Ana Sobral*

Visibility beyond the Visible
The Poetic Discourse of American Transcendentalism
Volume 196 – *By Albena Bakratcheva*

Ræd and Frofer: Christian Poetics in the Old English *Froferboc* Meters
Volume 195 – *By Karmen Lenz*

Ways of Being Free: Authenticity and Community in Selected Works of
Rushdie, Ondaatje, and Okri
Volume 194 – *By Adnan Mahmutovic*

More titles: www.rodopi.nl